For Nana and Grampy – the steady constants that have comforted us through every storm. Thank you for your patience as my chief taste testers, enduring every kitchen experience – the good, the bad and the 'maybe we shouldn't talk about that one'. This book is a tribute to your love, laughter and the countless meals shared around the dinner table. Forever my rocks and forever in my heart.

COMFORT
IN ONE

COMFORT IN ONE

Simple, joyful one pot meals

HARI BEAVIS

Carnival

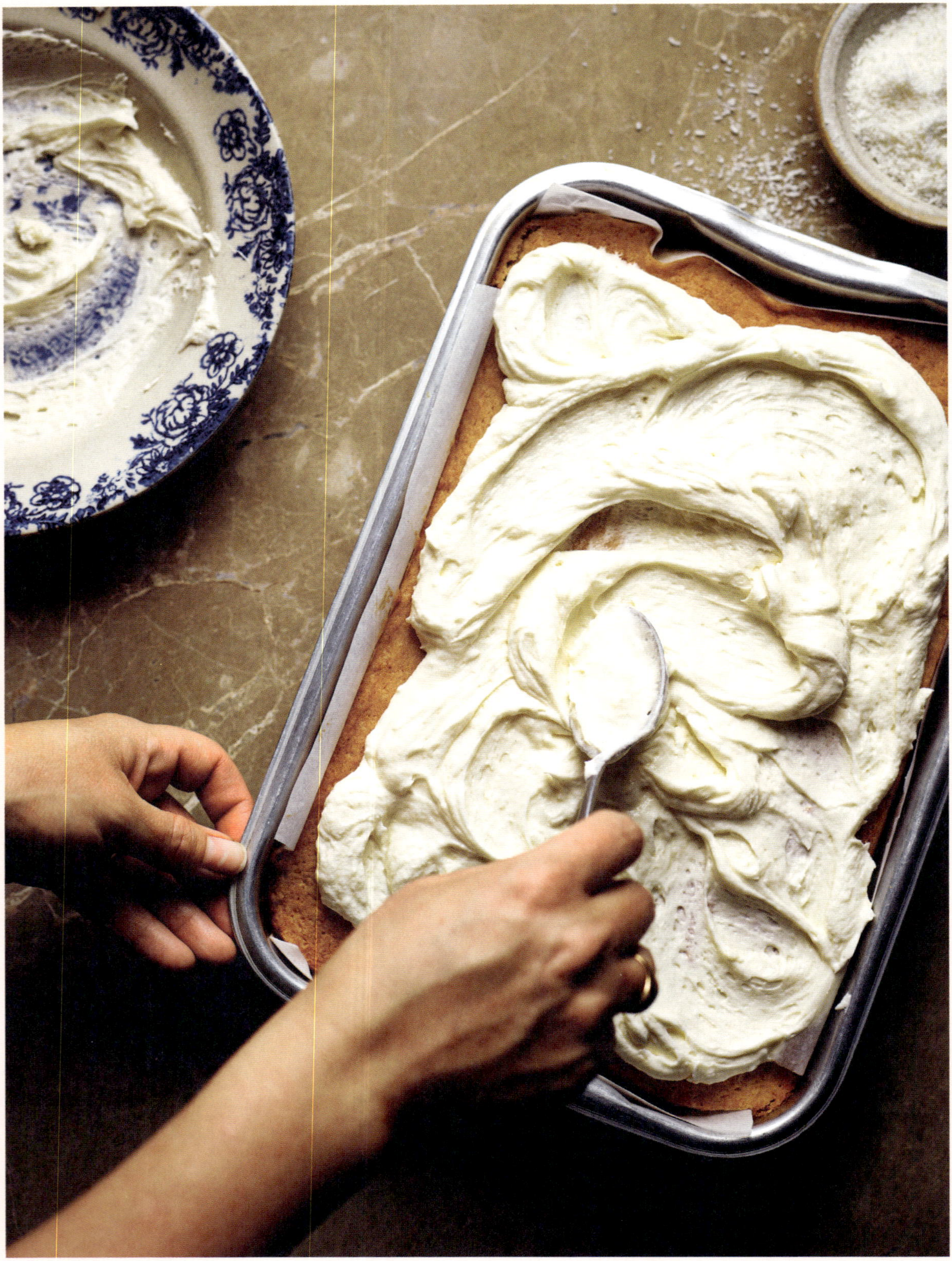

6
Introduction

12
One Pan

58
One Tray

104
One Pot

148
One Salad Bowl

180
One Tin

214
The Perfect Comfort Dinner

216
Index

221
Acknowledgements

222
About the Author

INTRODUCTION

Introduction

Wow, I can't believe this is my second book! This is truly what dreams are made of. I've always loved creating and cooking and, after seeing how much love my debut cookbook *Country Comfort* received, my team and I quickly decided to bring *Comfort in One* to life.

We listened to all the feedback from *Country Comfort*, which included:

'We love the aesthetic of this book.'
'Every recipe is one we actually want to cook.'
'There is a recipe for everyone.'

We knew we had to bring that same energy to *Comfort in One*.

This book is all about making life easier, whether you need a quick weeknight dinner, a cake for your grandparent's birthday, a Mother's Day lunch or an impromptu dinner in the garden with friends. Every recipe is designed to keep washing-up to a minimum, cut out the faff and come together quickly, so you can spend more time with the people you love and less time hovering over the stove. Basically, I wanted to make sure the pot, pan, tray, tin or bowl does the hard work for you.

The five chapters take you through the seasons, so no matter the weather, there will be a dish that brings comfort and puts a smile on everyone's face. Food is deeply emotive to me, and I truly believe there's no right or wrong way to cook (despite what some might say!). If you can combine flavours and textures you love, and finish a meal feeling happier, satisfied and excited for the next bite, then congratulations – to me, you're a certified home cook! Part of the magic of cooking is that you never know when you're on the brink of something delicious.

Each chapter in this book has been lovingly put together with one goal in mind: to make sure that no matter what you've got planned for lunch, dinner, or even a quick snack with friends and family, you can always whip something up using just one pan, pot, tray, bowl or tin. These recipes are all about ease, comfort and flavour, with minimal washing up and maximum enjoyment.

Whether it's a midweek dinner, a cake for a lazy Sunday afternoon or simply throwing together a salad on a warm summer evening with a chilled bottle of rosé, this book has you covered. Every recipe is designed to bring joy to your kitchen and warmth to your table; to be shared, enjoyed and remembered. Now, let's make some memories!

ONE PAN

This chapter is all about comfort food at its finest (faff-free). Most of these recipes can be made in under half an hour, and some even faster, but they never compromise on flavour. Whether it's a light summer dinner like the Spicy Tomato Orzo with Toasted Pine Nuts and Feta (page 16) or Rosé Prawn Pasta (page 18) or a cosy, grey-day dinner to curl up on the sofa with, like the Friday Night Red Thai Curry (page 31) or Green Goddess Winter Pie (page 36), there's something here for every season, mood and situation.

These dishes are made to be thrown into one pan or popped on the stove and then served with love. Perfect for dinner with your partner, family meals, or even a quick solo comfort dish, just chuck everything into one pan and you're done!

ONE TRAY

Ah, the beauty of the one-tray dinner! They're a personal favourite of mine (partly thanks to a bit of well-earned laziness). These are the meals you chuck onto a tray, slide into the oven and then let the oven do the work while you crack on with that never-ending to-do list or simply put your feet up.

These recipes are also made with friendly gatherings in mind, so you can spend time with your loved ones instead of hovering in the kitchen (a fault of mine). They're packed with flavour and made for sharing, from the show stopping Garlic Butter Spatchcocked Chicken (page 65), to the crowd-pleasing Cheeseburger Nachos (a perfect weekend sports day snack or lunch – page 92) or the comforting Mother's Day Lamb (page 89) – the perfect way to show your mum a little love.

And for those evenings when it's just you or two, the Peri Peri Salmon, Potato and Broccoli Traybake (page 76) or BBQ Tofu and Chips (page 94) are simple, satisfying and delicious. There's truly something for everyone, no matter the occasion.

ONE POT

This is your go-to chapter for slow-moving, cosy carb goodness. The kind of meals made for chilly evenings, big blankets and your favourite film. Think creamy, rich and full of depth, like the Creamy 'Marry Me' Chicken (page 108), Warming Meatballs and Onion Gravy (page 114) or a bowl of Simple Coconut Curry (page 134).

But don't worry, it's not all winter warmers. There are lighter, brighter dishes too, like the Summertime Tomato Stew (page 121) or the seaside-inspired On the Coast 'Rock' Mussels (page 122) perfect for al fresco summer evenings. These recipes are made to hug you and those you love from the inside out.

ONE SALAD BOWL

At home, I'm not a fan of using a hundred different bowls. The dishwasher's always full and the washing-up pile never ends! So, I've perfected the art of one-bowl salads. Dressings made right in the bowl, then loaded with all sorts of delicious bits that come together in five minutes but taste like so much more.

If you're new to salads or feel a little unsure, don't worry, I ease you in with simple but flavourful options like the Spicy Tuna Salad with Pesto Croutons (page 168) or the Avocado and Smoked Salmon on Toast Salad (page 174) – flavours you for sure would've had before, so you know they work! For those wanting to be a bit more adventurous, try the Chimichurri Chicken Salad (page 167) or the Goat's Cheese, Fig and Parma Ham Salad (page 152) – they're vibrant, beautiful and guaranteed to impress. These are perfect for sharing, showing off at a party, or simply for making something fresh and delicious for yourself with no bother at all.

ONE TIN

This final chapter is for those sweet, comforting bakes that come together quickly when you need a little magic. Whether it's a Sunday morning and your friends are popping round for a cup of tea or the kids are getting restless and need something fun to help with, these cakes and bakes are just the thing.

All made in one bowl and baked in one tin, they're low-mess (ideal), high-reward treats that bring joy every time. Some of my long-standing favourites include the Creamy Coconut Cake (page 192), the beautifully nostalgic 1920s Pineapple Upside Down Cake (page 195) and a family winner, the All the Best Bits of Banoffee Pie in a Cake (page 208) – P.S. This last one looks more impressive the messier you make it!

Every single bake is a crowd-pleaser, easy, comforting and guaranteed to bring smiles, satisfied sighs and lots of 'ooohs' and 'aahhhs'.

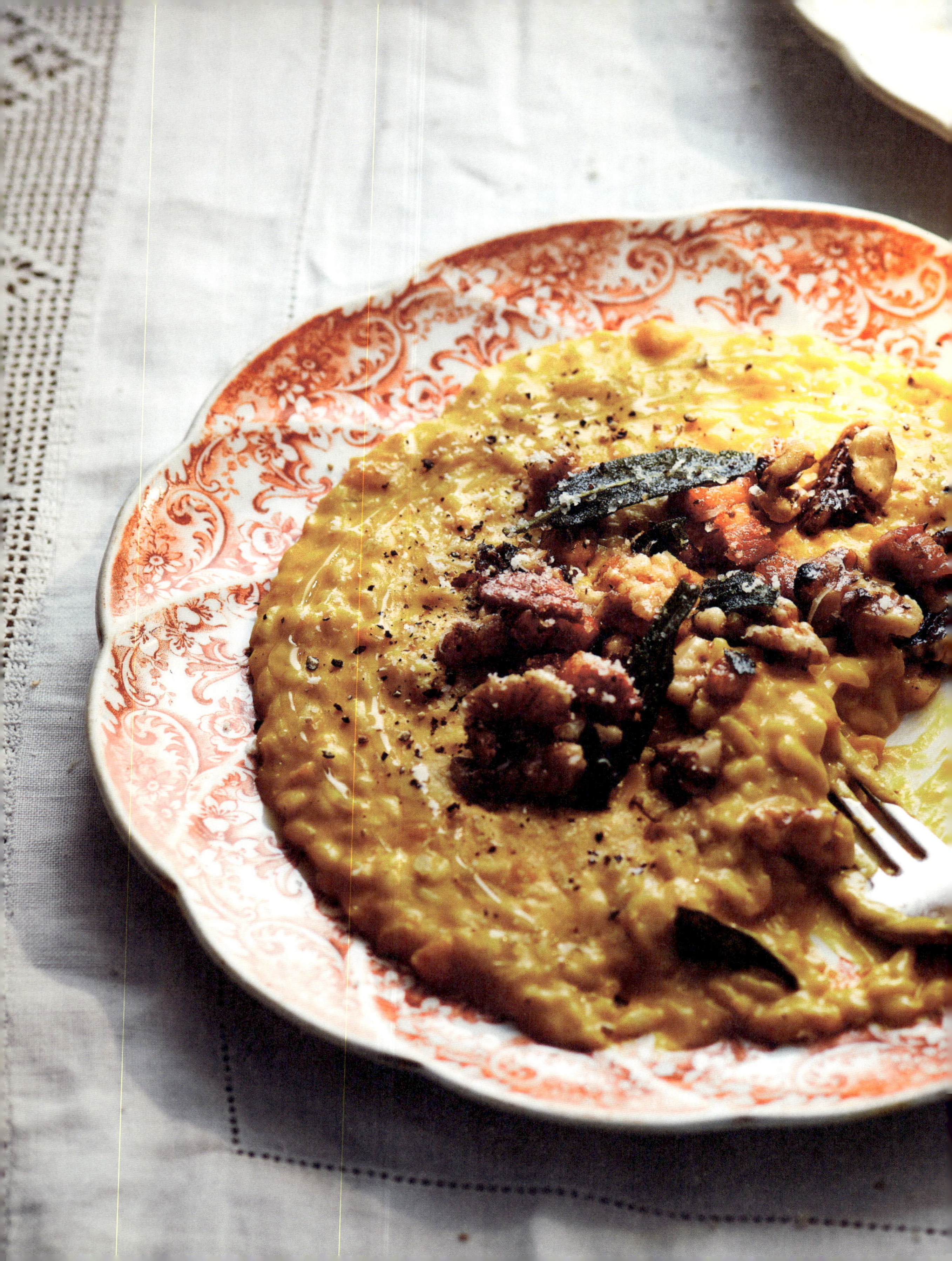

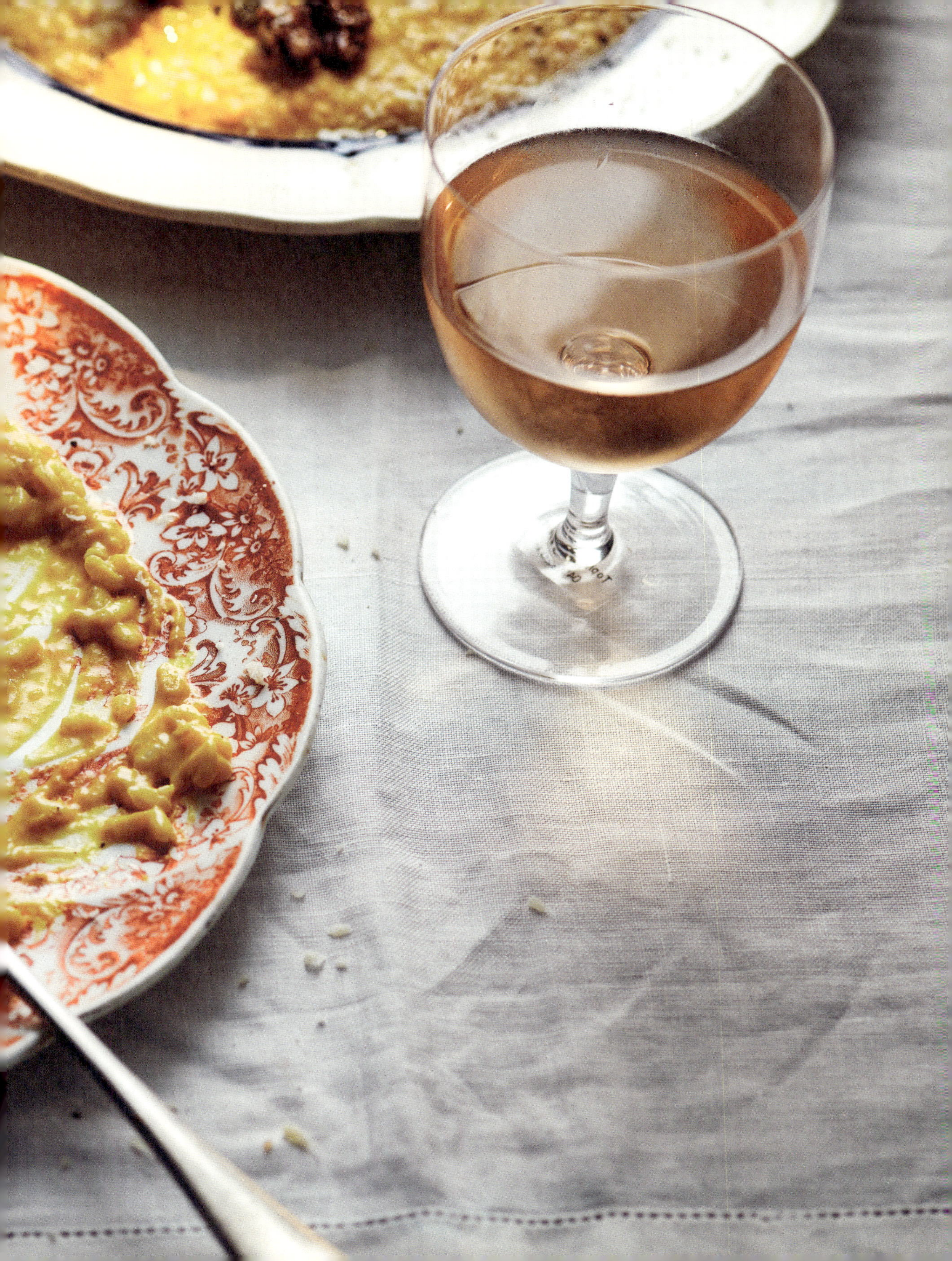

ONE PAN

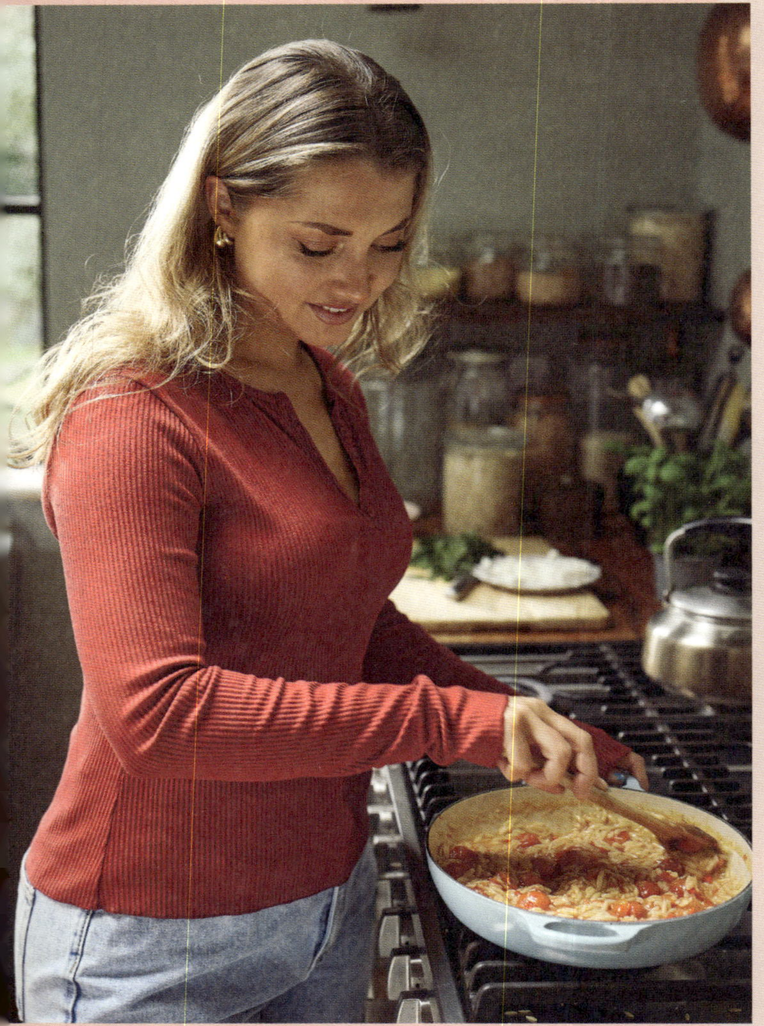

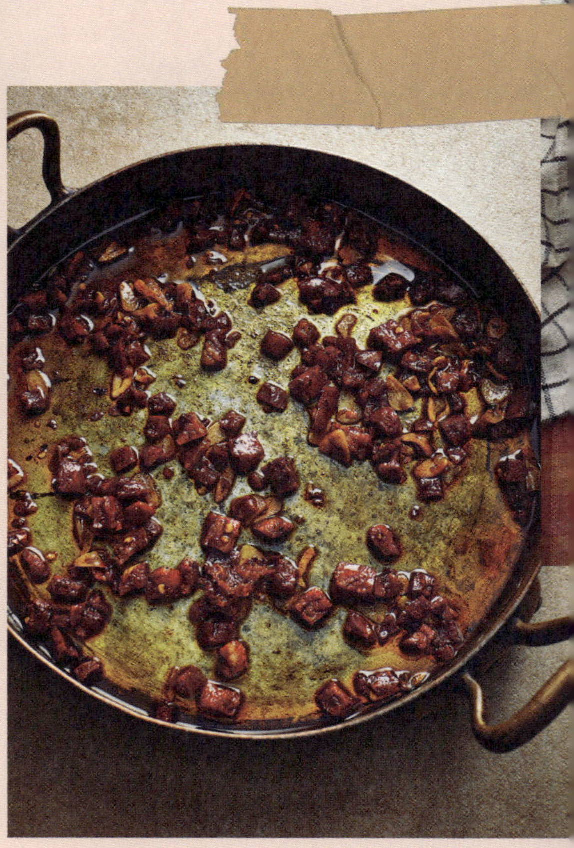

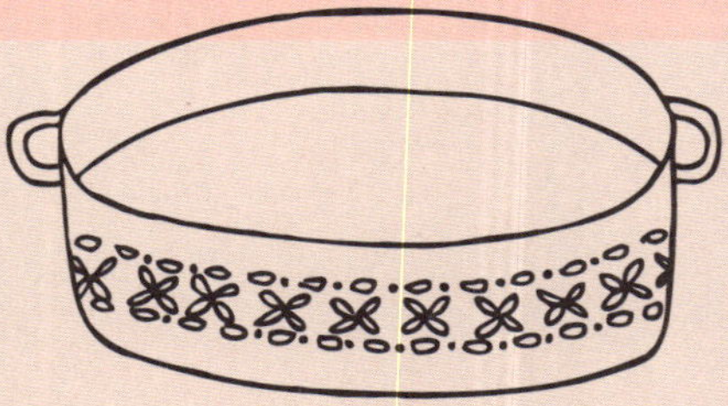

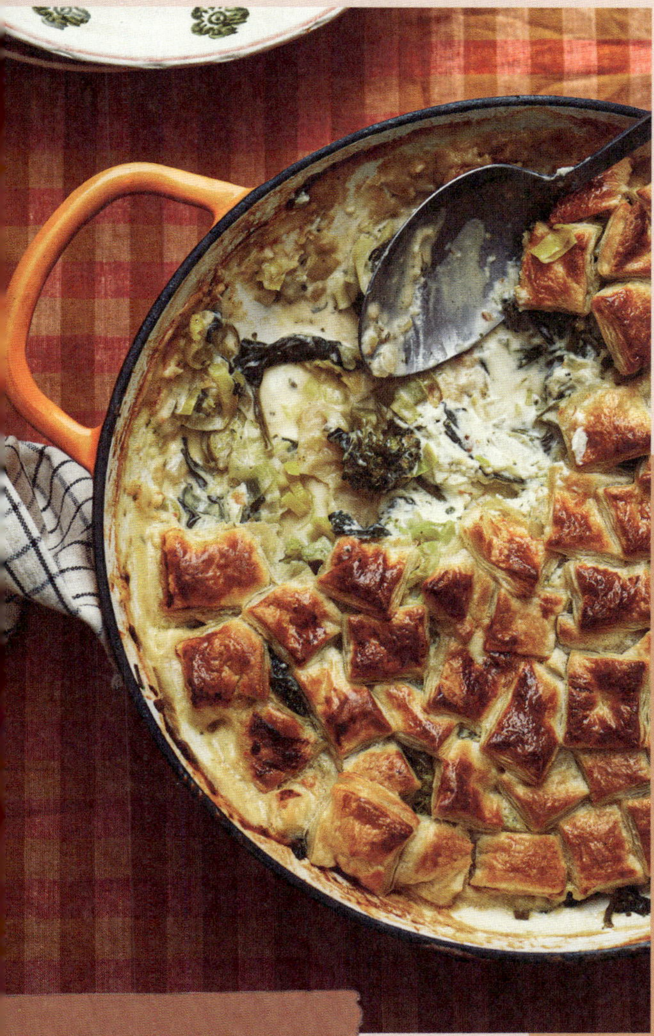

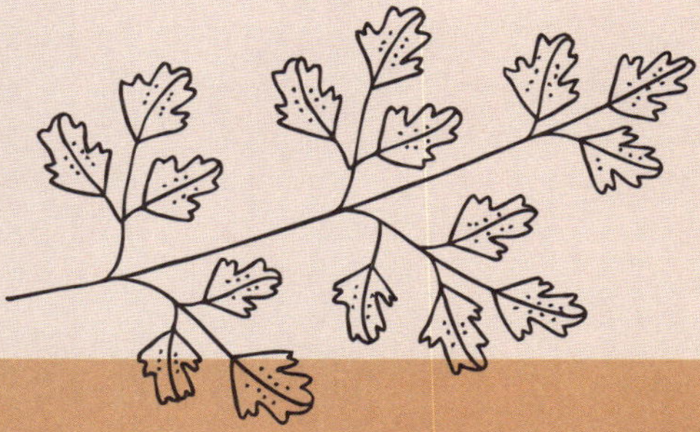

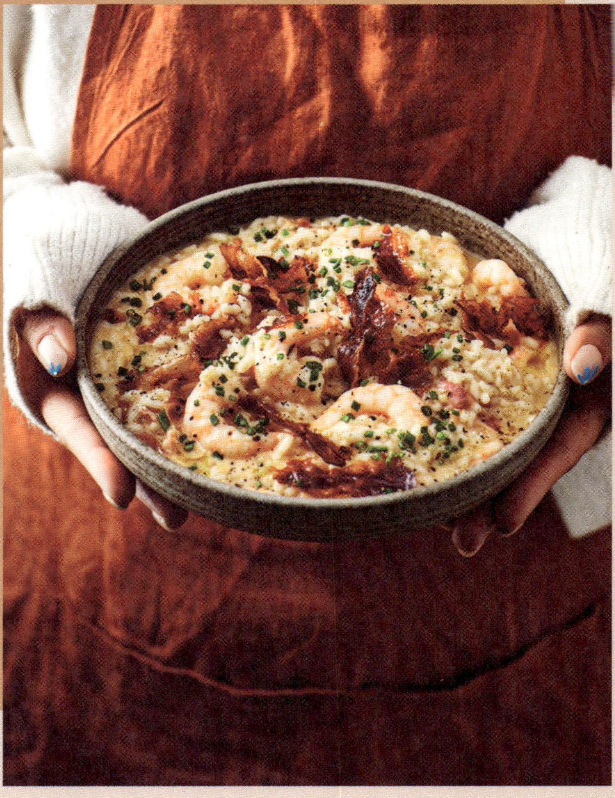

Spicy Tomato Orzo with Toasted Pine Nuts & Feta

SERVES 2
TOTAL TIME: 30 MINUTES

This dish is a year round winner, light enough for a summer evening but cosy enough to warm you through on a cold rainy evening. The orzo is cooked in a rich, garlic and tomato sauce meaning that it soaks up all of those flavours. Pine nuts sprinkled on top add a nutty, buttery texture along with the bursts of creamy salty feta. It's vibrant and always, always delivers. Don't forget to add a drizzle of olive oil over the top just before serving to bring everything together.

50g (1¾oz/⅜ cup) pine nuts
1–2 tbsp extra virgin olive oil, plus extra to serve
6 garlic cloves, finely chopped
1 red chilli, finely chopped
300–350g (10½–12oz) cherry tomatoes on the vine
150g (5½oz/¾ cup) orzo
350–400ml (12–14fl oz/1½–generous 1½ cups) vegetable or chicken stock
handful of chopped basil, plus extra leaves to serve
150g (5½oz) feta, crumbled, to serve
freshly ground black pepper, to serve

EQUIPMENT
chopping board—knife—deep frying pan with a lid—wooden spoon

1. Place a dry frying pan over a medium heat and toast the pine nuts for 3–5 minutes, stirring constantly. They catch quickly, so when they're golden brown and toasted, remove them from the pan immediately.

2. Put the oil, garlic and chilli into the same pan and let them become fragrant, then add in the tomatoes. Cook for 10 minutes until softening – we want to be able to squash them with the back of a spoon to release the juices, creating a sauce.

3. When you have a lovely tomato sauce, add the orzo and stock. Cover and cook for 8–10 minutes until the orzo has soaked up the stock and is cooked. Remove the pan from the heat and mix through the chopped basil.

4. Serve sprinkled with the feta along with a crack of black pepper, remaining basil, toasted pine nuts and drizzled with olive oil.

ONE PAN 17

Rosé Prawn Pasta

SERVES 2
TOTAL TIME: 15 MINUTES

This pink pasta is given its pretty hue by rosé wine. It is delicious and super quick to whip up. Perfect for date night or for having the girls over. Bucatini is my favourite type of pasta; it is like spaghetti but thicker and hollow like a tube, meaning every mouthful is filled with that beautiful creamy sauce.

Serve yourself a glass of rosé while cooking this for ultimate relaxation and comfort.

180g (6½oz) bucatini pasta
1 tbsp salted butter
6 garlic cloves, finely chopped
100–150ml (3½–5fl oz/scant ½–²⁄₃ cup) rosé wine
190g (6¾oz) shop-bought tomato and mascarpone sauce
50g (1¾oz) parmesan, grated, plus extra to serve
300–400g (10½–14oz) raw peeled king prawns (jumbo shrimp)
a handful of chopped parsley, to serve

EQUIPMENT
large saucepan—chopping board—knife
deep frying pan—wooden spoon—grater

1. Bring a large saucepan of water to the boil and cook the bucatini according to the packet instructions.

2. Meanwhile, melt the butter in a deep frying pan over a medium heat then throw in the garlic and fry for 2 minutes – you want to get those aromas going. Pour in the rosé and let the alcohol cook off for a minute or two, then add the tomato and mascarpone sauce and parmesan, along with a ladle of the pasta cooking water. Let the sauce thicken, then add the prawns and cook for 1–2 minutes until pink and opaque – be careful not to overcook them otherwise they can become rubbery. When the prawns have been on the heat for a minute, drain the bucatini and add it to the sauce, stirring well to make sure it's fully coated.

3. Serve with a generous sprinkling of parmesan and parsley over the top.

ALTERNATIVE INGREDIENTS
King prawns (jumbo shrimp): use a bag of frozen mixed seafood – it will just need a minute or two longer to cook
Tomato and mascarpone sauce: any creamy tomato sauce, such as tomato and ricotta

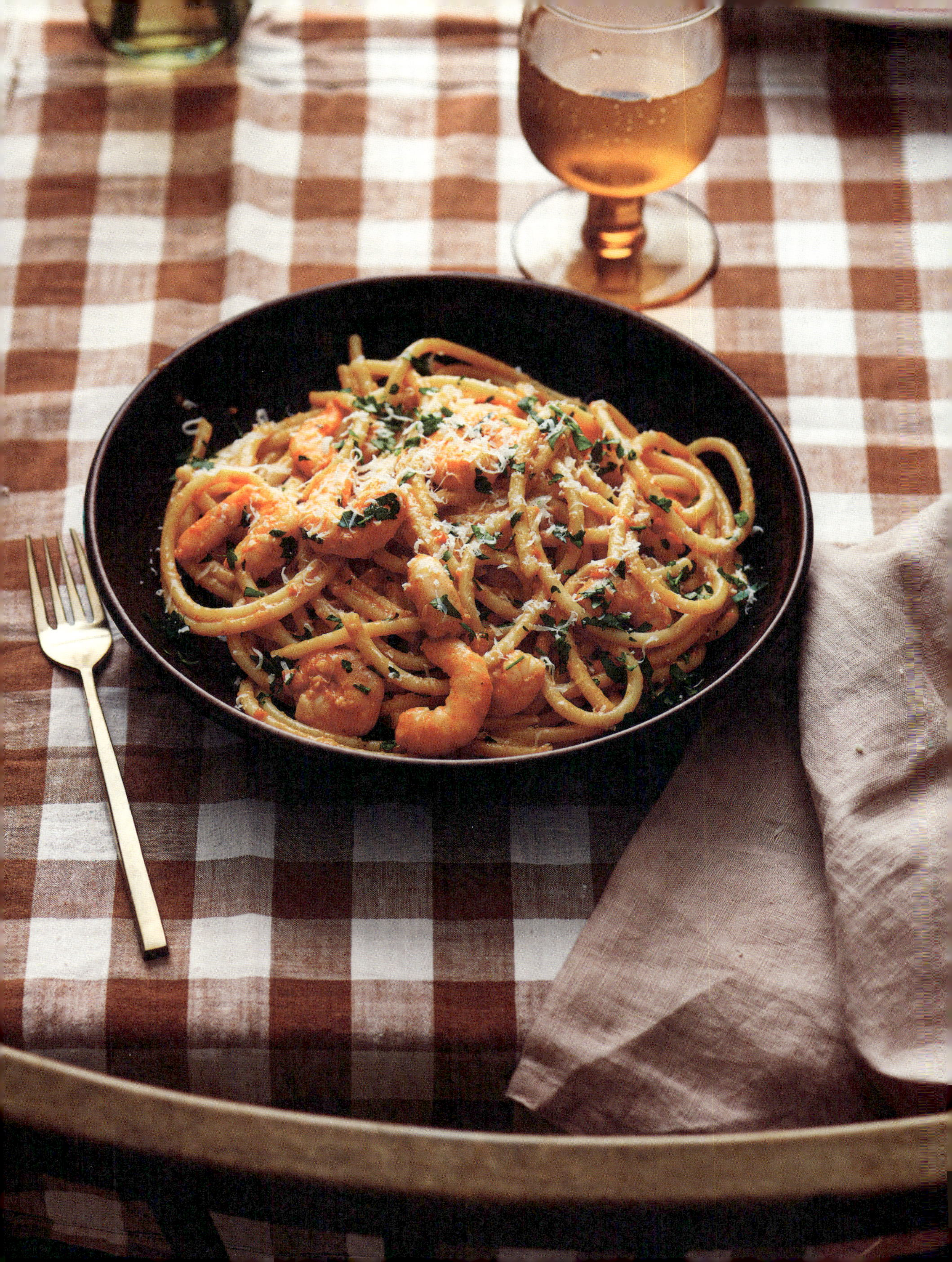

ONE PAN

Chicken Pot Pie

SERVES 4
TOTAL TIME: 35-40 MINUTES

Chicken pot pie is one of those dishes that immediately come to mind when you think about comfort food – and to me, this means it should also be easy to cook and on the plate in under an hour, ready to be enjoyed with those you love. My Nana and Gramps were the first to try this recipe and they have hinted at me making another one every week since!

2 tbsp olive oil or 1 large knob of butter
1 large onion, finely diced
2 carrots, finely diced
2 celery sticks, finely diced
300g (10½oz) chestnut (cremini) mushrooms, thinly sliced
600g (1lb 5oz) boneless, skinless chicken thighs, diced
1 tsp fine sea salt
1 tsp freshly ground black pepper
300ml (10fl oz/1¼ cups) double (heavy) cream
1 chicken stock pot
150g (5½oz) parmesan, grated
a few sprigs of fresh thyme, plus extra for the top
60g (2oz/½ cup) frozen peas
60g (2oz/scant ½ cup) frozen sweetcorn
320g (11¼oz) ready-rolled puff pastry
1 medium egg, beaten

EQUIPMENT
chopping board—knife—deep, ovenproof frying pan—wooden spoon—grater pastry brush

1. Preheat the oven to 220°C (200°C fan/425°F/gas mark 7).

2. Place a deep, ovenproof frying pan over a medium-high heat, add the olive oil or butter and then throw in the onion, carrots, celery and mushrooms. Cook for 10 minutes, stirring occasionally, until the vegetables have softened and started to caramelize.

3. Next, add the chicken and cook for about 5 minutes, then add the salt and pepper, followed by the cream, stock pot, parmesan and thyme. Stir for a few minutes until you have a thick sauce, then add the peas and sweetcorn. Remove from the heat.

4. Place the puff pastry sheet over the top of the mixture so that and it is overlapping the edge of the pan and crimp it around the edge. Make a little slit in the middle and stuff a few sprigs of thyme through it to allow the hot air to release, which will ensure your pie doesn't explode. Brush with the beaten egg.

5. Pop the pie in the oven and cook for 15–20 minutes until the pastry is golden brown. Serve hot with mash and greens of your choice.

ALTERNATIVE INGREDIENTS
Chicken thighs: use chicken breasts (but it won't be as juicy)
Cream and parmesan: use crème fraîche or cream cheese
Make it veggie: remove the chicken thighs, use vegetarian parmesan and swap the chicken stock with vegetable stock

Sea Bass with Mixed Beans

SERVES 2
TOTAL TIME: 15 MINUTES

This dish can be whipped up in just 15 minutes and is beautifully balanced, with light white fish paired with creamy butter (lima) beans and salty chorizo. It's a real crowd pleaser.

The crispier you can get your chorizo the yummier each mouthful of this dish will be because the softness of the beans mixed with crispy, chewy morsels of chorizo really packs a flavour punch.

If you want to save a few pennies, have a walk down the frozen fish aisle: there are usually some really cheap alternatives, such as basa fillets.

2 tbsp olive oil
1 tbsp salted butter
2 skin-on sea bass fillets
2 banana shallots, sliced
6 garlic cloves, finely chopped
225g (8oz) Spanish chorizo, diced
570g (1lb 4½oz) drained mixed jarred beans (I like to use butter/lima beans and queen butter beans but you could also use cannellini)
1–2 tbsp crème fraîche
60g (2oz) parmesan, grated
1 tsp freshly ground black pepper
finely chopped parsley, to serve

EQUIPMENT
chopping board—knife—frying pan
tongs—wooden spoon—grater

1. Heat the oil in a frying pan over a high heat, then add the butter and when the butter has melted, get the fish in, skin-side down. Sear for 90 seconds on each side until it is golden brown and crispy. Remove from the pan.

2. Reduce the heat to medium and throw in the shallots, garlic and chorizo. Fry for 3–4 minutes until the chorizo is crispy up and has released its oils, then add the beans, crème fraîche, parmesan and black pepper and mix well. Simmer for a further 3–4 minutes until warm through.

3. To serve, spoon the beans into a bowl, place the fish on top and scatter with the chopped parsley.

ALTERNATIVE INGREDIENTS
Chorizo: use pancetta
Sea bass: use halibut, salmon, cod or trout, adjusting the cooking time accordingly

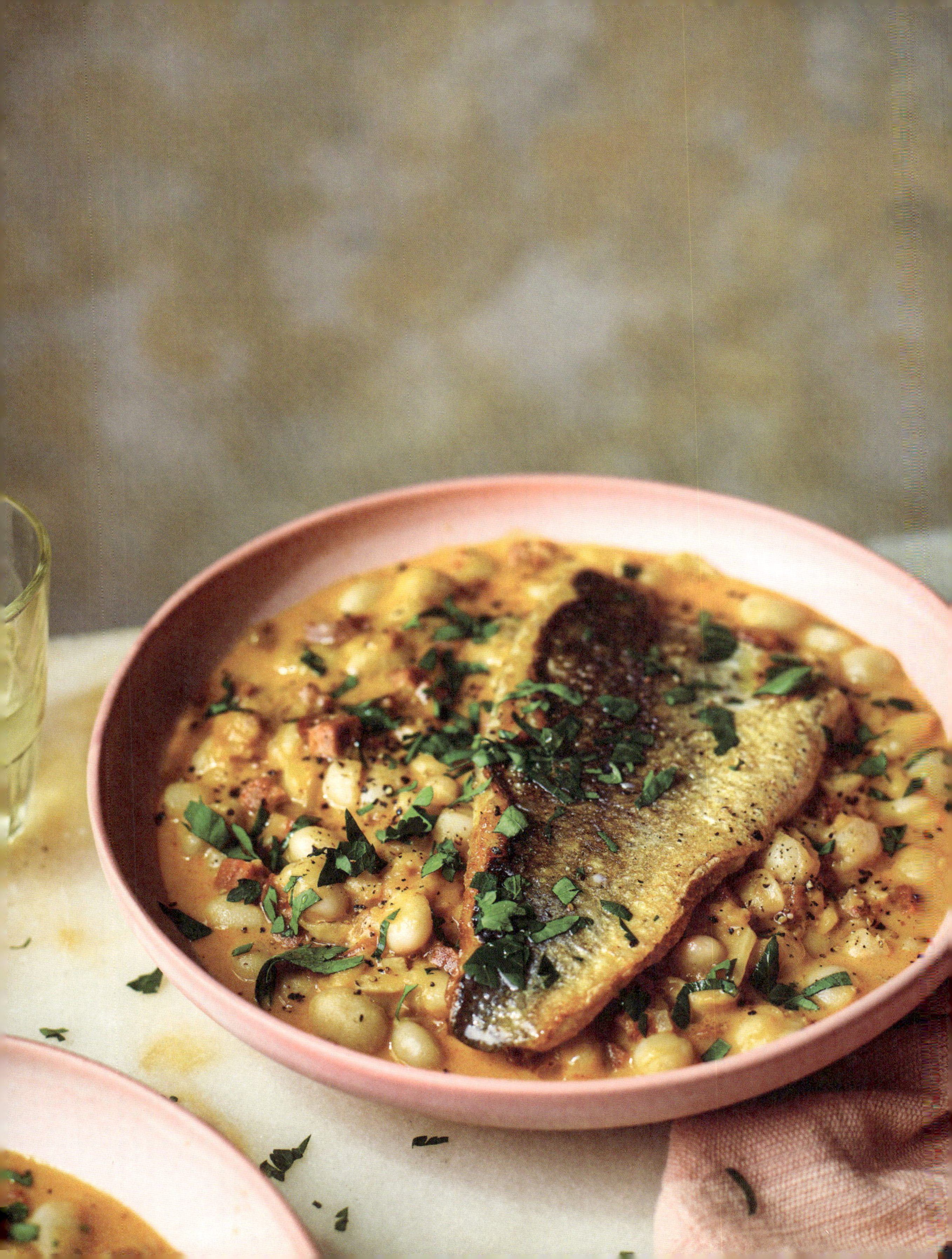

ONE PAN

Spicy Jerk-style Chicken, Black Beans & Rice

SERVES 4
TOTAL TIME: 45–50 MINUTES

If you're someone who loves bold flavours filled with warmth and spice this dish is just what you need. Packed with rich depth of flavours, it comes together effortlessly in just one pan in under an hour. It makes a delicious and satifying dinner and the leftovers taste even better.

If you can, marinate the chicken overnight as it will be even more flavourful.

For fluffier rice, be sure to wash it until the water runs clear before cooking.

8 boneless, skin-on chicken thighs
2 tbsp jerk seasoning powder or paste
1 tsp fine sea salt
1 tsp freshly ground black pepper
4 tbsp vegetable oil
1 onion, diced
8 garlic cloves, finely chopped
1 red chilli, deseeded and finely chopped
5cm (2in) piece of ginger, finely chopped
4 tbsp tomato purée (paste)
4 sprigs of thyme
3 red (bell) peppers, diced
400g (14oz) tin of black beans, drained
400g (14oz/2 cups) long-grain white rice, washed
500ml (17fl oz/generous 2 cups) coconut milk
500ml (17fl oz/generous 2 cups) chicken stock
4 spring onions (scallions), chopped, to serve
lime wedges, to serve

EQUIPMENT
mixing bowl—deep frying pan with a lid
chopping board—knife—wooden spoon

1. Put the chicken thighs into a bowl with the jerk seasoning, salt and pepper and mix well.

2. Heat the oil in a large, deep frying pan over a medium-high heat. Add the chicken thighs, skin-side down, and cook for 4–6 minutes until the skin is crispy and golden brown, then flip and cook for a few more minutes until they're 75 per cent cooked. Remove the thighs from the pan and set aside.

3. Add the onion, garlic, chilli and ginger to the same pan and cook for a few minutes until they have softened. Next, stir in the tomato purée and add in the thyme, peppers and black beans. Cook for 5 minutes to soften the peppers.

4. Stir in the rice, coconut milk and chicken stock, then place the chicken thighs on top, skin-side up, so that the skin stays crispy while allowing the rice to fluff up and absorb all the flavours and stock. Reduce the heat to medium-low, cover and cook for 15 minutes until the rice is fluffy and the chicken is cooked through. Serve with lots of chopped spring onions on top and lime wedges to sqeeeze over.

ALTERNATIVE INGREDIENTS
Chicken thighs: use breast or skinless chicken thighs
(Bell) peppers: use peas or sweetcorn
Black beans: use red kidney beans

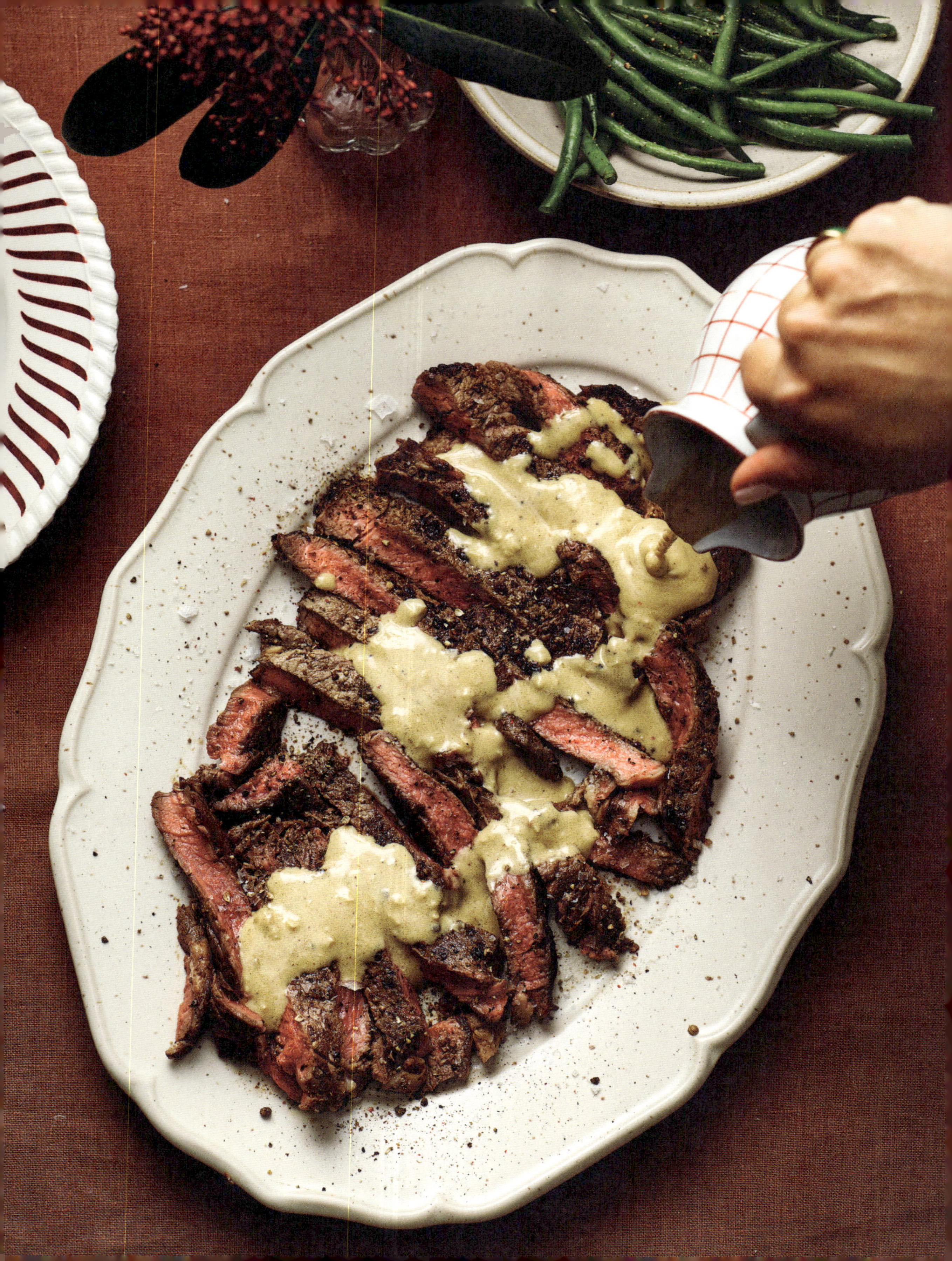

Peppered Steak with Whisky Sauce

SERVES 2
TOTAL TIME: 15 MINUTES

If you've got an occasion coming up, this is a dish to earmark and turn the corner down on. This is one of my partner's absolute favourites and it's easy to see why. The rich, velvety whisky sauce adds a touch of warmth while the peppercorns bring a spiced kick. It gives off fancy vibes but its so simple to whip up. Serve it with a buttery potato dauphinoise and green beans for a beautiful dinner at home.

2 tbsp crushed peppercorns (I like to mix it up with white and black but it's up to you)
2 large pinches of flaked sea salt
1 tbsp Dijon mustard
2 rib-eye steaks (or another steak of your choice), at room temperature
20g (¾oz) salted butter
1 tbsp olive oil
4 garlic cloves, finely chopped
50–100ml (1¾–3½fl oz/scant ¼–scant ½ cup) whisky (according to taste)
200ml (7fl oz/generous ¾ cup) double (heavy) cream
50g (1¾oz) parmesan, grated
vegetables of your choice, to serve

EQUIPMENT
frying pan—pastry brush (optional)—tongs chopping board—knife—whisk—grater

1. Place a dry frying pan over a high heat. Mix together the crushed peppercorns and salt in a small bowl.

2. Brush or smear the mustard over the steaks, then sprinkle them with the pepper and salt mixture, pressing it into both sides of the steaks. Try to mop up as much of the pepper and salt as you can with the meat.

3. Add the butter and olive oil to the hot pan, and when the butter starts to foam, place the steaks in the pan. Cook for 2–3 minutes on each side, depending on how you like your steak cooked. I find the perfect time for thick rib-eye is 2 minutes 20 seconds on each side. Once cooked, remove the steaks from the pan and set aside to rest while you make the sauce.

4. Add the garlic and whisky to the pan and let this simmer for a minute or two. We want the garlic to be fragrant and for the alcohol to cook off. Next, whisk in the double cream and parmesan. Keep whisking for about 2 minutes until the sauce thickens.

5. Serve the steaks with the sauce and vegetables of your choice.

ALTERNATIVE INGREDIENTS
Dijon mustard: you won't really be able to taste the mustard as it is just a light coating to help the salt and pepper stick, but you can also use horseradish sauce, mayonnaise or another condiment
Whisky: use white wine, Madeira or brandy – or, if you're looking for a non-alcoholic alternative, stock or a dash of apple cider vinegar works too

ONE PAN

Creamy Pesto, Mushroom & Courgette Pasta

SERVES 4
TOTAL TIME: 20 MINUTES

This is such a wonderful comfort food dinner. It's creamy and the pesto and courgette add pops of freshness. It's beautiful on its own but you can throw in any extra protein, like pulled chicken or turkey, or any veggies you like. It comes together in under 20 minutes so is perfect for weeknight dinners.

I really recommend taking your time with the mushrooms and giving them as long as you can so that they're almost crispy.

If you're making this for friends or want to make it a little more special, try using a mixture of different kinds of mushrooms. It will really intensify the flavour.

50g (1¾oz/⅜ cup) pine nuts
1 tbsp salted butter
500g (1lb 2oz) chestnut (cremini) mushrooms, thinly sliced
300g (10½oz) spaghetti
190g (6¾oz) basil pesto
150g (5½oz) garlic and herb soft cheese
2 courgettes (zucchini; about 500g/1lb 2oz), made into courgetti or thinly sliced on a mandoline
large handful of basil leaves
fine sea salt
freshly ground black pepper

EQUIPMENT
large, deep frying pan—chopping board knife—wooden spoon—large saucepan

1. Put your pine nuts into a large, deep frying pan over a medium heat and toast them for 3–5 minutes, keeping an eye on them as they catch easily, until they are golden brown and fragrant. Remove from the pan and pop in a little bowl to one side.

2. Next, add the butter and mushrooms to the same pan and cook for 5–10 minutes. Take your time – you want the mushrooms to be well browned so they have a gorgeous nutty flavour to them.

3. Meanwhile, bring a large saucepan of water to the boil and cook the spaghetti according to the packet instructions.

4. Add the pesto and garlic and herb soft cheese to the pan with the mushrooms along with a splash of the pasta cooking water to loosen the sauce. Now add the courgettes and cook for 1–2 minutes, then finally drain and add the spaghetti. Mix the courgette and spaghetti through the sauce until they are fully coated.

5. Throw in the basil, then taste and season as needed. Finish off with a sprinkling of toasted pine nuts.

ALTERNATIVE INGREDIENTS
Pesto: use red pesto
Garlic and herb soft cheese: use 600ml (20fl oz/2½ cups) double (heavy) cream and 100g (3½oz) grated parmesan, or light crème fraîche works well for a lighter midweek option

ONE PAN

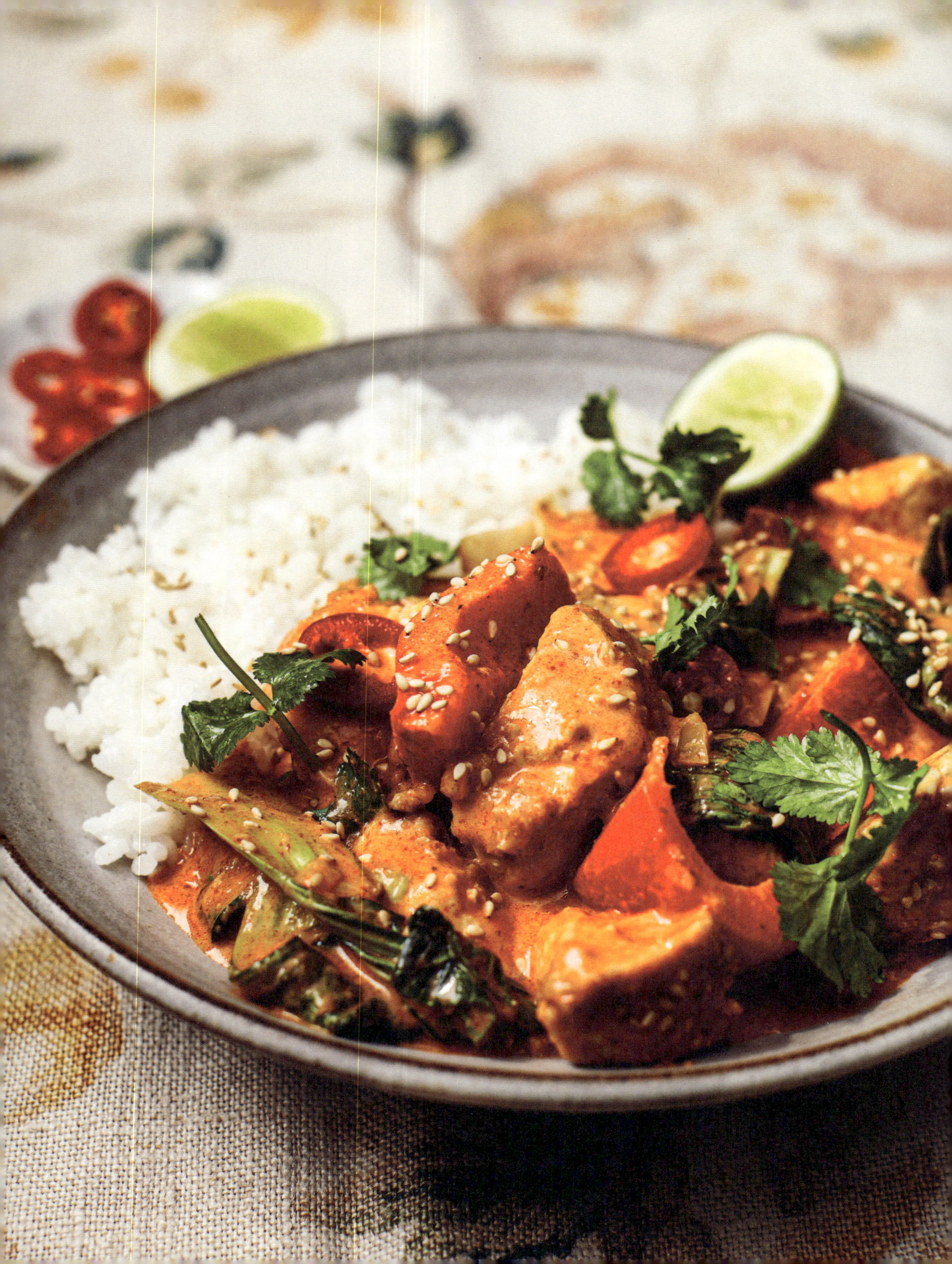

Friday Night Red Thai Curry

SERVES 2
TOTAL TIME: 20–30 MINUTES

I almost think this recipe is cheating! You don't have to do anything – just throw a few tins and jars and fresh ingredients into a pan and you're left with the most delicious, fragrant curry. You know when you want something jam-packed with flavour on a Friday night that keeps everyone happy? This is going to be that dish for you!

To elevate this dish further you can add in a few other fancy bits like lemongrass, lime leaves and other Thai herbs and spices – perfect for when you're hosting friends and want to impress.

1 tbsp vegetable oil
1 onion, diced
6–7 garlic cloves, finely chopped
5cm (2in) piece of ginger, finely chopped
1 red chilli, finely chopped, plus extra to serve
2 large chicken breasts (or 4 boneless and skinless chicken thighs), diced
170g (6oz) Thai red curry paste
400ml (14fl oz/generous 1½ cups) coconut milk
2 red (bell) peppers, diced
2 pak choi (bok choy), diced

TO SERVE
cooked jasmine rice
lime wedges
chopped coriander (cilantro)
sesame seeds

EQUIPMENT
chopping board—knife—saucepan
wooden spoon

1. Heat the oil in a saucepan over a medium heat, then add the onion, garlic, ginger and chilli and fry for about 5 minutes until the onion has softened.

2. Next, add the chicken and fry for 5–7 minutes until coloured and almost cooked through. Throw in the curry paste and stir well to coat everything, then pour in the coconut milk and bring to a gentle simmer. Once simmering, add the peppers and pak choi, then gently simmer for a few minutes until the vegetables have softened a little but still have nice crunch.

3. Serve over fluffy jasmine rice with a good squeeze of lime juice and a sprinkling of coriander, chilli and sesame seeds. Tuck in!

ALTERNATIVE INGREDIENTS
Ginger and chilli: use ground ginger and dried chilli (hot pepper) flakes
Chicken: use strips of beef, turkey or prawns (shrimp)
Thai red curry paste: use green, panang or massaman curry paste

ONE PAN

Gambas Pil Pil

SERVES 2
TOTAL TIME: 10–15 MINUTES

If I see these big prawns (shrimp) on a menu I will be ordering them. They're a flavour explosion and such a great starter. Using some bread to soak up all the juices and oil is something I thoroughly enjoy – you might even call it a hobby of mine. This dish is ideal for summertime, served with a crisp glass of rosé outside on the patio, but the warm spices mean it's equally delicious eaten while cuddling up in the winter. A perfect year-round dish.

The oily base for this dish is a beautiful start for flavours, so feel free to try adding other herbs and spices that you enjoy.

4 tbsp olive oil
120g (4oz) Spanish chorizo, finely diced
6 garlic cloves, finely chopped or sliced
15g (½ oz) salted butter
½ tsp chilli (hot pepper) flakes
½ tsp smoked paprika
600g (1lb 5oz) raw shell-on king prawns (jumbo shrimp)
1 lemon
large pinch of flaked sea salt
a handful of chopped parsley
lots of warm sliced baguette and butter, to serve

EQUIPMENT
chopping board—knife—frying pan
wooden spoon or spatula

1. Heat the oil in a frying pan over a medium-high heat, then throw in the chorizo and cook for 3–5 minutes until it starts to crisp up and release its lovely red oil.

2. Now add the garlic, butter, chilli flakes and paprika. Mix together, then add the prawns and let them cook in the oil for about 3 minutes until they turn pink – be careful not to overcook them otherwise they can become rubbery. Once the prawns are cooked, remove the pan from the heat and transfer to a bowl, then squeeze lemon over the top along with a pinch of salt and a sprinkle of parsley. Tuck in, not forgetting to mop up all the juices up with some lovely warm bread.

ALTERNATIVE INGREDIENTS
Chorizo: use bacon lardons or pancetta

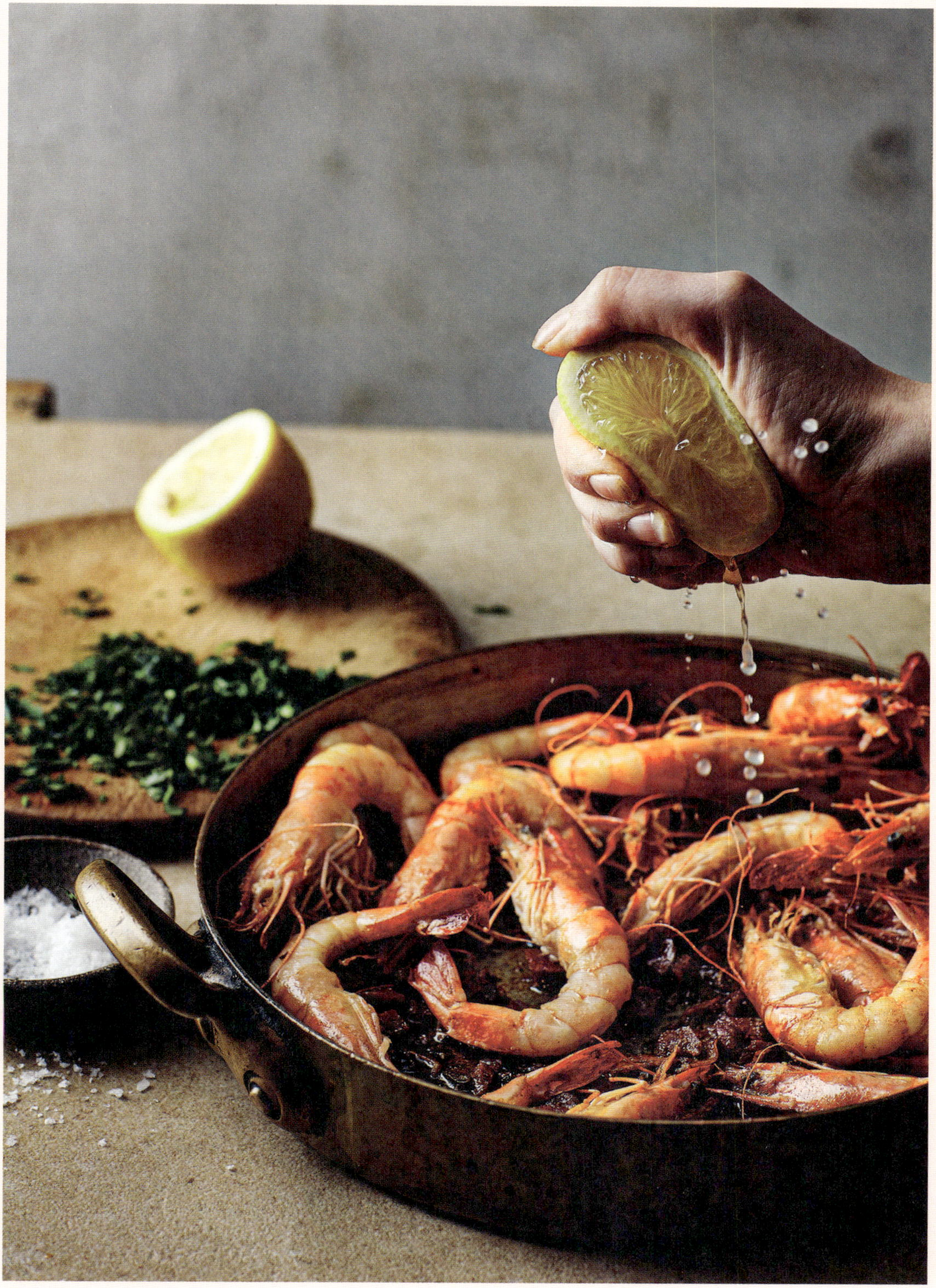

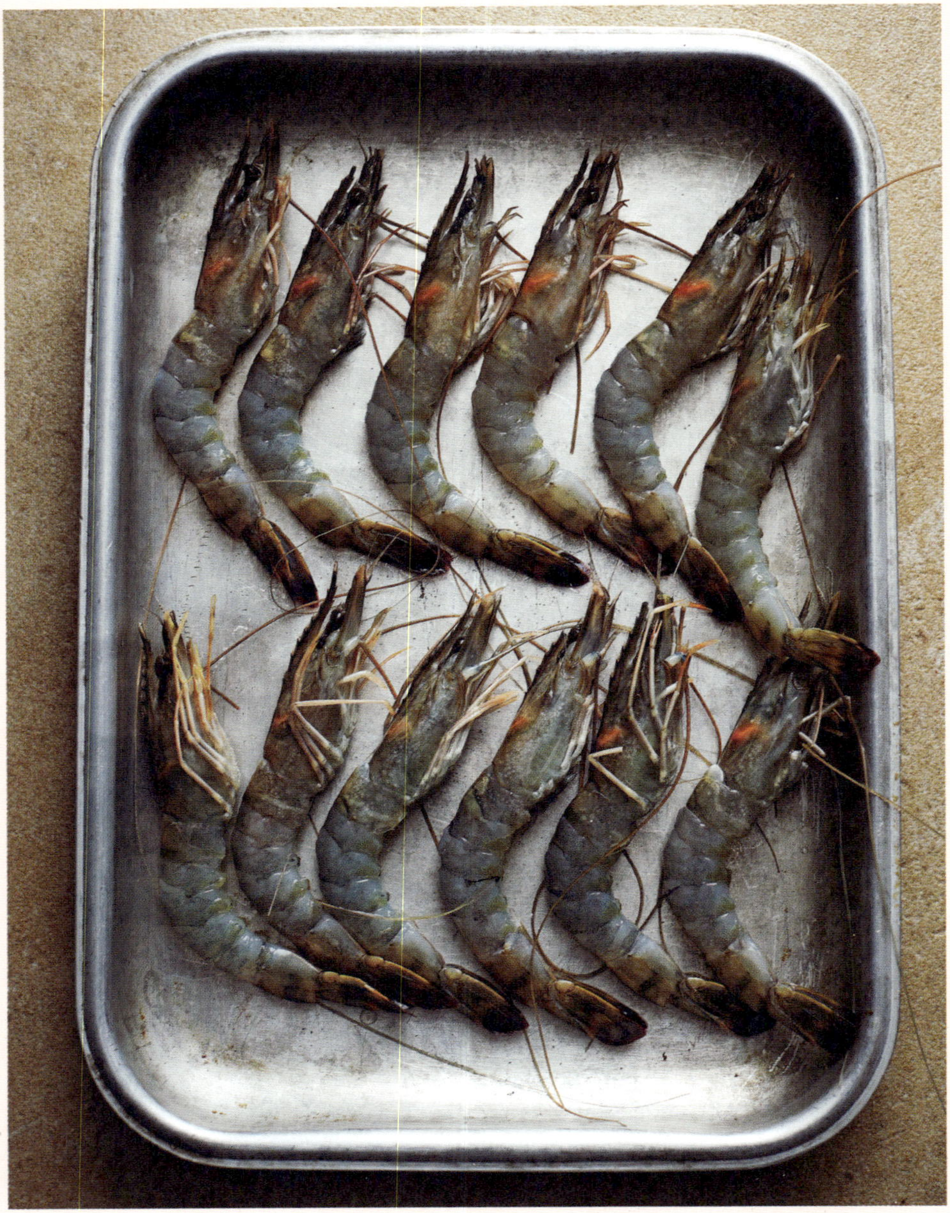

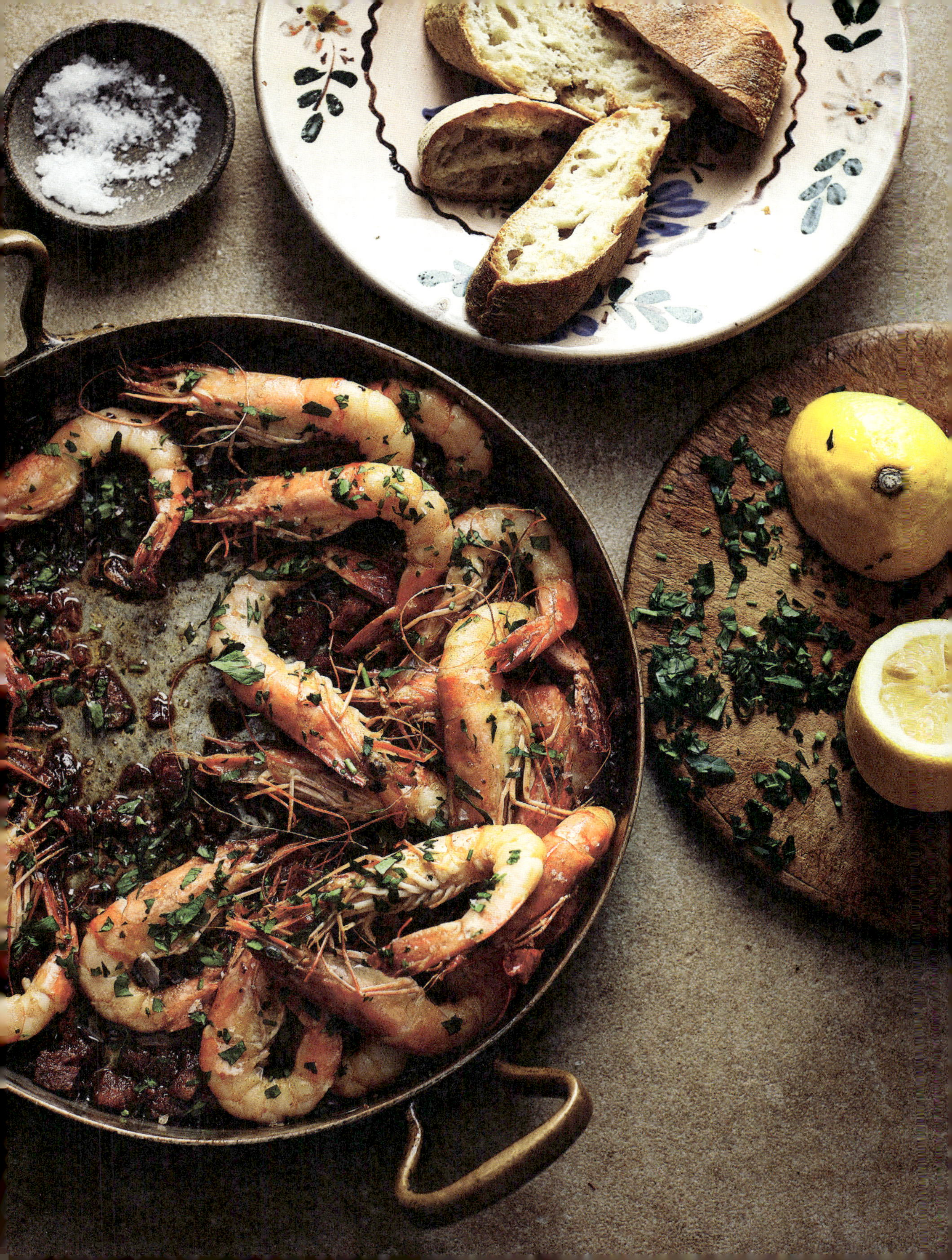

Green Goddess Winter Pie

SERVES 4
TOTAL TIME: 40–50 MINUTES

This lighter take on a beautiful winter warmer pie uses little pillows of pastry on top rather than the usual sheet. Filled with dark greens, it has so much goodness while also being utterly delicious. I like to throw in leftover roast chicken to add a little more protein if I have it, but it is wonderful as a veggie option just as it is. It's also a brilliant side dish – I actually first developed the recipe when I made it as an accompaniment for a Sunday roast dinner. I used up all the bits from the week that needed eating and added some scraps of pastry. When soaked in gravy, the pie made a gorgeous addition to the table.

2 tbsp olive oil
1 onion, diced
6–8 garlic cloves, finely chopped
2–3 leeks (about 400g/14oz), thinly sliced
1 broccoli (about 300g/10½oz), diced
200ml (7fl oz/generous ¾ cup) chicken or vegetable stock
240g (8½oz) spinach
300g (10½oz) garlic and herb soft cheese
100g (3½oz) parmesan, grated
320g (11¼oz) ready-rolled puff pastry, cut into 2cm (¾in) squares
1 medium egg, beaten

EQUIPMENT
chopping board—knife—casserole dish (Dutch oven), pie dish or ovenproof frying pan—wooden spoon—grater—pastry brush

1. Preheat the oven to 200°C (180°C fan/400°F/gas mark 6)

2. Heat the oil in an casserole dish, pie dish or ovenproof frying pan over a medium heat, then add the onion and garlic and fry for 4–6 minutes until translucent and softened. Add the leeks and broccoli and let these cook for 2 minutes, then add the stock and increase the heat to high. We want the stock to be bubbling so that it continues to soften the leeks and broccoli. After 10 minutes, throw in the spinach and cook until wilted.

3. Once the vegetables are soft and the spinach has wilted, add the soft cheese and parmesan. Stir until you have a delicious sauce coating all the greens. Remove from the heat.

4. Finally, place the squares of pastry over the top of the dish or pan so that the greens are completely covered and brush the pastry with the beaten egg. Transfer the pie to the oven and bake for 15 minutes until the pastry is golden brown and puffed up. Remove from the oven, get a big spoon and tuck right in! Absolutely delicious.

ONE PAN

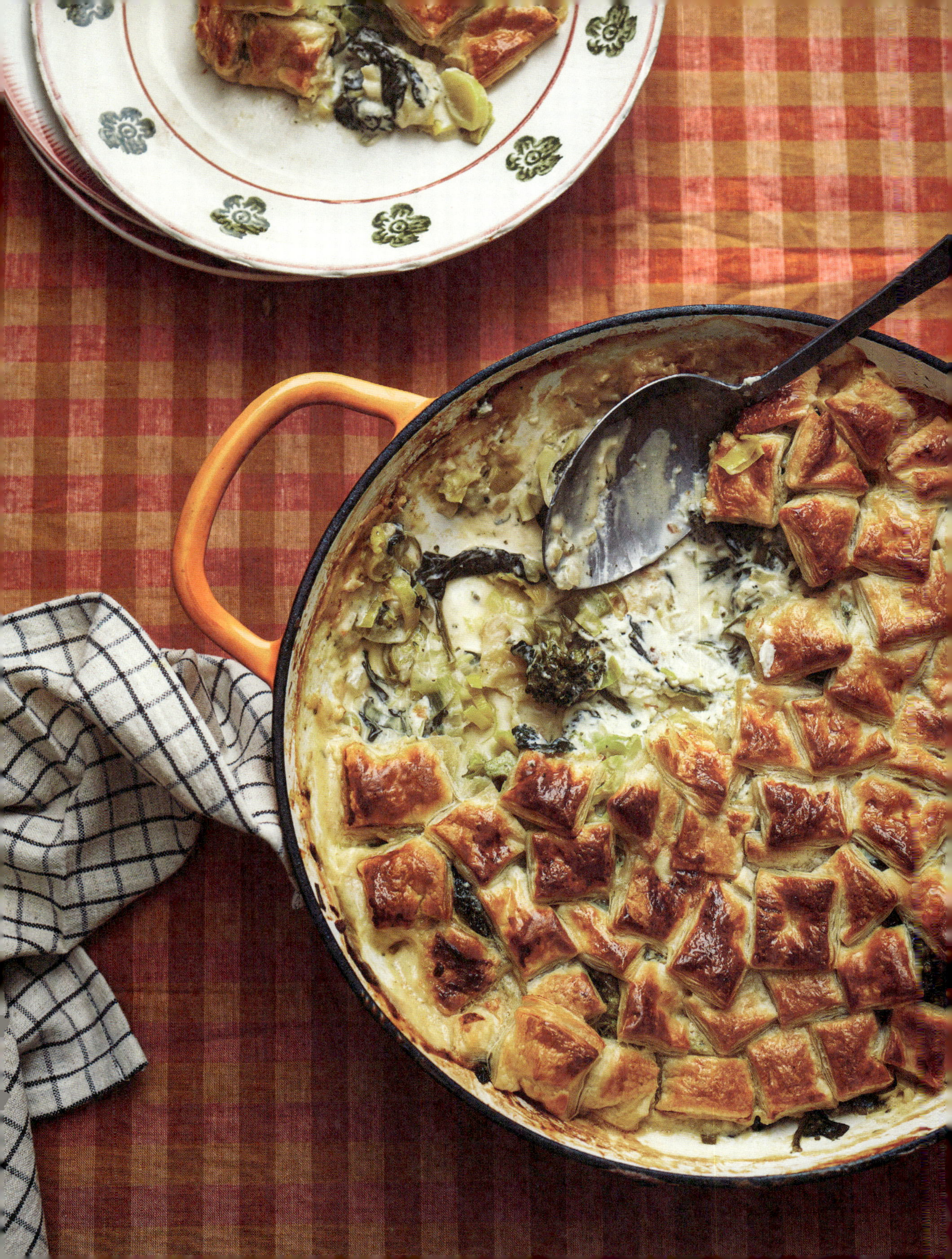

ONE PAN

Butter Bean & Broccoli Alfredo

SERVES 2
TOTAL TIME: 15 MINUTES

This indulgent butter (lima) bean dish is for anyone who always ends up eating a whole loaf of bread with anything saucy. It's creamy and dunkable and filled with soft, melt-in-the-mouth butter beans (I really recommend using Bold Bean Co or other high-quality butter beans for this dish, as it makes all the difference!). This has to be eaten with warm, crunchy sourdough bread, slathered with butter!

1 chicken stock pot
1 broccoli (about 300g/10½oz), florets diced
500g (1lb 2oz) drained jarred butter (lima) beans
250ml (8fl oz/1 cup) double (heavy) cream
150–200g (5½–7oz) parmesan, grated, plus extra to serve
½ tsp garlic granules
½ tsp fine sea salt
½ tsp freshly ground black pepper, plus extra to serve
generously buttered sourdough toast, to serve

EQUIPMENT
chopping board—knife—deep frying pan
wooden spoon—grater

1. Pour the chicken stock pot into a deep frying over a medium-high heat then throw in the broccoli. The broccoli needs to be chopped up pretty small so that it softens quickly and has a similar texture to the butter beans by the time the dish is served. Next add the butter beans, cream and parmesan along with the garlic granules, salt and pepper. Taste and adjust the seasoning if necessary. Simmer for 15 minutes until the sauce is thick and creamy.

2. Serve sprinkled with more black pepper and with generously buttered toast to scoop through that creamy sauce.

ALTERNATIVE INGREDIENTS
Make it vegan: replace the cream with vegan cream, the parmesan with 2 tablespoons nutritional yeast and the chicken stock with vegetable stock
Butter (lima) beans: use cannellini beans

Sloppy Joe Pasta

SERVES 4–6
TOTAL TIME: 45 MINUTES

If you follow me on my socials you may have seen this recipe pop up already, but now, after a few tweaks, I think I have found the formula for the best ever Sloppy Joe pasta. Sloppy Joe has sweet, tangy undertones, which makes its flavour different from a bolognese, however if you love the tomato base and ground meat element of a bolognese, this is one for you to try. It's perfect for a quick lunch or family dinner when you want to please everyone, but it can also be a slow-cooking, bottom-of-the-oven kind of tea for cold winter days.

2 tbsp olive oil
2 onions, diced
1 bulb of garlic, cloves finely chopped
200g (7oz) chestnut (cremini) mushrooms, very finely chopped
500g (1lb 2oz) minced (ground) beef
2 x 400g (14oz) tins of good-quality chopped tomatoes
1 beef stock pot
1 tsp Worcestershire sauce
1 tsp light brown sugar
large pinch of fine sea salt
a good glug of milk
100g (3½oz) parmesan, grated
350g (12½oz) macaroni
cheese of your choice, grated (I like sharp cheddar)

EQUIPMENT
chopping board—knife—large, deep frying pan—wooden spoon—saucepan—grater

1. Heat the oil in a large, deep frying pan over a medium heat, then add the onions and garlic and fry for 4–6 minutes until softened. Throw in the mushrooms and let them wilt down and cook for a further 5 minutes, then add the beef. Brown the beef, breaking it up with a wooden spoon, for about 6–8 minutes until it is cooked. Now add the chopped tomatoes, stock pot, Worcestershire sauce, brown sugar and salt. Let this simmer together for 5–10 minutes.

2. Meanwhile, bring a large saucepan of water to the boil and cook the macaroni according to the packet instructions. Drain and set aside.

3. Once the sauce has reduced a little, add the milk and parmesan and cook a for a further 5 minutes until you have a thick, well-reduced sauce. Stir the pasta into the sauce, then sprinkle over as much cheese as you like!

ALTERNATIVE INGREDIENTS
Mushrooms: use grated courgette or aubergine (aubergine)
Chopped tomatoes: use fresh chopped tomatoes or passata (sieved tomatoes)
Minced (ground) beef: use half beef and half pork
Milk: use single (light) or double (heavy) cream

ONE PAN

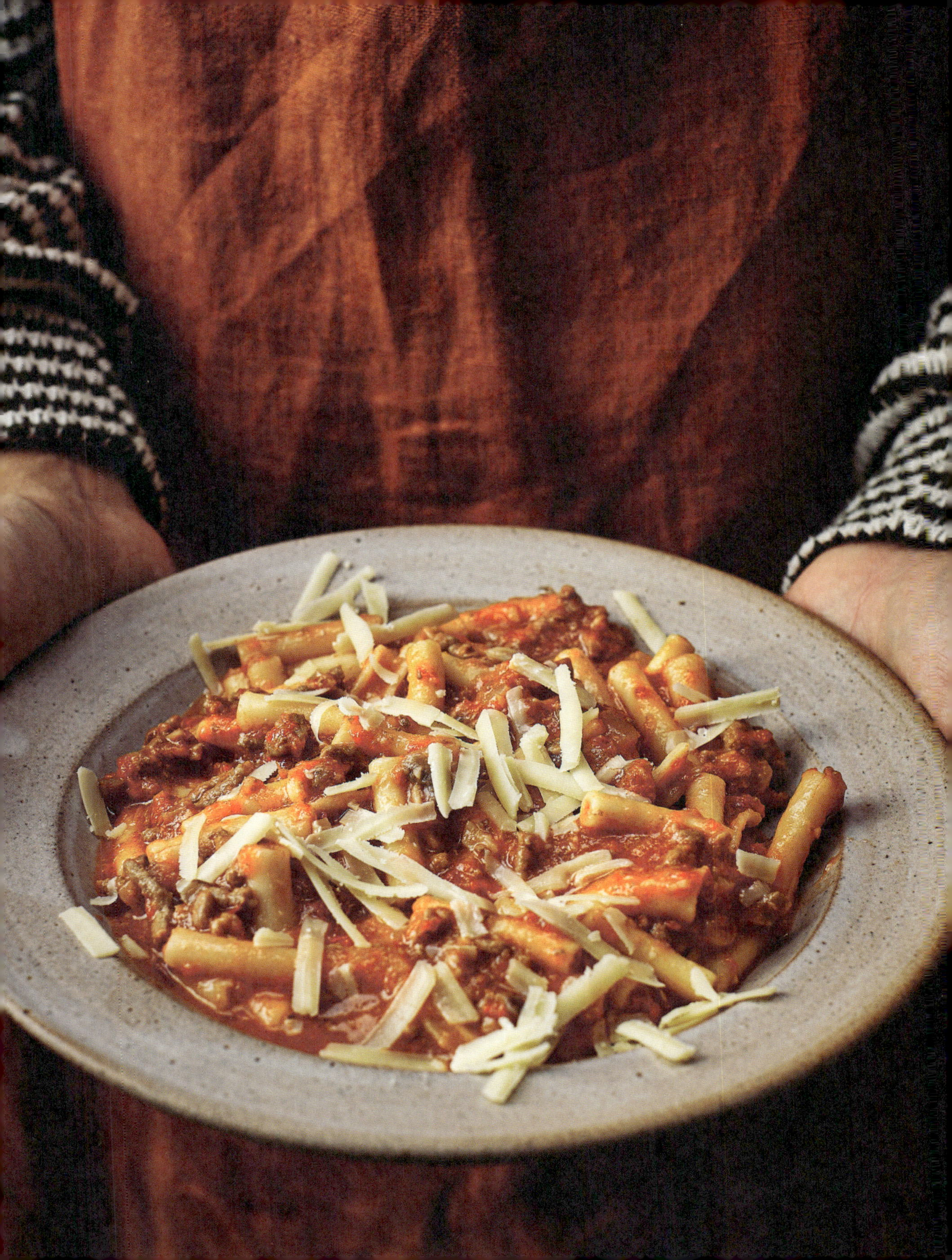

Haddock Kedgeree with Jammy Eggs

SERVES 4
TOTAL TIME: 30 MINUTES

There is something deeply comforting about a warm bowl of kedgeree, tender flakes of smoked haddock with fragrant spiced rice feels like a hug in a bowl. Kedgeree is a curried rice dish made with flaked fish and usually topped with boiled eggs. As a child, this was my worst nightmare, but as an adult, I love it! This one-pan version has a few non-traditional elements that make it speedy and delicious. It's a midweek favourite that I always look forward to making. Although the jammy eggs are optional here, I do recommend making them as they add an extra element of flavour which really lifts the dish.

2 large eggs (optional)
2 tbsp olive oil
2 onions, finely diced
6 garlic cloves, finely chopped
1 red or green chilli, finely chopped
2 tsp medium curry powder
2 tsp garam masala
4 smoked haddock fillets
200g raw peeled king prawns (jumbo shrimp)
500g (1lb 2oz) microwavable basmati rice
120g (4oz/¾ cup) frozen peas
zest of 1 lemon, plus a squeeze of juice
a handful of chopped coriander (cilantro) leaves, to serve
freshly ground black pepper, to serve

EQUIPMENT
chopping board—knife—large saucepan or casserole dish (Dutch oven)—wooden spoon—small saucepan—zester

1. Make the jammy eggs, if using. Bring a large saucepan or casserole dish of water to the boil, then reduce to a gentle boil. Carefully add the eggs and cook for 7 minutes. As they're cooking, fill a bowl with ice-cold water. After 7 minutes, remove the eggs from the pan and pop them straight into the iced water. Set aside for 4–5 minutes.

2. Heat the oil in the same pan over a medium heat and fry the onion, garlic and chilli for 5 minutes, then stir in the curry powder and garam masala. Add the haddock and cook for 5 minutes, then break up the rice and add it along with the prawns, peas, lemon zest and a good squeeze of lemon juice.

3. Peel the eggs and slice them into eighths, then scatter on top of the kedgeree along with a sprinkling of coriander and back pepper.

ALTERNATIVE INGREDIENTS
Haddock: use any meaty, flavourful fish, such as cod, kippers or salmon
Garam masala: use a teaspoon each of ground coriander and cumin (or just use curry powder)

ONE PAN

ONE PAN 43

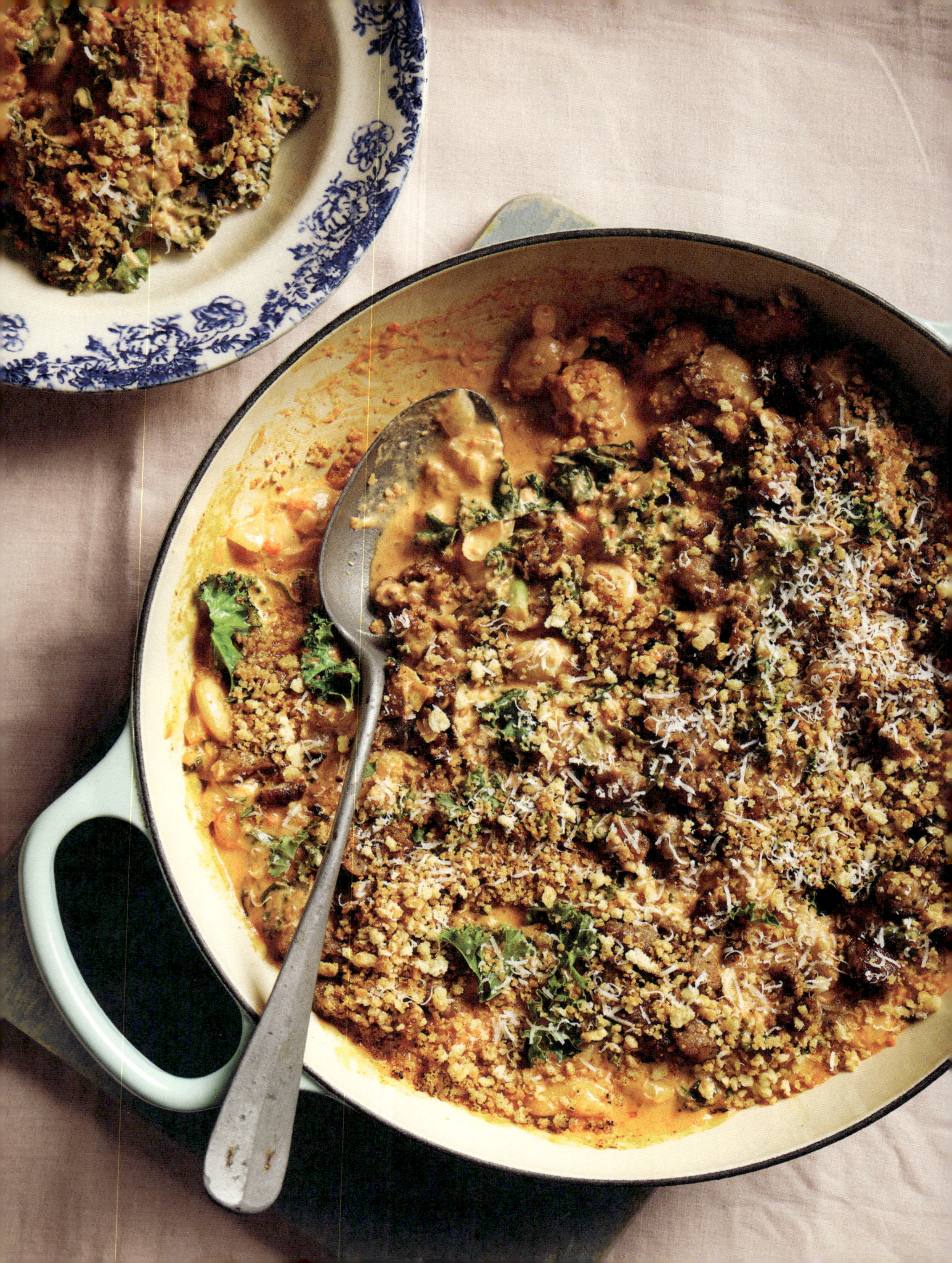

Creamy Sausage & Bean Bake with a Crunchy Topping

SERVES 2
TOTAL TIME: 30 MINUTES

Next time you're having a lazy weekend at home and are wondering what sort of lunch or dinner you can make that you can eat with a big spoon in your favourite bowl, this is it. One of my favourite things to do is get some warm, fresh bread and scoop creamy beans onto it. It's so indulgent and delicious.

Try mixing the breadcrumbs with parmesan, garlic granules, salt or any other herbs and spices to elevate the crunchy topping.

1 tbsp olive oil
2 onions, diced
6–7 garlic cloves, finely chopped
4–6 pork sausages
400g (14oz) tin of chopped tomatoes
500–600g (1lb 2–5oz) drained jarred beans of your choice (butter/lima beans, queen chickpeas/garbanzo beans and cannellini beans are my favourite)
400g (14oz) spinach or kale
large pinch of smoked sea salt
300ml (10fl oz/1¼ cups) double (heavy) cream
60g (2oz) parmesan, grated, plus extra to serve
250g (9oz/2½ cups) panko breadcrumbs

EQUIPMENT
chopping board—knife—casserole dish (Dutch oven)—wooden spoon—grater

1. Preheat the oven to 180°C (160°C fan/350°F/gas mark 4).

2. Heat the oil in a casserole dish, then add the onion and garlic and soften for 5 minutes. Tear the sausages into bite-size pieces and throw them into the pan, then fry for 6–8 minutes until cooked through with crispy, browned edges.

3. Next, add the chopped tomatoes, beans, spinach, smoked sea salt, double cream and parmesan. Cook for 5 minutes until thickened, then sprinkle over the breadcrumbs.

4. Pop the dish in the oven and cook for 8–10 minutes until the breadcrumbs are crispy. Sprinkle with more parmesan.

ALTERNATIVE INGREDIENTS
Sausages: use minced (ground) chicken, beef or pork
Make it veggie: use chunks of halloumi instead of sausages and use vegetarian parmesan

ONE PAN

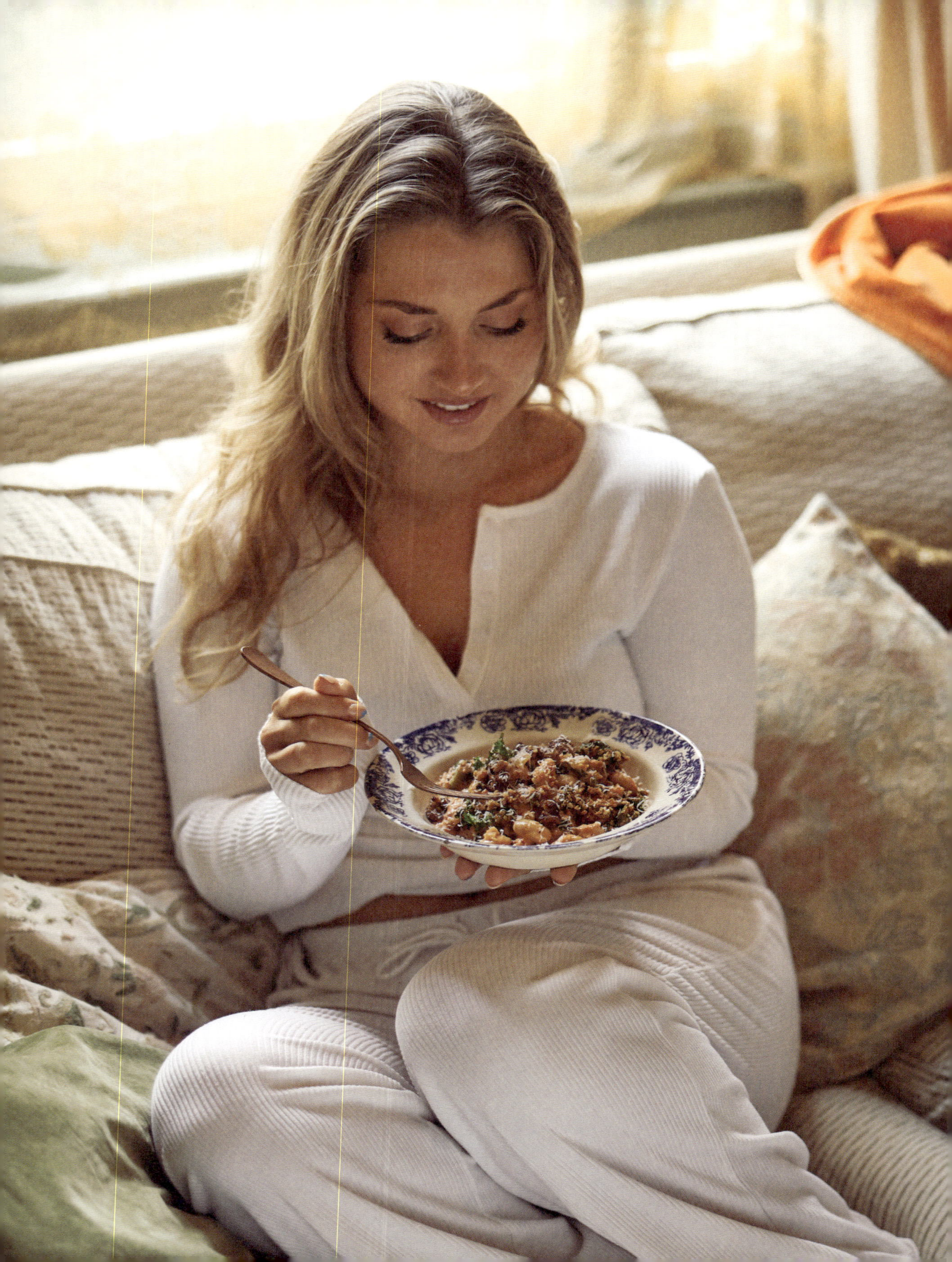

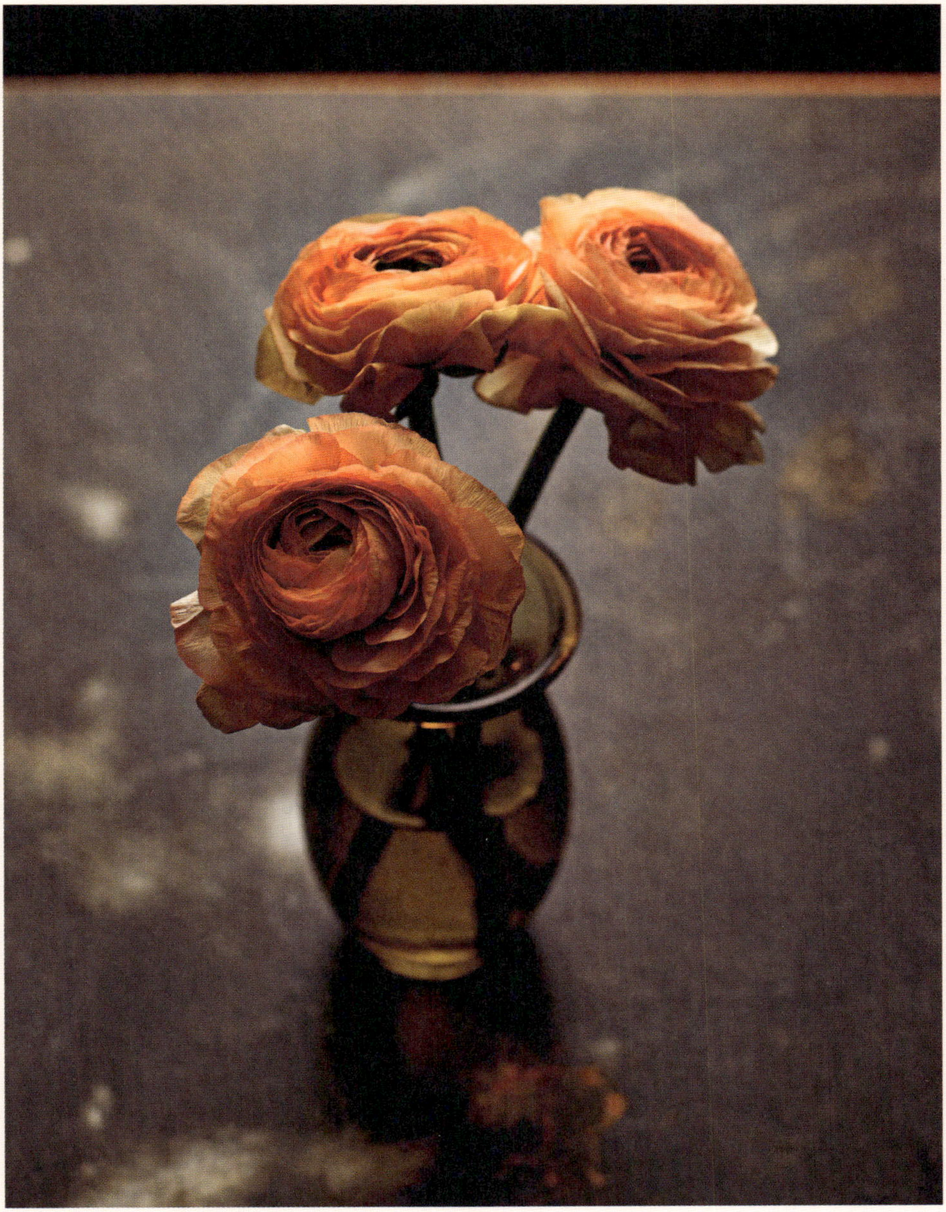

Spicy Peanut Butter Noodles

SERVES 2
TOTAL TIME: 10–15 MINUTES

This is the perfect go to meal especially when you need something quick and bursting with salty flavours. My fiancé loves these noodles so they're on rotation for our dinners in the week. This dish really does have everything: it's creamy, spicy and so easy to make. Next time you're craving rich, flavourful noodles, don't get take out … make these instead.

The finer you chop the shallots, garlic, ginger and chilli, the quicker they will soften. While the noodles are cooking, chop up all your garnishes so you can tuck in while it's piping hot.

2 tsp sesame oil
2 banana shallots, finely chopped
6–8 garlic cloves, finely chopped
5cm (2in) piece of ginger, finely chopped
1 red chilli, deseeded and finely chopped
1 heaped tbsp smooth peanut butter
2–3 tbsp light soy sauce
2 tbsp maple syrup
700–750ml (1½–1¾ pints/3–3¼ cups) chicken or vegetable stock
250g (9oz) ramen noodles

TO SERVE
chopped spring onions (scallions)
crispy fried onions
chopped coriander (cilantro)
sliced red chilli
lime wedges
crispy chilli oil

EQUIPMENT
chopping board—knife—large saucepan
whisk or wooden spoon

1. Heat the sesame oil in a large saucepan over a medium heat and throw in the shallots, garlic, ginger and chilli. Let this cook until fragrant and the shallots are starting to soften, making sure that the garlic doesn't catch.

2. Add the peanut butter, soy sauce and maple syrup and mix to form a paste. Next, slowly add the stock (doing this slowly means the peanut butter will be evenly distributed). Throw in the ramen noodles and cook for 3–4 minutes.

3. Serve the noodles and broth topped with chopped spring onions, crispy onions, coriander, sliced red chilli, a squeeze of lime juice and lots of chilli oil.

ALTERNATIVE INGREDIENTS
Sesame oil: use olive, vegetable or coconut oil
Shallots: use onions (but the taste will be a bit stronger)
Smooth peanut butter: use crunchy peanut butter
Maple syrup: use honey
Ramen noodles: use egg noodles

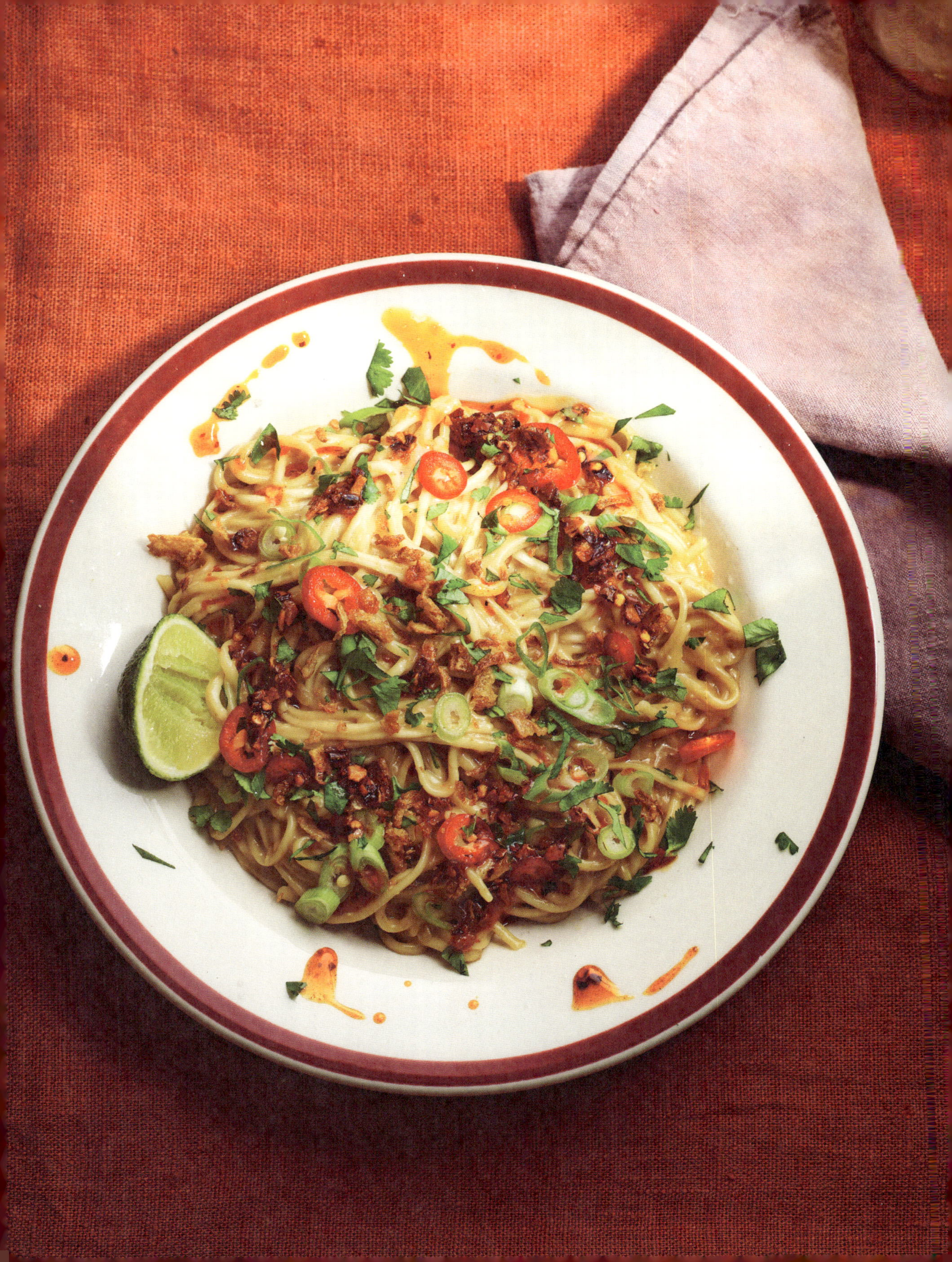

Prawn & Pancetta Risotto

SERVES 4
TOTAL TIME: 25–30 MINUTES

A creamy indulgent risotto is probably in every family favourite cookbook for a reason. In my version, I dot salty bites of pancetta throughout the velvety, rich parmesan sauce which brings every bite together. Adding a splash of dry white wine or prosecco adds a touch of elegance perfect to be cooked on date nights or to treat your mum, sister or cousin. It's simple enough for a night in but with the truffle oil on top you can really impress with this dish.

150g (5½oz) pancetta, roughly chopped
1 tbsp butter
1 onion, diced
6 garlic cloves, finely chopped
½ tsp paprika
½ tsp freshly ground black pepper, plus extra to serve
1 tbsp chopped chives
400g (14oz/generous 1¾ cups) risotto rice
750ml (25fl oz/3 cups) chicken stock
150ml (5fl oz/⅔ cup) dry white wine or prosecco
300ml (10fl oz/1¼ cups) double (heavy) cream
200g (7oz) parmesan, grated, plus extra to serve
350g (12oz) raw peeled king prawns (jumbo shrimp)
drizzle of truffle oil or extra virgin olive oil, to serve

EQUIPMENT
saucepan with a lid—chopping board knife wooden spoon—grater

1. Put the pancetta into a saucepan over a medium heat and fry for 4–6 minutes until golden and crisp, so that it has released all of its fatty flavours.

2. Remove the pancetta from the pan and set it aside, then throw in the butter, onion and garlic and fry for 4–6 minutes until the onion is soft and the garlic is fragrant. Now add the paprika, black pepper and half the chopped chives. Stir in the rice, then add the stock, wine and cream. Stir to combine then cover and cook for 10–12 minutes.

3. When the rice is 90 per cent cooked and has absorbed all of the flavours from the stock, pancetta and cream, mix through the parmesan and prawns. Cook for a further 2 minutes until the prawns are pink and opaque and the rice is perfectly cooked.

4. Serve scattered with the pancetta, remaining chives, some grated parmesan, black pepper and the oil of your choice.

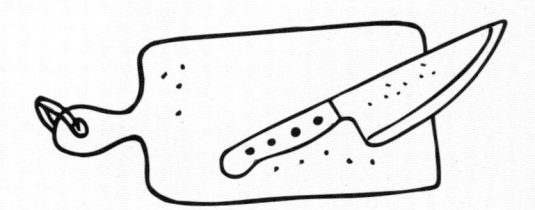

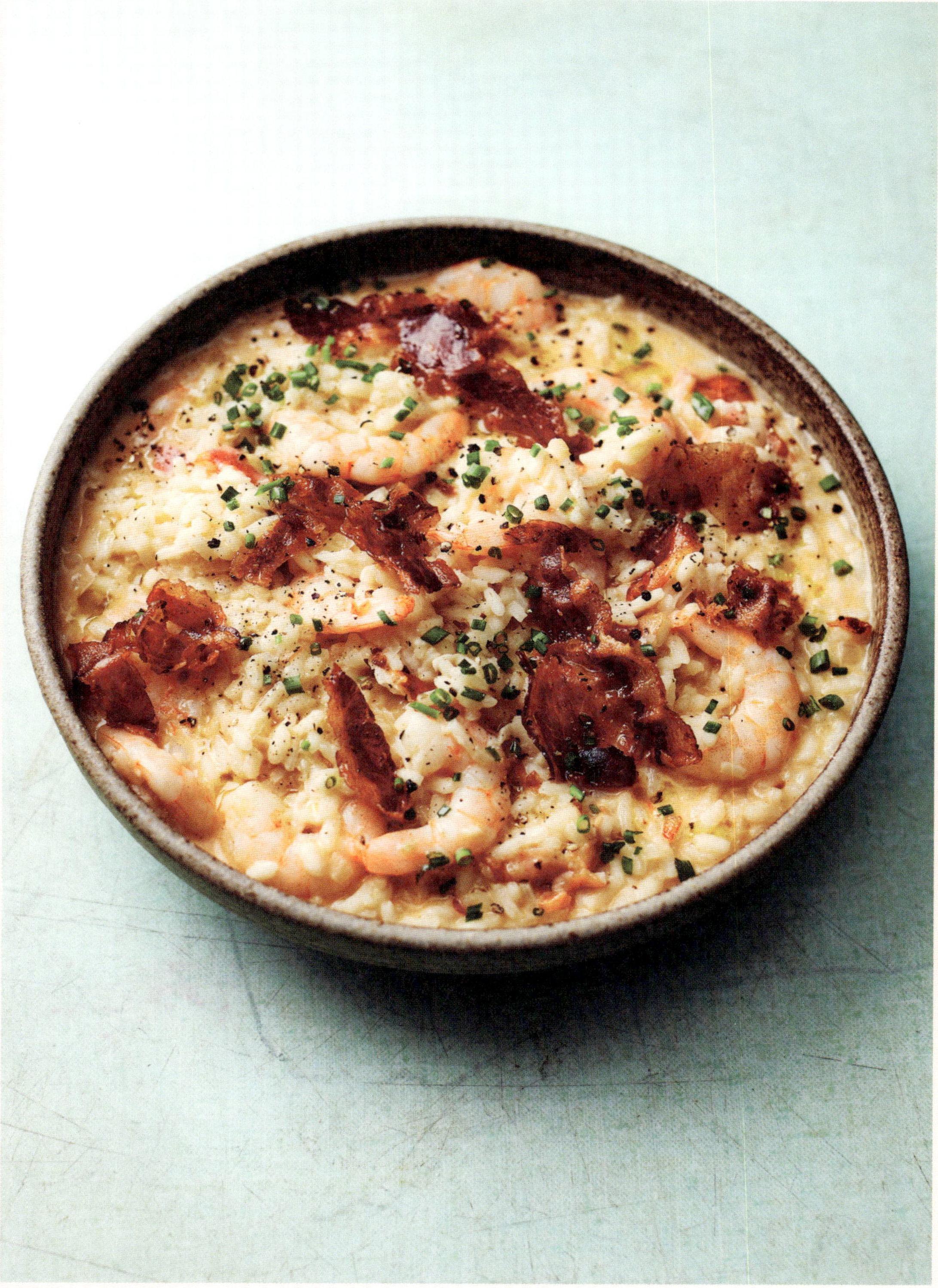

Georgie's Creamy Prawn Orzo

SERVES 2
TOTAL TIME: 20 MINUTES

My sister has always been a sucker for a good pasta dish and when I introduced her to orzo, pasta that you can spoon into your mouth without making a mess, she was sold! When I started working on my second book it was natural that her beloved prawn orzo made the cut, it's something she whips up most weeks and it is perfect. It delivers big on flavour with tender prawns, silky orzo and a creamy sauce that binds everything together. The definition of comfort in a bowl.

2–4 tbsp extra virgin olive oil, plus extra to serve
1 banana shallot, finely diced
6 garlic cloves, grated
250g (9oz) cherry tomatoes, halved
300ml (10fl oz/1¼ cups) double (heavy) cream
1 chicken stock pot
150ml (5fl oz/⅔ cup) white wine
zest and juice of 1 lemon, plus extra zest to serve
200g (7oz/1 cup) orzo
80g (2¾oz) parmesan, grated, plus extra to serve
a handful of chopped tarragon, plus extra to serve
200g (7oz) raw peeled king prawns (jumbo shrimp)
freshly ground black pepper

EQUIPMENT
chopping board—knife—saucepan with a lid—zester—wooden spoon—grater

1. Heat the oil in a saucepan over a medium heat, then add the shallot and garlic and fry for a minute or two until fragrant. Now throw in the tomatoes and cook for 4–5 minutes, pressing the back of each tomato as they're cooking to release a sweet juice. Once you have a beautiful silky tomato sauce, reduce the heat to medium-low. Add the cream, stock pot, white wine, lemon zest and juice and orzo. Cover and cook for 6 minutes until the orzo is three-quarters cooked.

2. Remove the lid and stir in the parmesan, tarragon and prawns. Cover again and cook for a further 2–3 minutes until the prawns and orzo are cooked through. Garnish with extra parmesan, black pepper, lemon zest, chopped tarragon or olive oil – your choice!

Juicy Spiced Chicken Legs

SERVES 4
TOTAL TIME: 45 MINUTES

This is something I make during summer, in those wonderful periods when I'm making myself a mocktail or cocktail or pouring a crisp glass of rosé every weekend, when I've been sitting outside in the garden every day for dinner and waking up to see sunshine. Serve this with baguette or garlic bread because the pan juices are unbelievable. It's also great with a salad (see pages 148–178) in the garden for friends for a stunning dinner.

3 tbsp olive oil
2 banana shallots, finely chopped
1 red chilli, deseeded and finely chopped
6 garlic cloves, grated
2 sprigs of rosemary
2 sprigs of thyme
100ml (3½fl oz/scant ½ cup) chicken stock
4 large chicken legs
1 tsp ground cumin
1 tsp ground coriander
1 tsp ground ginger
1 tsp garlic granules
1 tsp onion granules
1 tsp paprika
1 tsp ground turmeric
1 tsp dried oregano
large pinch of fine sea salt
large pinch of freshly ground black pepper
zest and juice of 2 lemons

TO SERVE
chopped parsley
baguette or garlic bread

EQUIPMENT
chopping board—knife—zester—large ovenproof frying pan—wooden spoon

1. Preheat the oven to 200°C (180°C fan/400°F/gas mark 6).

2. Heat the oil in a large ovenproof frying pan over a medium heat, then add the shallots, chilli and garlic and fry for 4–6 minutes until the shallots and garlic have softened. Now throw in the sprigs of rosemary and thyme along and pour in the chicken stock.

3. Meanwhile, pat the chicken legs dry with paper towels, then coat the chicken with the spices – you don't need another bowl for this; you can do it in the packet the chicken has come in.

4. Place the chicken in the pan skin-side up (this is going to get the skin crispy), shake any excess spices into the pan, then add the salt and pepper and the lemon zest.

5. Roast this in the oven for 35–40 minutes until the chicken is crispy and cooked through. Remove the pan from the heat and squeeze over the lemon juice, then finish with a sprinkle of parsley serve. Now tuck in, soaking up all the juices in the pan with some baguette or garlic bread!

54 ONE PAN

Love at First Bite Cannellini Beans with Dollops of Pesto

SERVES 2
TOTAL TIME: 20 MINUTES

Who says a big bowl of comfort food can't be meat free? I set out to create a vegetarian twist on the popular 'Marry Me Chicken' and this recipe was born. Pairing creamy cannellini beans with a rich tomato and cream sauce with aromatic basil, I pulled at the basil strings and included dollops of pesto to the top for an added punch. Scoop these beans up with some buttered sourdough toast and I promise it will win over anyone.

Using as many different types and colours of tomatoes as you can really brightens up this dish and you will notice a sweeter hum of flavour, too.

1 tbsp extra virgin olive oil, plus extra to serve
1 red or brown onion, diced
6 garlic cloves, finely chopped
200g (7oz) mixed tomatoes (red, orange, yellow, green), roughly chopped
1–2 Romano peppers, diced
2 large tbsp tomato purée (paste)
150ml (5fl oz/⅔ cup) double (heavy) cream, plus extra to serve
400–500g (14oz–1lb 2oz) drained jarred butter (lima) beans
60g (2oz/) parmesan, grated
large pinch of smoked sea salt
handful of basil leaves, plus extra to serve
100g (3½oz) basil pesto
sourdough bread, to serve

EQUIPMENT
chopping board—knife—deep frying pan wooden spoon—grater

1 Heat the oil in a deep frying pan over medium heat, then add the onion and garlic and fry for 4–6 minutes until softened. Next, add the tomatoes and peppers and cook for a further 5 minutes until softening and releasing some juices. Add the tomato purée and cream along with the parmesan and stir until well combined and you have a lovely sauce, then throw in the butter beans, salt and basil. Let this bubble away for 3–5 minutes until thickened and warm through.

2 Serve with dollops of pesto over the top with a generous drizzle of olive oil, more cream and some basil leaves. Tuck in with lots of sourdough bread.

ALTERNATIVE INGREDIENTS
Butter (lima) beans: use cannellini beans
Basil pesto: use red pesto
Mixed tomatoes: use tinned chopped tomatoes
Double (heavy) cream: use crème fraîche or cream cheese, or try single (light) cream (I would recommend adding more parmesan)

Taco Tuesday Pan Dinner

SERVES 4
TOTAL TIME: 30 MINUTES

Once a week, my fiancé Jake and I will have fajitas, tacos or enchiladas for dinner. We both love a bit of spice and anything packed with flavour, and the shop-bought kits are so convenient. I know some people may think that using these little packets is 'cheating', but if you can grab something that makes cooking delicious comfort food easier (we all have busy schedules) then in my eyes you're winning!

This is perfect for meal prep, as you can make the sauce in advance then add tortilla chips and toppings as you need.

2 tbsp olive oil
1 onion, diced
6–7 garlic cloves, finely chopped
1 red chilli, finely chopped
400g (14oz) 15% fat minced (ground) beef
20–30g (¾–1oz) taco seasoning of your choice
1 tsp fine sea salt
1 tsp freshly ground black pepper
400g (14oz) black beans, drained
300g (10½oz) salsa of your choice, or to taste

TOPPINGS
tortilla chips
grated mature cheddar or red Leicester
sliced avocado
lime wedges
coriander (cilantro)

EQUIPMENT
chopping board—knife—deep frying pan
wooden spoon—grater

1. Heat the oil in a deep frying pan, then add the onion and garlic and fry for 4–6 minutes until softened. Add the chilli and cook for a further 2 minutes, then throw in the beef mince and let it brown, about 8–10 minutes.

2. Once the beef is browned, add the taco seasoning, salt and pepper and stir well, then add the black beans and salsa and let this cook for 5–7 minutes until the beans are soft.

3. Serve in bowls with the toppings of your choice – I love to have mine with tortilla chips, LOTS of cheese (Jake knows how much lots of cheese is for me!), avocado and a big squeeze of lime, then all sprinkled with coriander.

ALTERNATIVE INGREDIENTS

Minced (ground) beef: I find that 15 per cent fat beef has more flavour, but you can use a leaner mince, or use minced chicken
Taco seasoning: use a mixture of seasonings that you have in your cupboard instead (try 1 teaspoon garlic granules, 1 teaspoon onion granules, 2 teaspoons smoked paprika, 2 teaspoons ground cumin, 2 teaspoons ground coriander and ½ teaspoon dried oregano)
Black beans: use red kidney beans or even sweetcorn
Salsa: use good-quality tinned chopped tomatoes

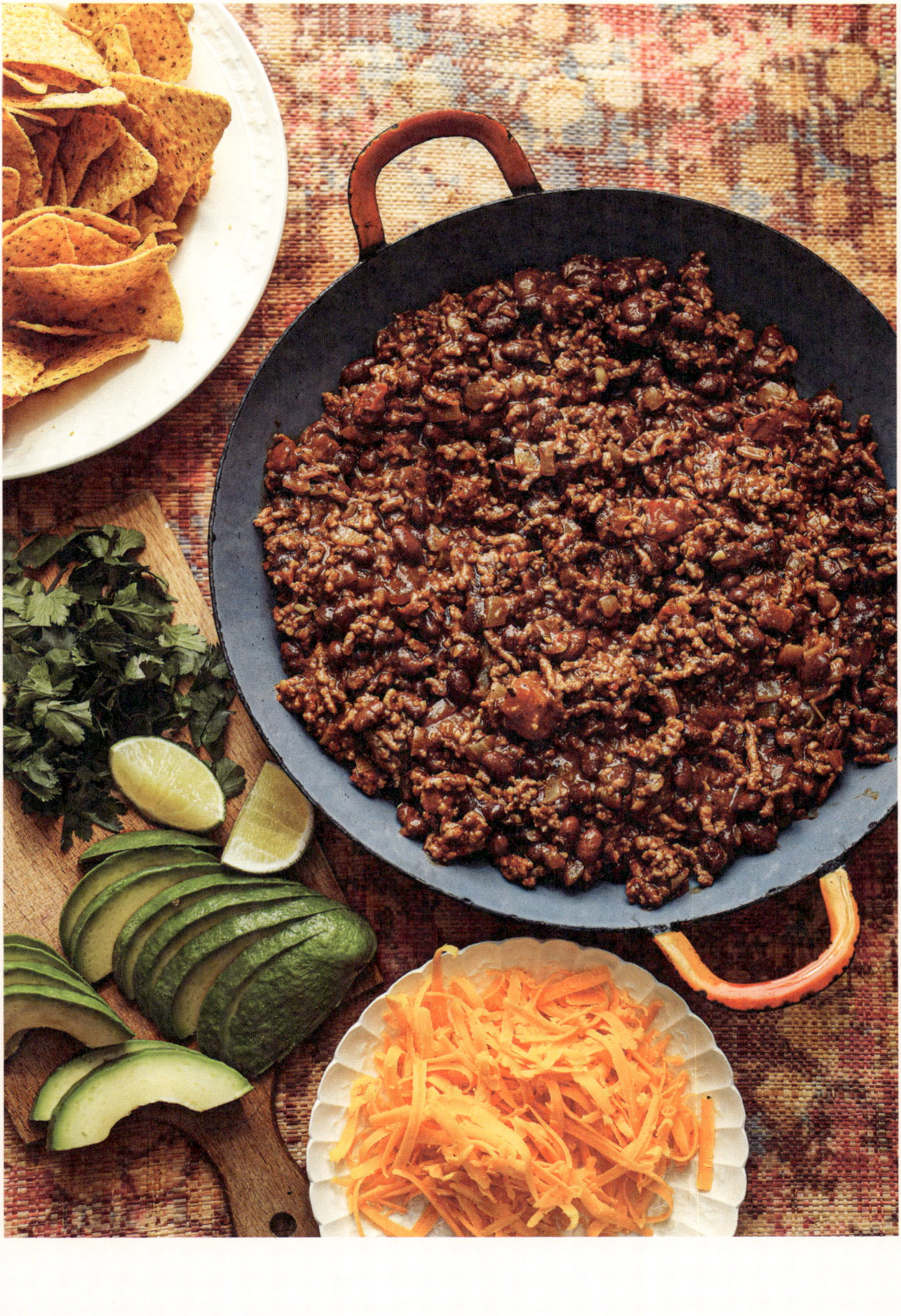

ONE TRAY

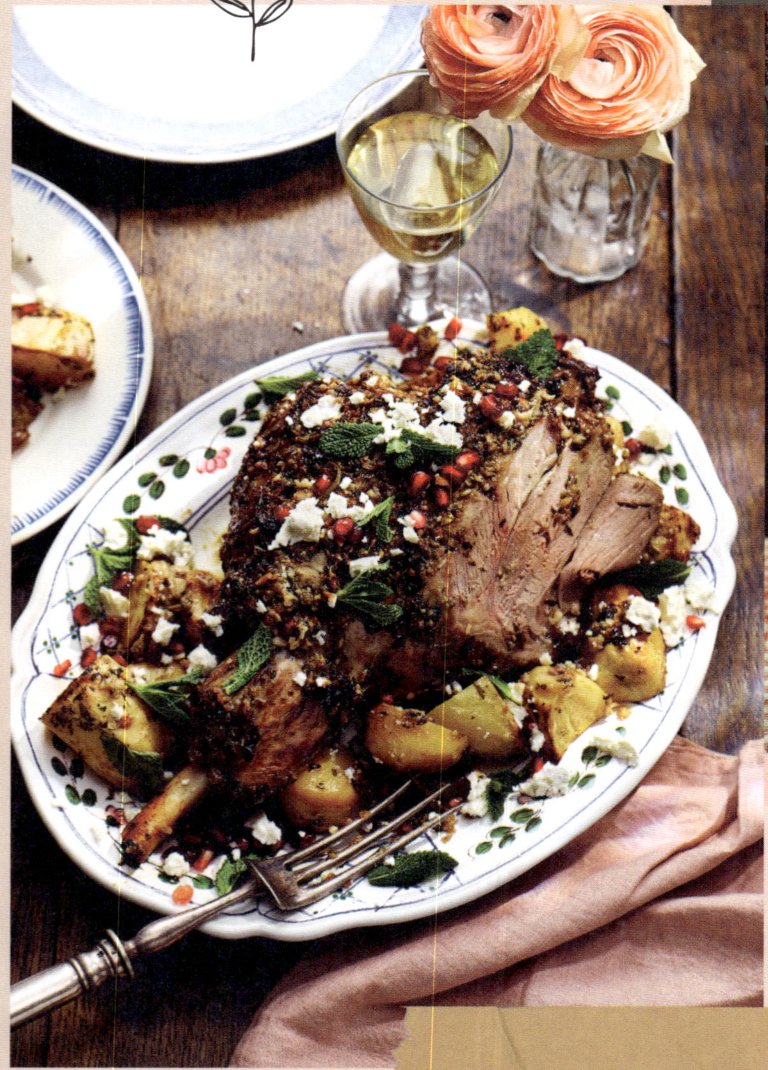

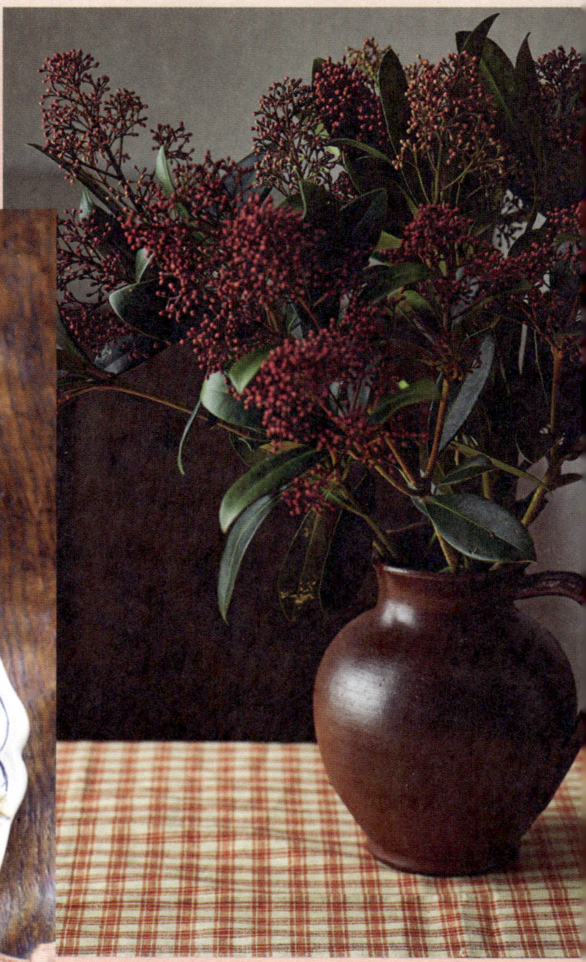

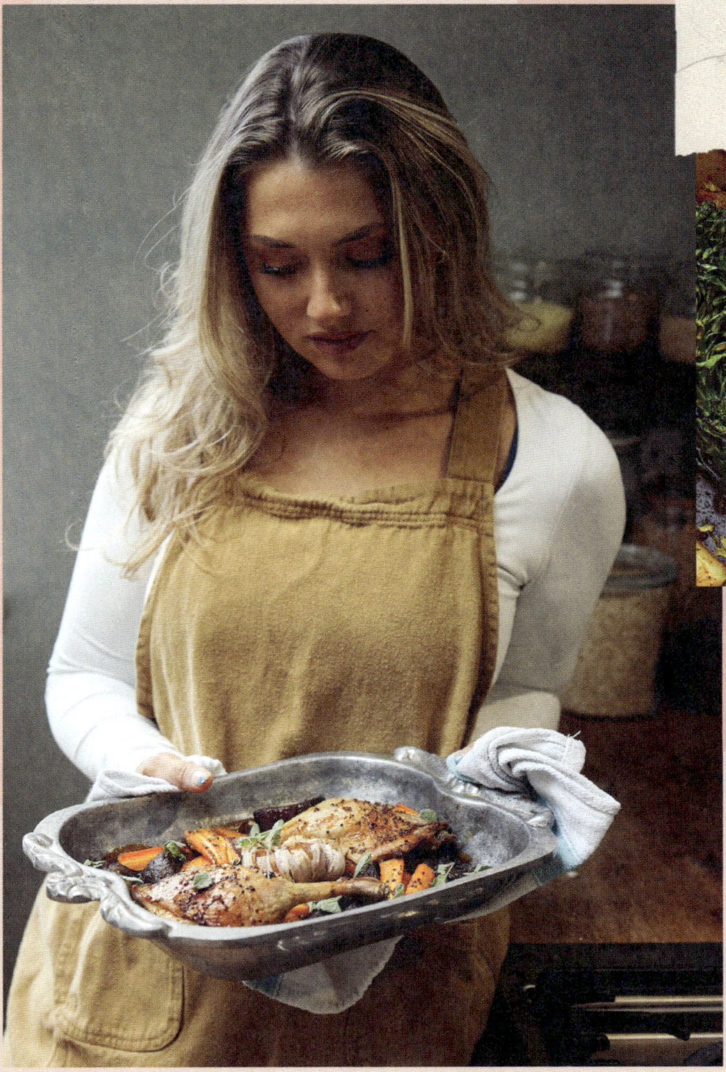

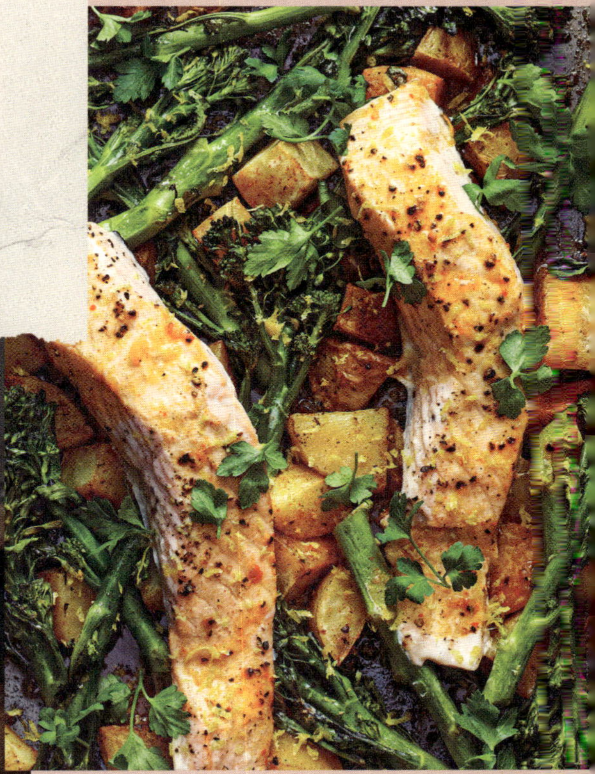

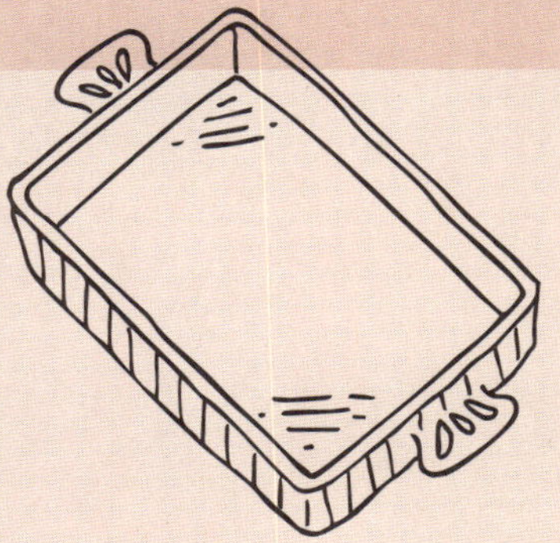

Maple-roasted Duck Leg and Veggie Traybake

SERVES 2
TOTAL TIME: 50 MINUTES

This is a gorgeous recipe that I like to make as autumn approaches – when the colours of the trees turn to oranges, reds and yellows, I know it's time to get the maple-roasted recipes out. The sweetness of the maple syrup is complemented beautifully by the seasonal vegetables. And all you need to do is put it in a tray and let the oven do the work.

6 carrots, sliced lengthways and then in half
4 cooked beetroots (beets), quartered
2 red onions, cut into eighths
2 skin-on duck legs
4–6 tbsp olive oil, plus extra for drizzling
3 tbsp maple syrup
1 tbsp wholegrain mustard
zest and juice of 1 orange
large pinch of fine sea salt
plenty of freshly ground black pepper
1 bulb of garlic
oregano leaves, to serve (optional)

EQUIPMENT
chopping board—knife—roasting tin
jug (pitcher)—zester—whisk

1. Preheat the oven to 200°C (180°C fan/400°F/gas mark 6).

2. Put the carrots, beetroots and onions into a roasting tin and place the duck legs on top.

3. In a bowl or a jug (pitcher), whisk together the oil, maple syrup, mustard, orange zest and juice, then drizzle this over everything in the tin. Sprinkle with the salt and pepper. Now get your hands in there and mix everything together so the maple syrup and seasoning is evenly spread out over all the veggies and your duck (give an extra little sprinkle of salt and pepper to the skin of each duck leg).

4. Cut the top off the bulb of garlic off and place it in the middle of the tin, then drizzle it with olive oil (this roast garlic is going to give the dish the most delicious, delicate hum of garlic).

5. Place the tin in the oven and roast for 35–40 minutes until the duck legs are crispy and cooked through. Remove the tin from the oven, squeeze out the soft garlic and mix it with the vegetables. Sprinkle with the oregano, if using, then serve.

ALTERNATIVE INGREDIENTS

Vegetables: use any seasonable vegetables that are suitable for roasting
Seasonings: add or take away whatever you'd like: a little hint of chilli is always a lovely addition
Maple syrup: use honey or golden syrup

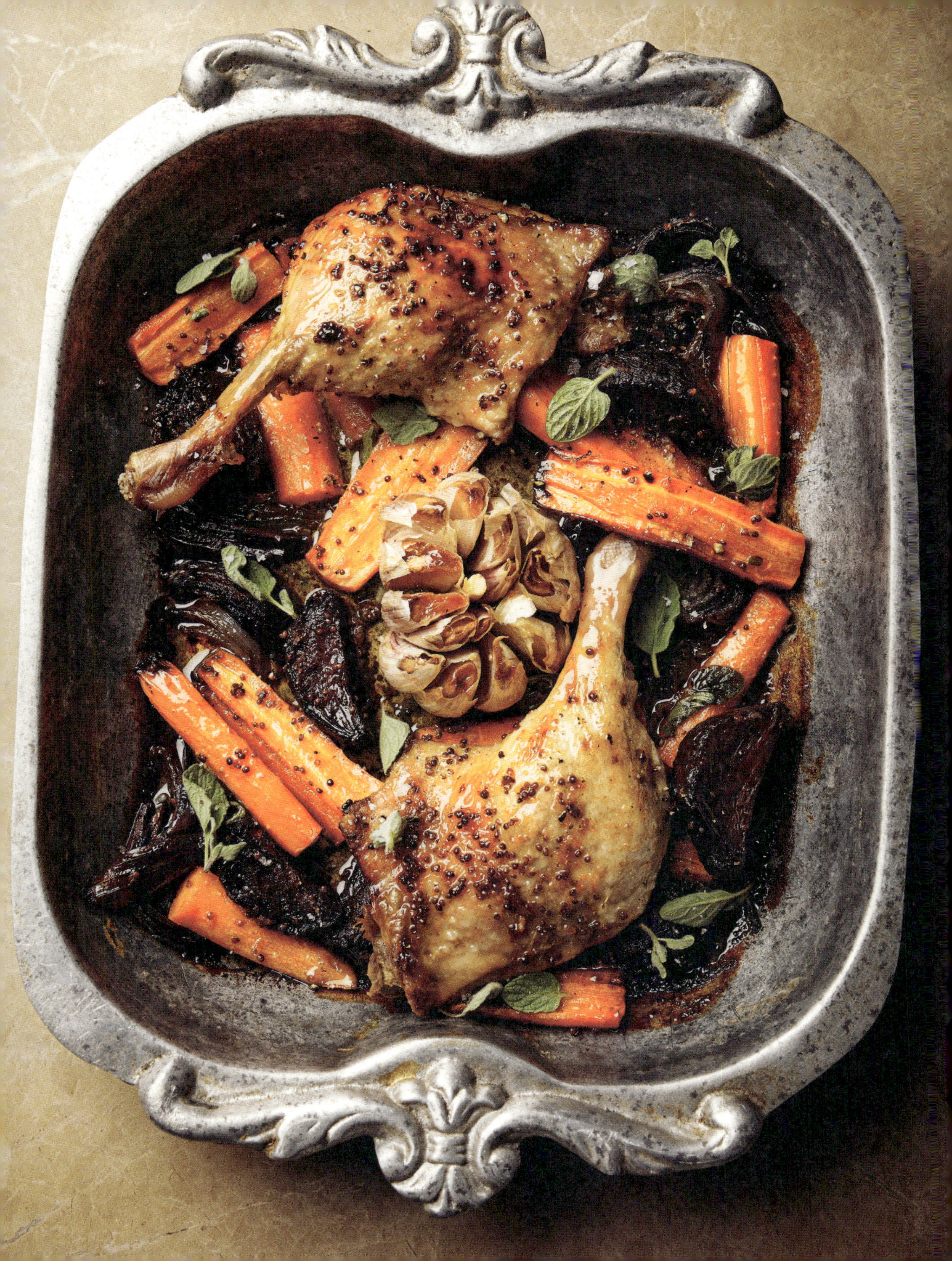

Cheesy Pesto Chicken Bake

SERVES 4
TOTAL TIME: 35 MINUTES

If you're craving something really cheesy, this pesto chicken is the recipe for you. It takes 30 minutes in the oven and you don't have to stress about it at all. Serve it on top of some cosy carbs like pasta or rice or with fresh vegetables or salad – utter comfort food that is great in winter or when the weather is warm!

If you're going to serve this with pasta, I really recommend mixing the pasta through the remaining sauce in the tray and serving the cheesy chicken on top. Or, if you're making a salad, whack this in with some mixed leaves, toasted pine nuts, Parma ham and lots of parmesan – such a delicious combination.

2 tbsp Greek yoghurt
190g (6½oz) basil pesto
100g (3½oz) parmesan, grated
½ tsp fine sea salt
½ tsp freshly ground black pepper
4 chicken breasts
250g (9oz) grated mozzarella (pre-grated works really well here)
handful of basil leaves

EQUIPMENT
grater—baking tray (pan)

1. Preheat the oven to 200°C (180°C fan/400°F/gas mark 6).

2. Put the Greek yoghurt, pesto, parmesan, salt and pepper into a baking tray and mix them together. Add the chicken breasts and coat each breast in the mixture so they're thickly coated. Sprinkle the mozzarella over the top of the chicken. Bake in the oven for 25–30 minutes until the chicken is cooked through. Remove the dish from the oven and serve with the basil leaves.

ALTERNATIVE INGREDIENTS
Basil pesto: use red pesto and throw a few cherry tomatoes in the tray (around 150–200g/5½–7oz).

Garlic Butter Spatchcocked Chicken

SERVES 4-6
TOTAL TIME: 1¼ HOURS

This recipe has a special place in my heart. I first made it a few years ago when I wanted to do something a little extra for the Sunday roast dinner, and since then I have been making it for almost every other meal! My partner and I often roast a chicken for the week because it provides several meals and sandwiches and makes those midweek meals that bit better. Don't be intimidated by spatchcocking – just get yourself a pair of scissors and take it step by step; with just a few snips you've done it and learned a new skill in the kitchen.

If you're struggling with spatchcocking, there are plenty of videos available online. You can save the spine to make a stock.

1 large chicken
250g (9oz) salted butter, softened
1 tbsp chopped rosemary
1 tbsp chopped parsley
1 tbsp chopped thyme
1 bulb of garlic, cloves chopped
large pinch of fine sea salt
200ml (7fl oz/generous ¾ cup) double (heavy) cream (optional)
80g (2¾oz) parmesan, grated (optional)

EQUIPMENT
chopping board—kitchen scissors—roasting tin—mixing bowl—wooden spoon—small saucepan—grater—whisk

1. Preheat the oven to 220°C (200°C fan/425°F/gas mark 7).

2. Start by spatchcocking the chicken. Place it breast side down on a board. Starting at the tail, use scissors to cut along both sides of the spine. Once you've done that, the spine should come away from the chicken. Flip the chicken over and use both hands to press down between the breasts until you hear a crack. Flatten the chicken out and place in a roasting tin. Easy!

3. Next, mix together the butter, rosemary, parsley, thyme, garlic and salt. If you want to make the sauce (I suggest you do!), set aside 1 tablespoon of this garlic butter.

4. Separate the chicken skin from the chicken by gently rubbing your finger between the skin and the breast, then push some of the garlic butter between the skin and breast and spread it out evenly underneath the skin. Use any remaining butter to smear evenly over the skin of the chicken. This is going to make the most moist chicken ever!

5. Roast the chicken in the oven for 45–50 minutes (depending on the size of your chicken). When cooked, the skin should be golden and crispy, and the juices should run clear.

6. Five minutes before the chicken is done, combine the cream, parmesan and reserved garlic butter in a small saucepan over a medium heat and whisk until thickened.

7. Remove the chicken from the oven and pour over the sauce.

ALTERNATIVE INGREDIENTS
Herbs: use any herbs that you like – I love tarragon
Chicken: you can also use this recipe for turkey, but it will need to cook for longer, so cover it with foil for the first 1½ hours

ONE TRAY

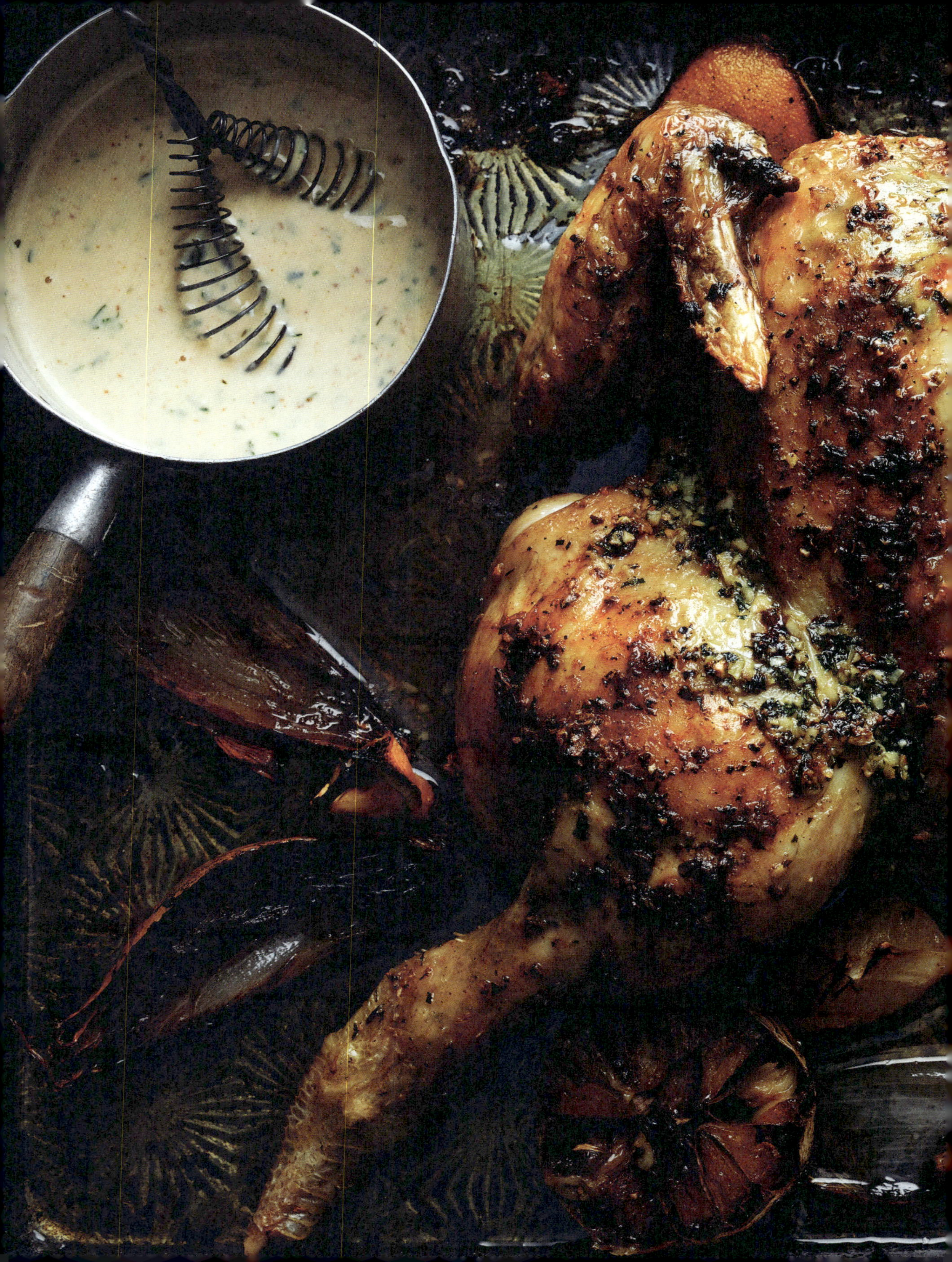

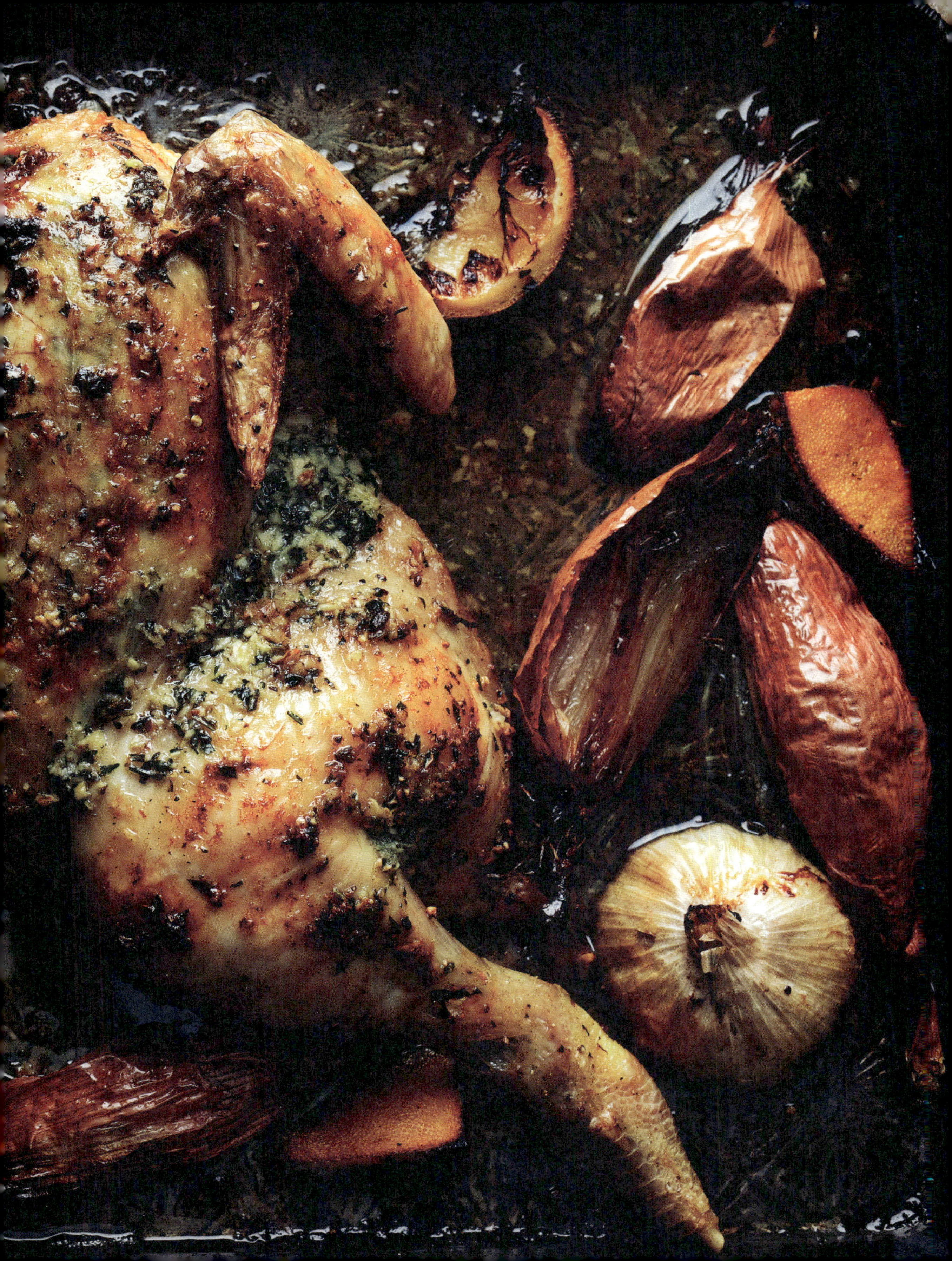

Baked Sausage & Tomato Gnocchi

SERVES 4
TOTAL TIME: 45 MINUTES

This recipe was a family favourite when I was younger. It's packed with flavour and a great one to throw together midweek when there are 101 other things to do. The breadcrumbs give a really lovely texture and bite to this dish – it's one of my favourite dinners to eat while curled up on the sofa.

I sometimes switch out the gnocchi for high-quality butter (lima) beans if I am looking for a lighter option, too.

400g (14oz) mixed tomatoes (red, orange, yellow, green), halved
400g (14oz) tin of chopped tomatoes
6 garlic cloves, finely chopped
540g (1lb 3½oz) uncooked cocktail sausages (see Alternative Ingredients if you can't find them uncooked)
500g (1lb 2oz) gnocchi
2 tbsp olive oil
120g (4oz/¾ cup) panko breadcrumbs
1 tbsp garlic granules
1 tsp fine sea salt
1 tbsp dried mixed herbs

EQUIPMENT
chopping board—knife—roasting tin (pan)—wooden spoon

1. Preheat the oven to 220°C (200°C fan/425°F/gas mark 7).

2. Put the tomatoes, tin of chopped tomatoes, garlic, sausages and gnocchi into a roasting tin and drizzle over the olive oil, then give it all a mix together before popping it into the oven to roast for 20 minutes.

3. While that's cooking, mix together the breadcrumbs, garlic granules, salt and mixed herbs. After 20 minutes, remove the tray from the oven and sprinkle over the breadcrumb mixture. Return to the oven and cook for a further 10–15 minutes until the breadcrumbs are golden brown and crispy. Remove from the oven and tuck in.

ALTERNATIVE INGREDIENTS
Gnocchi: use beans or pasta (if you're going to use pasta, add some stock or water to the tray too)
Sausages: use larger sausages, chorizo, halloumi or firm tofu

ONE TRAY 69

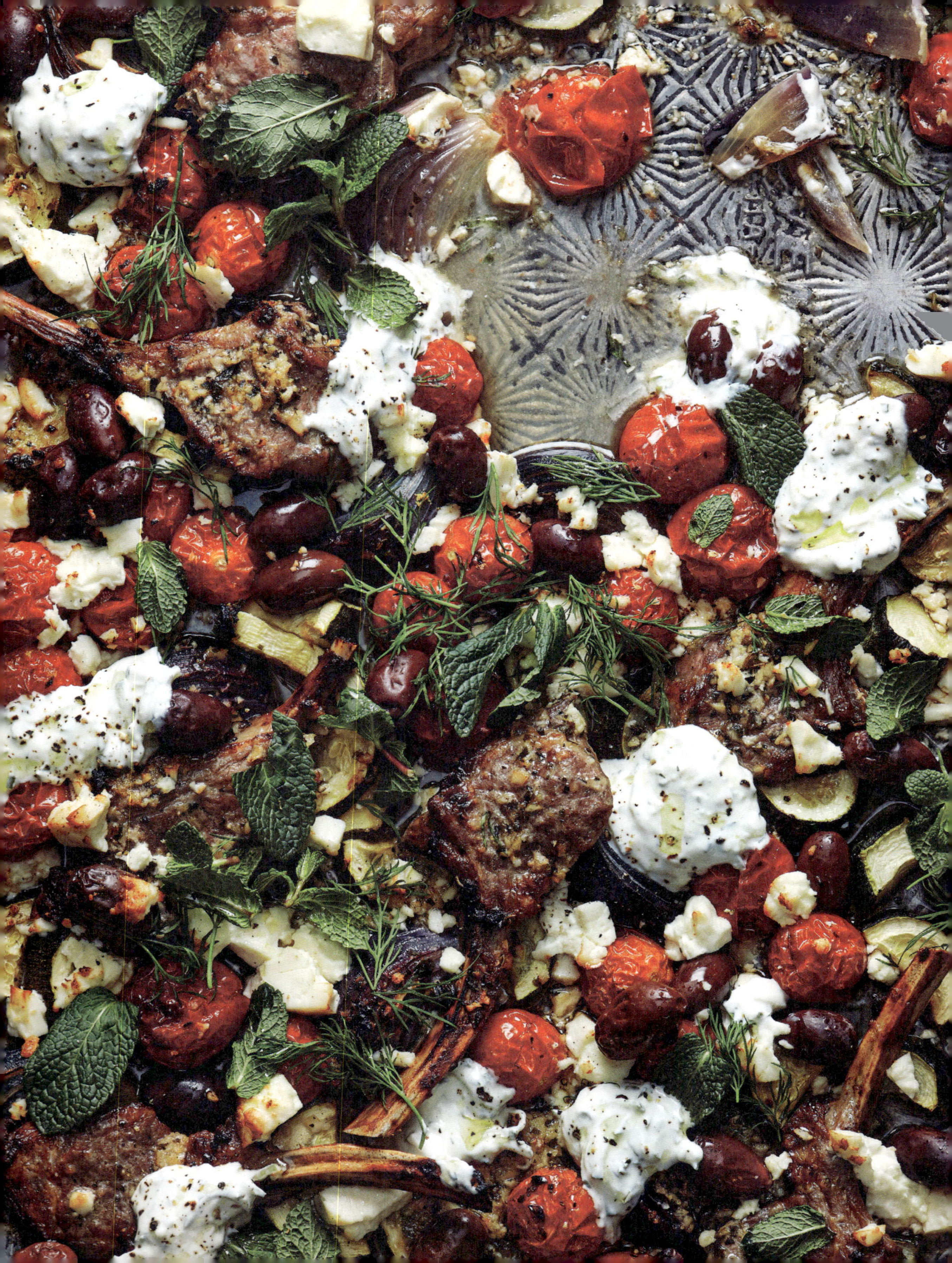

Greek Herby Roasted Lamb Sharing Platter

SERVES 4
TOTAL TIME: 45 MINUTES

This bite of sunshine brings back so many memories and reminds me of being on a Greek island. I created this recipe after returning from Greece in the summer of 2024, a trip filled with endless fizz, far too much feta and an engagement ring. Juicy lamb chops are accompanied by sweet cherry tomatoes, courgettes and briny olives all drizzled with sweet honey, crumbled feta and creamy tzatziki. Serve with warm pitta to scoop it up and share with your loved ones. This is a celebration on a tray.

2 red onions, cut into eighths
400g (14oz) cherry tomatoes (whole or halved, up to you)
200g (7oz) courgette (zucchini), cut into half-moons
4 garlic cloves, finely chopped
8 lamb chops
4–6 tbsp extra virgin olive oil, plus extra to serve
1 tbsp honey
zest and juice of 1 lemon
1 tbsp dried oregano
large pinch of fine sea salt
large pinch of freshly ground black pepper, plus extra to serve
200g (7oz) feta, crumbled
150–200g (5½–7oz) pitted kalamata olives
a handful of dill, finely chopped
a handful of mint, finely chopped
200g (7oz) tzatziki
pitta breads, to serve

EQUIPMENT
chopping board—knife—roasting tin (pan)—zester

1. Preheat the oven to 220°C (200°C fan/425°F/gas mark 7).

2. Put the onions, tomatoes, courgette and garlic into a roasting tin. Place the lamb chops on top and drizzle over the olive oil and honey. Add the lemon zest and juice, oregano, salt and pepper. Get your hands in there and make sure the vegetables and lamb chops are coated in all the seasonings.

3. Pop this in the oven and roast for 15 minutes, then remove from the oven and sprinkle over the feta, olives, half the dill and half the mint. Return to the oven and cook for 5–10 more minutes (depending on how you like your lamb chops to be cooked).

4. Finally, remove the tray from the oven and add the remaining dill and mint, more black pepper, a drizzle of olive oil then dollop over the tzatziki. Serve with pitta breads and enjoy the messiness as you scoop up this Mediterranean flavour-packed traybake.

ALTERNATIVE INGREDIENTS
Vegetables: You can swap these for any you like, or you can add butter (lima) beans or other pulses if you fancy
Lamb: use skin-on boneless chicken thighs, just account for extra cooking time

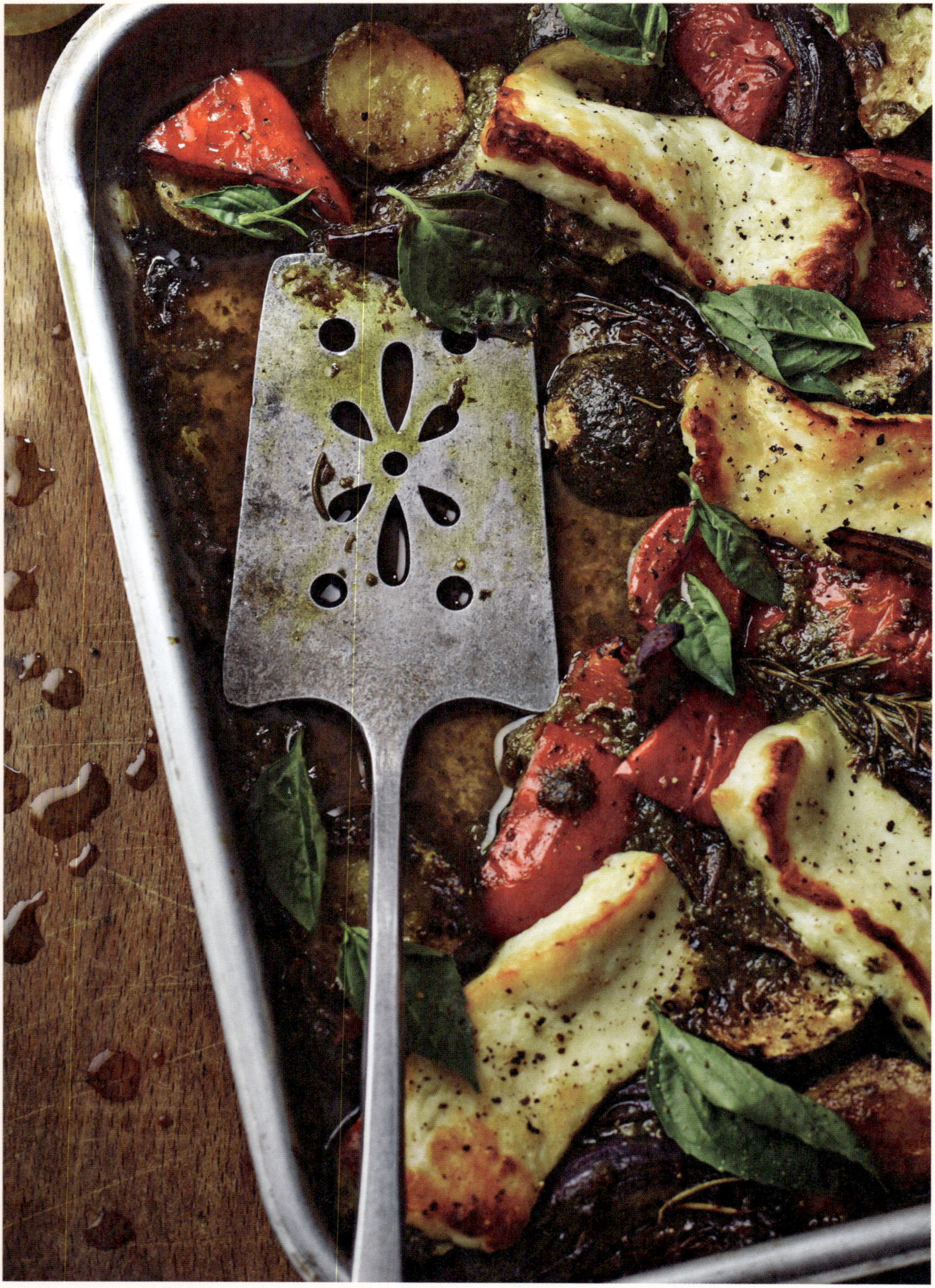

The Easiest Summertime Pesto and Halloumi Traybake

SERVES 2
TOTAL TIME: 30 MINUTES

During the summer, sometimes you just need a quick oven dinner that's easy peasy and delicious – no one wants to be stood over a hot oven when it's warm outside! Any time I have halloumi it reminds me of barbecues, so this halloumi and vegetable traybake is a great summery option.

1 red onion, roughly chopped
1 red (bell) pepper, roughly chopped
1 courgette (zucchini), roughly chopped
2 sprigs of rosemary
1 tsp dried oregano
1 tbsp balsamic vinegar
2 tbsp olive oil
190g (6¾oz) basil pesto
250g (9oz) halloumi, sliced
squeeze of lemon juice
basil leaves, to serve

EQUIPMENT
chopping board—knife—baking tray (pan) wooden spoon

1. Preheat the oven to 200°C (180°C fan/400°F/gas mark 6).

2. Put the red onion, pepper, courgette, rosemary sprigs, oregano, balsamic vinegar and olive oil into a baking tray. Mix together so that everything is coated, then roast in the oven for 15 minutes.

3. Remove the tray from the oven and turn on the grill (broiler). Add the pesto to the vegetables, mixing well to make sure everything is coated. Place the slices of halloumi on top, then place under the grill for 3–5 minutes until the halloumi has some colour.

4. Remove from the oven. Serve with a squeeze of lemon juice, then tear over some basil leaves.

ALTERNATIVE INGREDIENTS
Vegetables: any sort of Mediterranean vegetables can be used, such as aubergine (eggplant), tomatoes and potatoes (par-boil the potatoes beforehand so they're soft when you eat them)
Pesto and seasonings: mix it up with whatever you have in the cupboard, packet seasonings can be easy and simple, a mixed herb or a different kind of pesto works well too
Protein: add chicken thighs or a meaty fish on top for added protein

Chicken Shawarma-style Traybake

SERVES 2
TOTAL TIME: 30 MINUTES

Packed with flavour and spice, this is a recipe that I love to eat with friends while sharing a bottle of wine outside when the sun is shining (though when the winter months creep in it can be a warming option that takes the faff out of cooking too). All you need are some pittas or flatbreads to make a banquet. But remember, this is just a starting point – if you want to serve this on chips (fries) or with salad that's up to you. Tailor your meals to the season you're in – I am just guaranteeing delicious comfort food!

Marinate the chicken for up to 12 hours in the refrigerator (even 1 hour before will help) and the flavour will be next level.

6 skinless, boneless chicken thighs, diced
3 tbsp Greek yoghurt
2 tbsp olive oil
1 tbsp tomato purée (paste)
1–2 tbsp shawarma spice mix (see Alternative Ingredients if you want to make your own spice blend)
zest and juice of 1 lemon, plus 1 quartered, to serve
200g (7oz) hummus
3 spring onions (scallions), thinly sliced
chopped coriander (cilantro), to serve
flatbreads or pitta breads, to serve

EQUIPMENT
chopping board—knife
baking tray (pan)—zester

1. Preheat the oven to 200°C (180°C fan/400°F/gas mark 6).

2. Put the chicken, yoghurt, oil, tomato purée, spice mix and the lemon zest and juice into a baking tray. Mix together really well with your hands so that the chicken is fully coated. Pop this into the oven and roast for 20 minutes.

3. Once the chicken is cooked through, remove the tray from the oven. Top with dollops of hummus, then sprinkle with the spring onions. Serve sprinkled with coriander, the lemon quarters on the side for squeezing and plenty of flatbreads or pittas. We put the tray on the table and scoop up mouthfuls of chicken with our flatbreads – it's a finger food dinner.

ALTERNATIVE INGREDIENTS

Shawarma spice mix: to make your own, combine 1 tablespoon dried oregano, 1 teaspoon ground cumin, ½ teaspoon ground coriander, 1 teaspoon salt, ½ teaspoon ground cinnamon, ½ teaspoon ground nutmeg and 1 teaspoon paprika
Chicken: use lamb shoulder or rib-eye beef instead
Flatbreads: serve it with rice, chips (fries) or salad

ONE TRAY 75

Peri Peri Salmon, Potato & Broccoli Traybake

SERVES 2
TOTAL TIME: 45 MINUTES

This dish is wonderful – it epitomises everything I love about a traybake. We enjoy this in the summer and winter. It's colourful and appealing to the eye and your stomach at the same time. My Nana and Gramps get me salmon once a week from a fish man that delivers to the local pubs around us so I always have an excess of salmon, but you can make this with chicken or other meaty fishes, too.

If you boil the potatoes for 5 minutes first, they will be softer on the inside while still being crispy on the outside.

4 waxy potatoes, cubed
2 tbsp olive oil
2 tbsp peri peri seasoning
2 skin-on salmon fillets
200g (7oz) Tenderstem broccoli (broccolini)
peri peri sauce or mayonnaise, for brushing, plus extra to serve
freshly ground black pepper
zest and juice of 1 lemon, to serve
chopped parsley, to serve

EQUIPMENT
chopping board—knife—baking tray (pan)
pastry brush—zester

1. Preheat the oven to 200°C (180°C fan/400°F/gas mark 6).

2. Put the potatoes into a baking tray and drizzle over the olive oil and sprinkle on the peri peri seasoning. Pop them in the oven and roast for 30 minutes.

3. Meanwhile, brush the salmon with the peri peri sauce or mayonnaise and then sprinkle with plenty of black pepper. After the potatoes have been cooking for 30 minutes, remove the tray from the oven and add in the broccoli and place the salmon on top of the vegetables.

4. Return the tray to the oven for 10 minutes until the salmon and broccoli are cooked. Serve sprinkled with the lemon zest and juice and chopped parsley.

ALTERNATIVE INGREDIENTS
Potatoes: use butter (lima) beans or cannellini beans
Broccoli: use any green vegetables like asparagus or green beans
Salmon: use chicken, beef, cod, haddock or trout

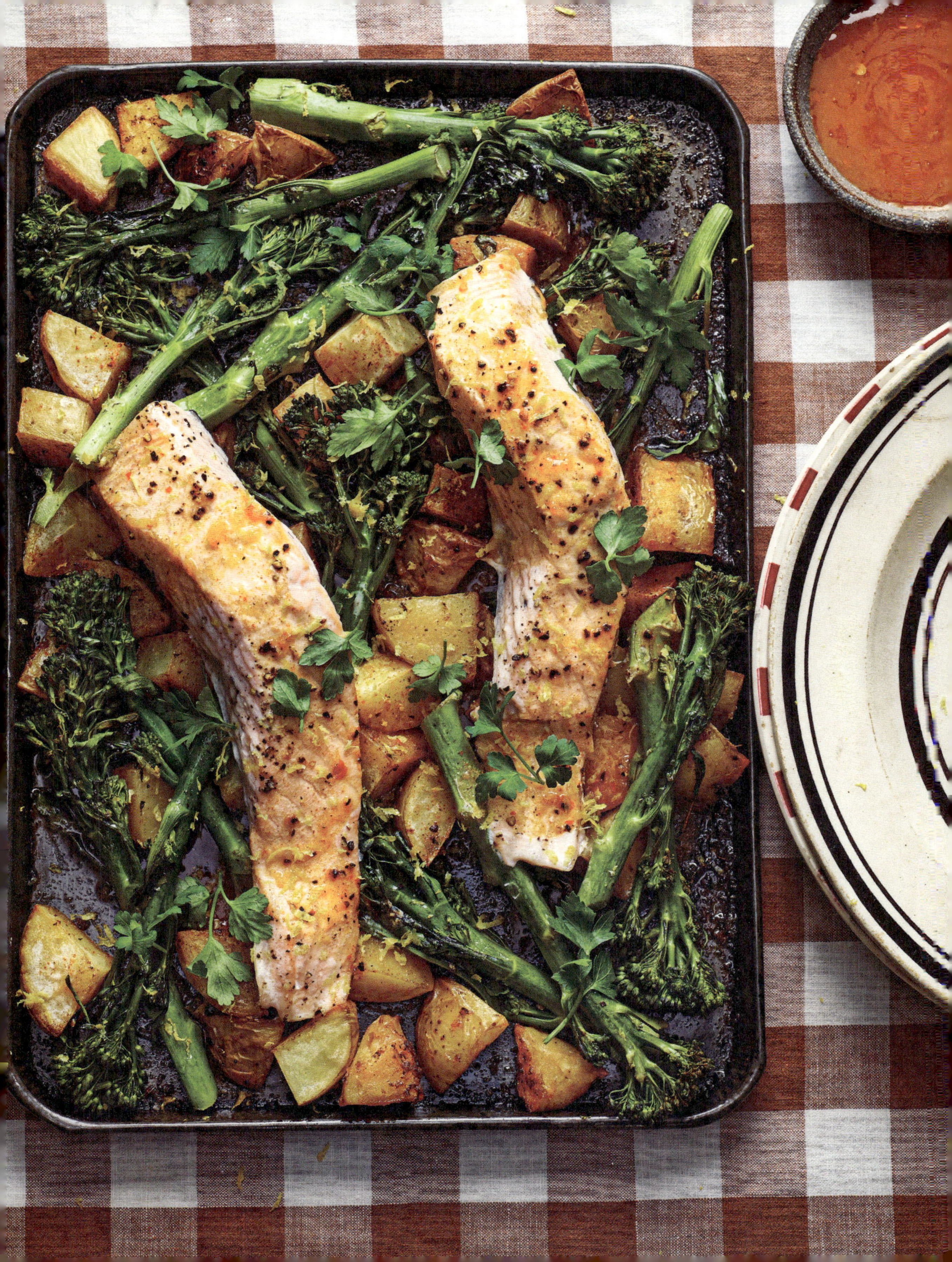

78 ONE TRAY

Parma Ham-wrapped Cod with Sweet Potato Traybake

SERVES 2
TOTAL TIME: 1 HOUR

This is such a perfect meal for summer – the salty Parma ham wrapped around the cod is so delicate and paired with some tomatoes, peppers and sweet potatoes, it's a really well-rounded dinner whether its midweek for you and your family or after work for friends on a Friday. It will make everyone happy!

If you're hosting, pre-wrap the cod in the Parma ham so that when your timer goes off, all you need to do is pop the fish on the tray and you're not spending time wrapping fish when you'd rather be drinking wine and socialising.

2 large sweet potatoes, diced
1 red onion, quartered
1 red (bell) pepper, roughly chopped
100g (3½oz) cherry tomatoes on the vine
4 tbsp olive oil
1 tbsp dried mixed herbs
large pinch of fine sea salt
2 skinless cod fillets
4–6 slices of Parma ham
80g (2¾oz) pitted kalamata olives

TO SERVE
a handful of basil leaves
2 tbsp crispy fried onions
freshly ground black pepper

EQUIPMENT
chopping board—knife—baking tray (pan) wooden spoon

1. Preheat the oven to 200°C (180°C fan/400°F/gas mark 6).

2. Put the potatoes, red onion, pepper and cherry tomatoes into a baking tray. Drizzle over the olive oil, add the mixed herbs and salt and mix everything together. Pop this in the oven and roast for 35 minutes.

3. Meanwhile, wrap the cod fillets with the Parma ham.

4. After the 35 minutes, remove the tray from the oven and add the wrapped cod and olives. Return to the oven for a further 15 minutes.

5. Remove from oven and serve scattered with basil and crispy onions and a crack of black pepper. Tuck in!

ALTERNATIVE INGREDIENTS
Sweet potatoes: use white potatoes. I also sometimes throw in a butternut squash around autumn time or a little bit of pumpkin
Cod: use any other meaty fish or chicken – I recommend using thighs over a breast so that it stays moist
Basil: throw on any fresh herbs you like

Honey & Mustard Chicken Thighs

SERVES 2–3
TOTAL TIME: 1 HOUR

My family all love honey and mustard sausages around Christmastime, so imagine if there was a one-pan recipe that celebrated those same flavours, which we could make when colder days start creeping up so that we have delicious comfort food on demand ... Oh, wait – there is! Follow this recipe once and I know you'll make it again and again.

If you have time, combine the chicken thighs with the marinade and set them aside to marinate for a few hours before cooking. The thighs will absorb as much flavour as they can before the cooking process has even started!

2 tbsp Dijon mustard
2 tbsp honey
1 tbsp red wine vinegar
1–2 tbsp olive oil
1 tsp garlic granules or garlic salt
1 tsp fine sea salt, plus extra as needed
500g (1lb 2oz) new (baby) potatoes, halved
1–2 red onions, roughly chopped
4–6 skin-on boneless chicken thighs
200ml (7fl oz/generous ¾ cup) chicken stock
a few sprigs of thyme
freshly ground black pepper
green salad, to serve (optional)

EQUIPMENT
chopping board—knife—jug (pitcher)
roasting tin

1. Preheat the oven to 200°C (180°C fan/400°F/gas mark 6).

2. Combine the mustard, honey, vinegar, olive oil, garlic granules and salt in a jug and mix well.

3. Put the potatoes and onions into a baking tray, then add the chicken thighs, skin-side up. Pour the stock into the side of the tin (this is going to help the potatoes to steam in the oven).

4. Drizzle the marinade over everything, then add the sprigs of thyme and a final sprinkle of salt and pepper. Roast in the oven for 45 minutes, then remove from the oven and serve with your favourite green salad.

ALTERNATIVE INGREDIENTS
Chicken thighs: use pork sausages

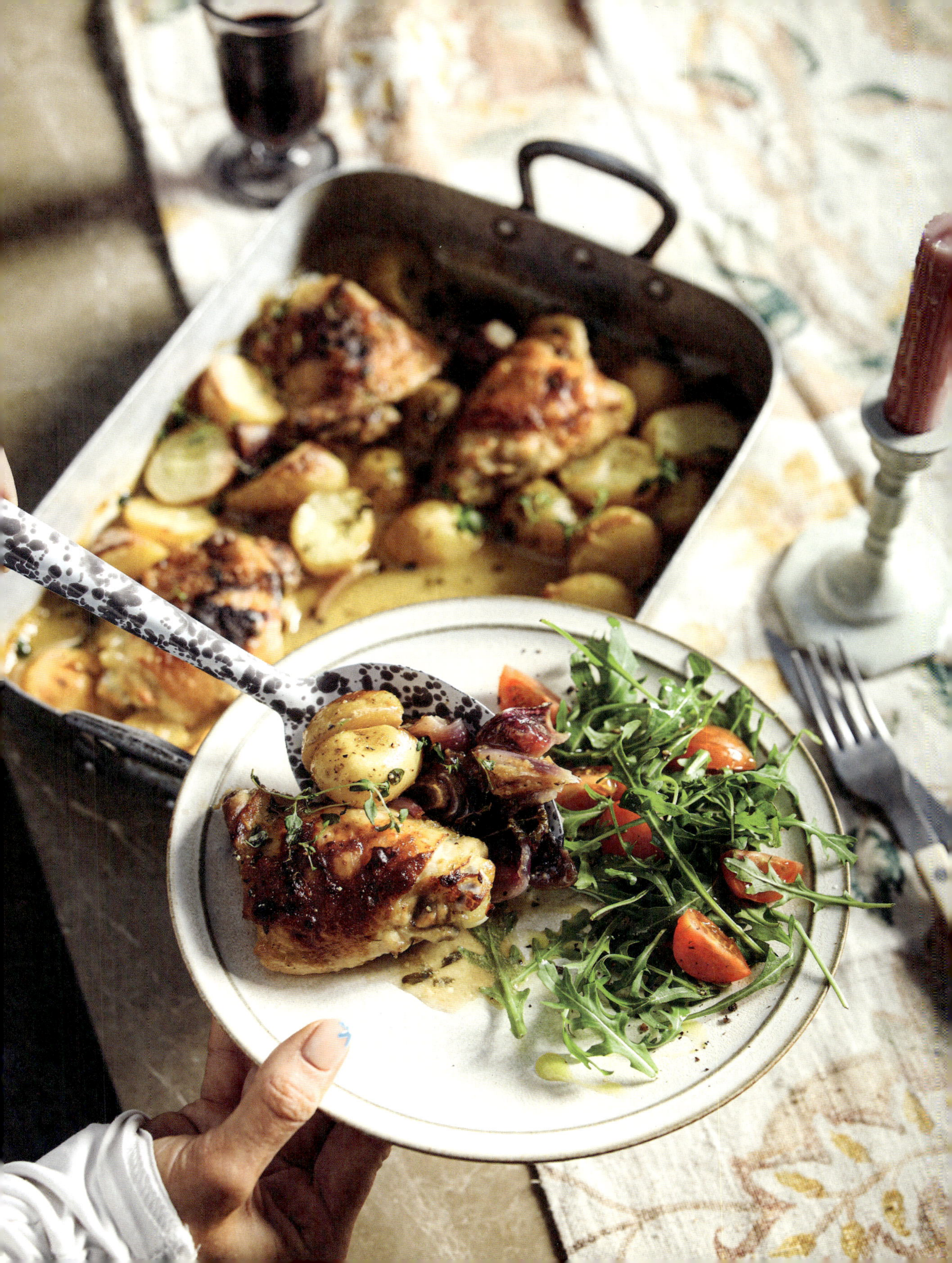

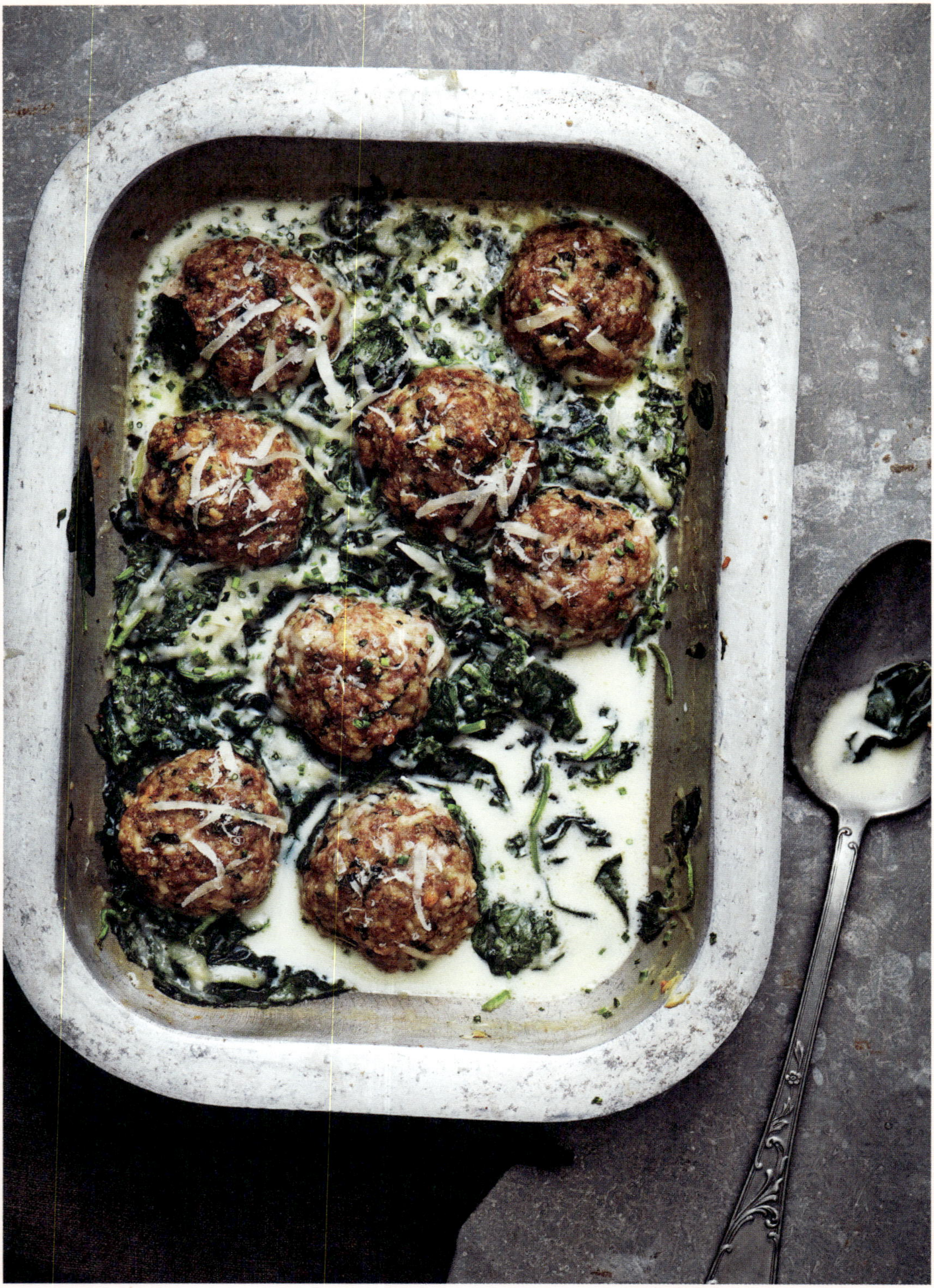

Creamy Spinach & Turkey Meatballs

SERVES 4
TOTAL TIME: 45 MINUTES

This recipe gets your hands a little bit dirty but it's a real family favourite and is wonderful to make whatever the weather. It's easy to increase the recipe quantities if there are more mouths to feed, too.

I sometimes like to add some butter (lima) beans at the same time as the spinach, which make a lovely additions.

500g (1lb 2oz) minced (ground) turkey
1 medium egg
1 tsp garlic granules
1 tbsp chopped basil
100g (3½oz/⅔ cup) panko breadcrumbs
1 tsp fine sea salt
1 tsp freshly ground black pepper
400g (14oz) spinach
150g (5½oz) garlic and herb soft cheese
150ml (5fl oz/⅔ cup) chicken or vegetable stock
50g (1¾oz) parmesan, grated, plus extra to serve
chopped chives, to serve

EQUIPMENT
large mixing bowl—roasting tin (pan)
wooden spoon—grater

1. Preheat the oven to 200°C (180°C fan/400°F/gas mark 6).

2. Put the turkey, egg, garlic granules, basil, half the breadcrumbs and salt and pepper into a bowl and combine with your hands. You'll need to almost knead the meat like you would dough to make sure the seasoning is evenly distributed.

3. Roll the mixture into bite-size balls and place in a roasting tin. Pop these in the oven for 15 minutes, then remove the tray from the oven and add the spinach, soft cheese and stock. Mix everything together and then return to the oven for 10 minutes. Finally, remove from the oven and mix through the parmesan.

4. Finish with a sprinkling of chives and parmesan before serving.

ALTERNATIVE INGREDIENTS
Turkey: use minced (ground) chicken or beef, or veggie mince

ONE TRAY

Chorizo, Manchego & Red Pepper Traybake

SERVES 4
TOTAL TIME: 45 MINUTES

My Nana used to make the most amazing chorizo and manchego buns, they were rich, salty and would leave me reaching for another one immediately. These inspired me to combine those same bold flavours that made me so happy and throw it into a hearty potato traybake, I just knew it was going to be a winner. Crispy golden potatoes, melty manchego and bursts of salty chewy chorizo this dish has comfort food written all over it!

If you want this to be extra cheesy, add in any of your favourite cheeses – a combination of parmesan, manchego and cheddar is unmatched for me!

1kg (2lb 4oz) waxy potatoes, diced
2 onions, diced
225g (8oz) Spanish chorizo, diced
2 red (bell) peppers, diced
2 tbsp olive oil
200g (7oz) manchego, grated
60ml (2fl oz/¼ cup) double (heavy) cream
flaked sea salt
chopped parsley, to serve
lemon wedges, to serve

EQUIPMENT
chopping board—knife—roasting tin
grater

1. Preheat the oven to 200°C (180°C fan/400°F/gas mark 6).

2. Place the potatoes, onions, chorizo and peppers into a roasting tin and drizzle with the olive oil. Transfer to the oven and roast for about 15 minutes. Remove from the oven and stir.

3. Pour over the cream and scatter over the manchego. Return to the oven and cook for 25 minutes.

4. Finally, remove the tray from the oven and sprinkle over some flaked sea salt and parsley. Serve with the lemon wedges then tuck in with a big spoon!

ALTERNATIVE INGREDIENTS
Spanish chorizo: use pancetta (this then starts feeling very 'tartiflette-y' to me, so if you're going to do that I recommend using reblochon cheese)

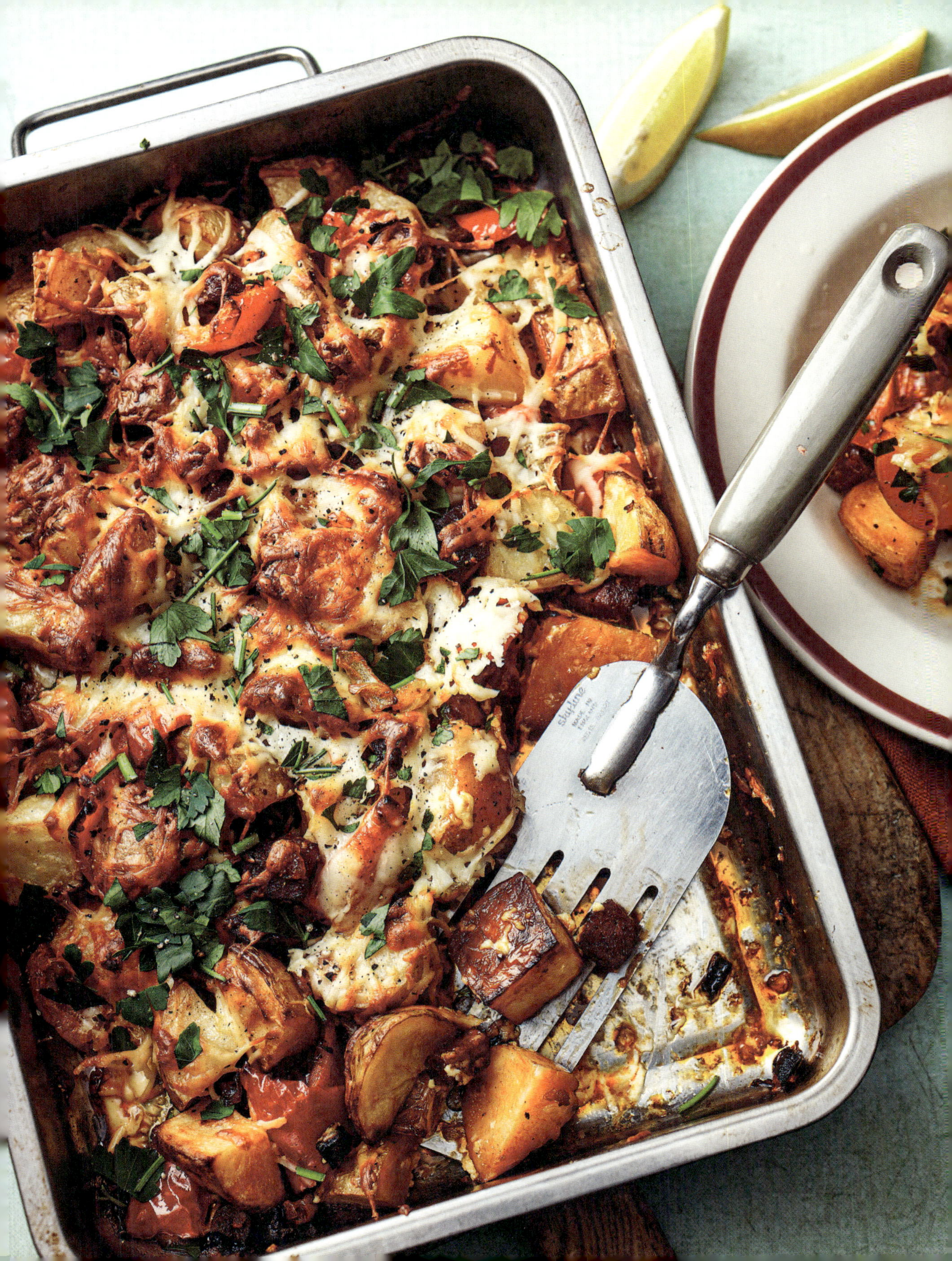

Cheesy Garlic-stuffed Chestnut Mushrooms

SERVES 4 AS A SIDE OR 2 AS A MAIN
TOTAL TIME: 30 MINUTES

In my household, mushrooms can only be eaten if they're disguised with other foods because I have a few picky eaters. These stuffed mushrooms are such a delicious way to maximise flavour and, if you're not a mushroom fan, a great way to break into the mushroom-loving stage of your life.

Serve this with mashed potatoes and green beans, spooning the cheesy, oily juices over the top – divine!

16 large chestnut (cremini) mushrooms, stalks removed
3 tbsp olive oil
100g (3½oz) mozzarella, grated
50g (1¾oz) parmesan, grated
handful of chopped parsley
6 garlic cloves, finely chopped
½ tsp chilli (hot pepper) flakes
fine sea salt
freshly ground black pepper

EQUIPMENT
chopping board—knife—baking tray (pan)
grater—small bowl—metal spoon

1. Preheat the oven to 200°C (180°C fan/400°F/gas mark 6).

2. Drizzle the mushrooms with the olive oil and sprinkle them with salt and pepper, then place on a baking tray.

3. Combine the mozzarella, parmesan, parsley, garlic and chilli flakes in a bowl and mix well, then form the mixture into eight even balls. Place each ball on top of a mushroom, then roast in the oven for 20 minutes until the cheese is bubbly and golden in places. Enjoy!

ALTERNATIVE INGREDIENTS
Mushrooms: use courgettes (zucchini) or aubergines (eggplants) halves
Make it vegan: use vegan cheese

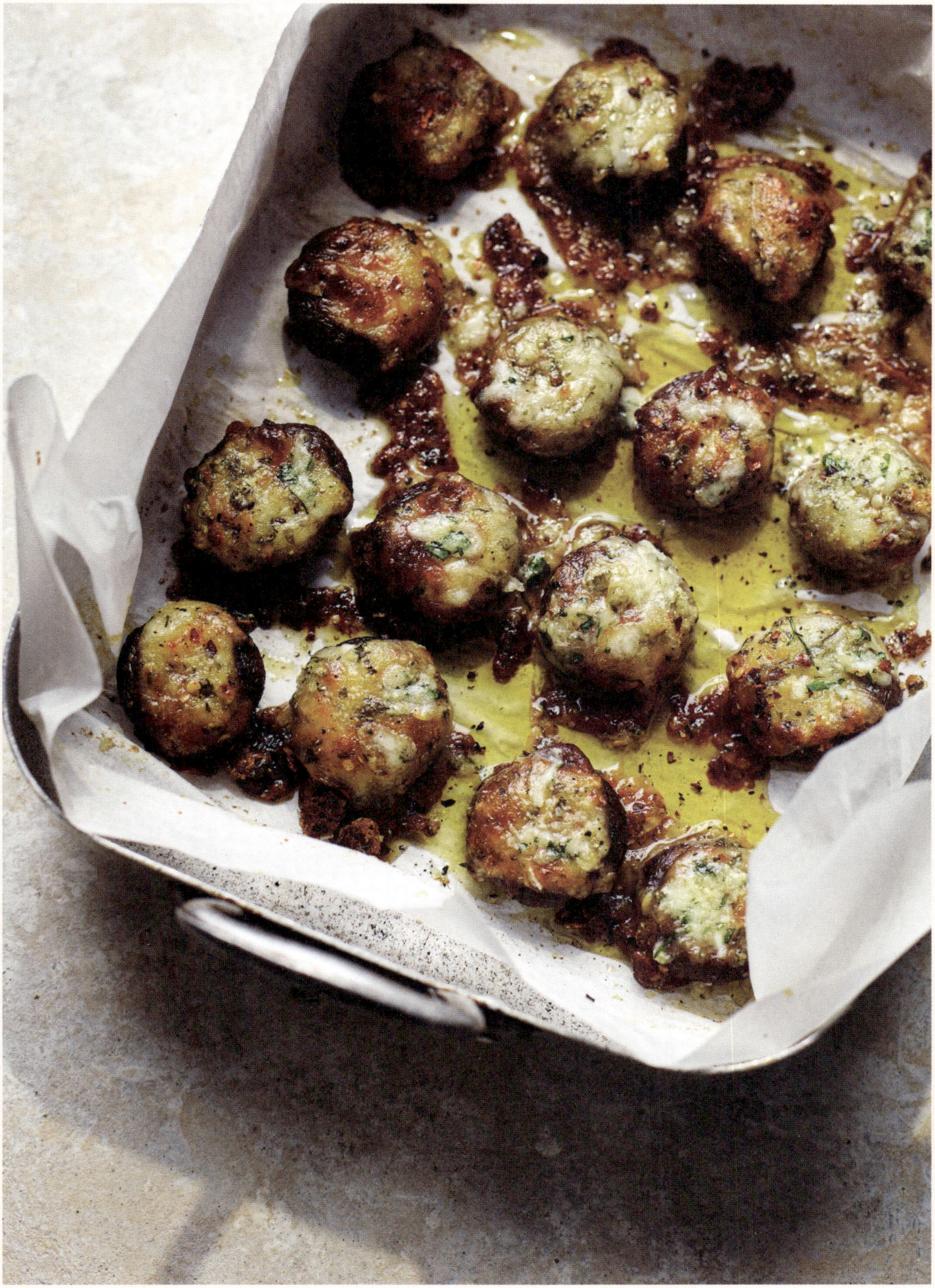

Caramelised Onion Pasta Traybake

SERVES 4
TOTAL TIME: 1 HOUR 20 MINUTES

I made caramelised onion pasta at the same time that everyone else was and it was so delicious, but it was during summer and I really didn't want to spend an hour sweating over the oven. I thought that surely you could just pop it in the oven instead … so I tried it, and you definitely could! So, if you're looking for a creamy, veggie pasta dish to make the family happy in the summer or in the winter, this is the one for you!

6–8 onions, thinly sliced
1 tbsp chilli oil
4 tbsp olive oil, plus extra for drizzling
a few shakes of Worcestershire sauce
large pinch of fine sea salt
juice of 1 lemon
1 bulb of garlic, top sliced off
200ml (7fl oz/generous ¾ cup) single (light) cream
60g (2oz) parmesan, grated
450g (1lb) bucatini (or any pasta shape)

EQUIPMENT
chopping board—knife—ceramic ovenproof dish—large saucepan—wooden spoon—grater

1. Preheat the oven to 200°C (180°C fan/400°F/gas mark 6).

2. Put the sliced onions, chilli oil, olive oil, Worcestershire sauce, salt and lemon juice into a ceramic ovenproof dish and toss to coat. Place the bulb of garlic in the middle and drizzle with a little more oil. Cover the dish with foil and roast in the oven for about 1 hour until the onions are soft and caramelised (it may need longer – all ovens are different).

3. When the onions have almost finished cooking, bring a large saucepan of water to the boil and cook the pasta according to the packet instructions, then drain, reserving a little of the pasta cooking water.

4. Once the onions are ready, remove the dish from the oven and squeeze out the garlic cloves from the bulb into the onions. Add the cream, parmesan and drained pasta, mixing well. If the sauce is a bit thick, add a little splash of pasta cooking water. Serve and enjoy.

ALTERNATIVE INGREDIENTS
Try adding sun-dried tomatoes or other veggies to this dish to add even more depth. I love adding some halved cherry tomatoes occasionally.

Mother's Day Lamb

SERVES 4–6
TOTAL TIME: 1½ HOURS

This was named 'Mother's Day lamb' in our household because when I first made it for Mum and Nana to celebrate Mother's Day they were obsessed, so it quickly became a tradition. You can make this for any family event throughout the year, though, or for those occasions when you want impress friends with minimal effort!

If you like your potatoes extra crispy, top them with some extra fat once they're in the roasting tin – olive oil, goose fat or duck fat all work well.

1.5kg (3lb 5oz) waxy potatoes, peeled and quartered
2.5–3kg (5½–6¾lbs) leg of lamb
150ml (5fl oz/⅔ cup) olive oil
1 bulb of garlic, cloves finely chopped
2 tbsp chopped rosemary
2 tbsp chopped mint, plus extra to serve
1 tsp fine sea salt
1 tsp freshly ground black pepper
1 tbsp red wine vinegar
200ml (7fl oz/generous ¾ cup) dry white wine
150g (5½oz) feta
150g (5½oz) pomegranate seeds

EQUIPMENT
chopping board—peeler—knife—roasting tin—bowl or jug (pitcher)

1. Preheat the oven to 200°C (180°C fan/400°F/gas mark 6).

2. Put the lamb into a deep roasting tin. Combine the oil, garlic, rosemary, mint, salt, pepper and red wine vinegar in a small bowl or jug (pitcher) and mix together. Pierce the lamb all over with a sharp knife, then smother the olive oil mixture all over the lamb, make sure to get as much garlic and herbs into the slits you made as possible.

3. Scatter the potatoes around the leg of lamb, mixing them through any excess oil and seasoning. Pour the white wine into the bottom of the tin and cover the whole tin in foil. Pop this in the oven and roast for 35 minutes, then remove the foil and continue to cook for a further 25 minutes until the potatoes and lamb are crisp and golden.

4. Remove from the oven, crumble over the feta and sprinkle with the pomegranate seeds, then finish with some more mint.

ALTERNATIVE INGREDIENT
Lamb: use a whole chicken
Potatoes: use carrots and parsnips

ONE TRAY

ONE TRAY

ONE TRAY 91

Cheeseburger Nachos

SERVES 2-4
TOTAL TIME: 30 MINUTES

We all love nachos so in the summertime and I love to whip up this cheeseburger version after we have had a barbecue. I often find that there are some burgers or toppings left over, and being able to use them up to reduce waste and make something super delicious is ideal!

200–250g (7–9oz) minced (ground) beef
1 tsp onion granules
1 tsp garlic granules
½ tsp fine sea salt
1 tsp freshly ground black pepper
100–150g (3½–5½oz) cheddar, grated
200g (7oz) lightly salted tortilla chips
½ onion, finely diced
a handful of chopped romaine or iceberg lettuce
2–3 gherkins (pickles), finely chopped
1–2 tbsp finely chopped jalapeños
a drizzle of ketchup
a drizzle of American mustard

EQUIPMENT
ovenproof frying pan—wooden spoon
grater—chopping board—knife

1. Preheat the oven to 200°C (180°C fan/400°F/gas mark 6).

2. Put the minced beef into an ovenproof frying pan and brown for 5 minutes, then throw in the onion granules, garlic granules and salt and pepper. Cook for a further 5–10 minutes until the mince is well browned and there is no more liquid in the pan. Remove from the heat.

3. Sprinkle the cheese over the beef, then pop this in the oven for 8–10 minutes, or until the cheese has melted. Remove the pan from the oven.

4. Place the tortilla chips on a serving dish and carefully spoon over the beef, being careful not to break up the cheese too much. Scatter over the onion, lettuce, gherkins and jalapeños, then drizzle over a little ketchup and mustard and tuck in.

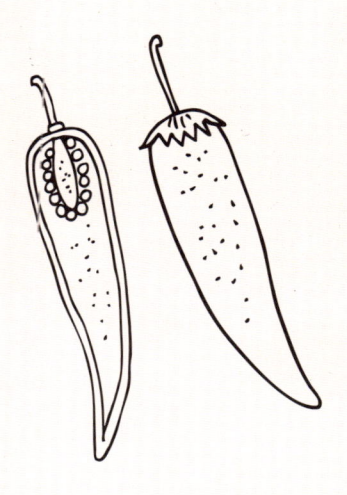

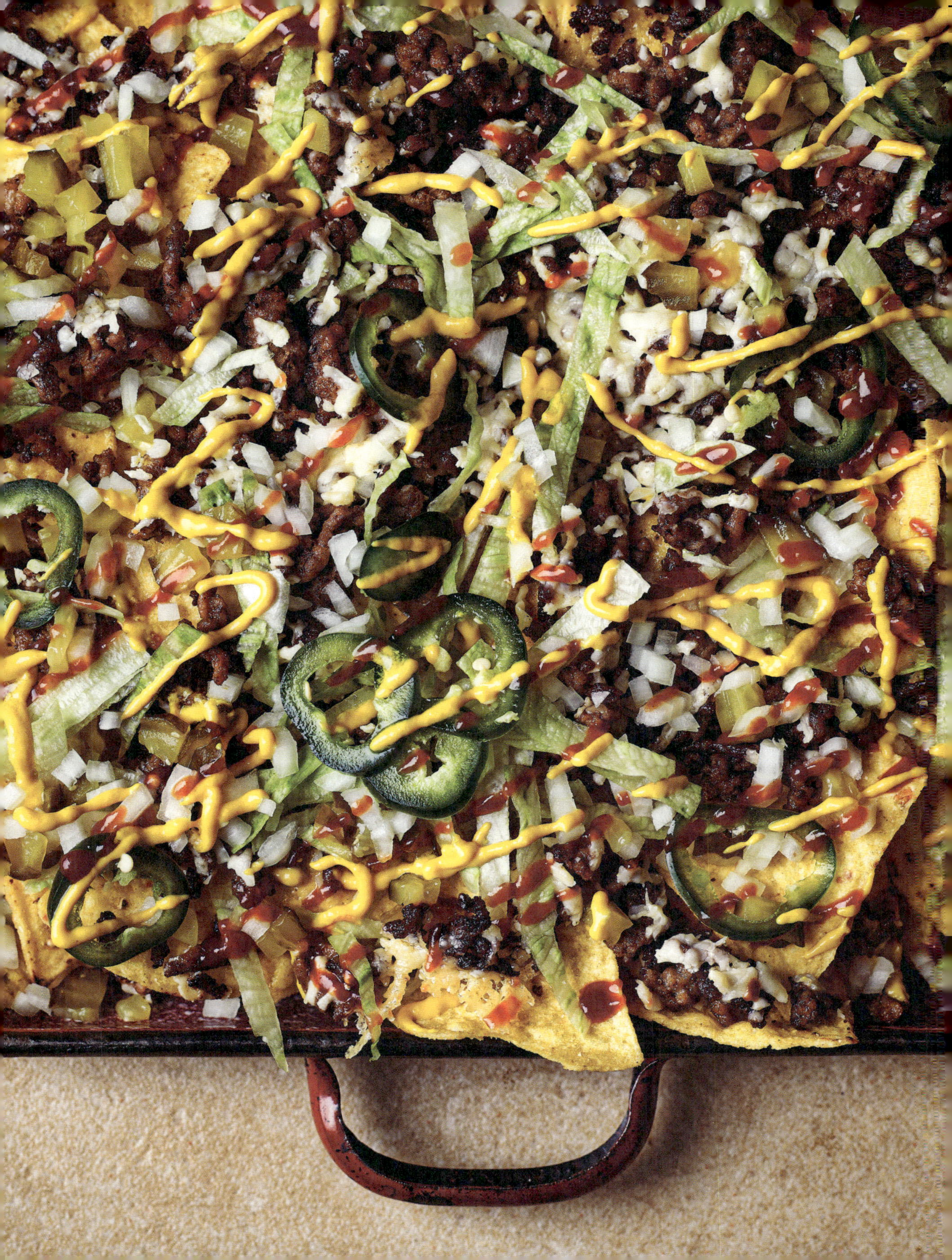

BBQ Tofu & Chips

SERVES 2
TOTAL TIME: 1¼ HOURS

When I was at university, my housemates (my best friends, who are now my bridesmaids) became rather obsessed with BBQ-flavoured food. Don't ask me why, but we started experimenting with all the things that worked best with BBQ sauce, and I am going to say it: this tofu and chips (fries) traybake was one of the best things ever. We just needed to chop everything up and chuck it onto a tray, but the flavours we had created made us feel like we were going out for dinner – only on a student budget!

280g (10oz) firm tofu
2–4 waxy potatoes, peeled and cubed (I use for 4 for bigger portions)
1 red onion, sliced
1 red (bell) pepper, sliced
2–3 tbsp olive oil
1 tsp garlic granules
1 tsp onion granules
1 tsp dried oregano
½ tsp paprika
large pinch of fine sea salt
large pinch of freshly ground black pepper
4 tbsp BBQ sauce (choose your favourite kind)

TO SERVE
sliced spring onions (scallions)
crispy fried onions
chopped coriander (cilantro)

EQUIPMENT
chopping board—knife—roasting tin

1 Preheat the oven to 200°C (180°C fan/400°F/gas mark 6).

2 Remove the tofu from the package and allow it to drain. Wrap some kitchen towel or a clean tea towel around it and squeeze for a few minutes to remove the excess liquid. Alternatively pop it on a flat surface and leave a heavy object on top of it for 10 minutes or so (the longer you press it the firmer it will get). Once you've left it for 10-15 minutes, pat dry then cut into bite-size cubes.

3 Put the tofu, potatoes, onion and pepper into a roasting tin, drizzle over the oil and sprinkle over the garlic granules, onion granules, oregano, paprika, salt and pepper. Massage the seasoning into the ingredients so everything is well coated.

4 Pop this in the oven for 15 minutes, then remove from the oven and toss everything through the BBQ sauce. Return to the oven for 20–25 minutes until potatoes are soft and everything is beautifully caramelised.

5 Remove the tray from the oven and sprinkle over the spring onions, crispy onions and chopped coriander before serving.

ONE TRAY

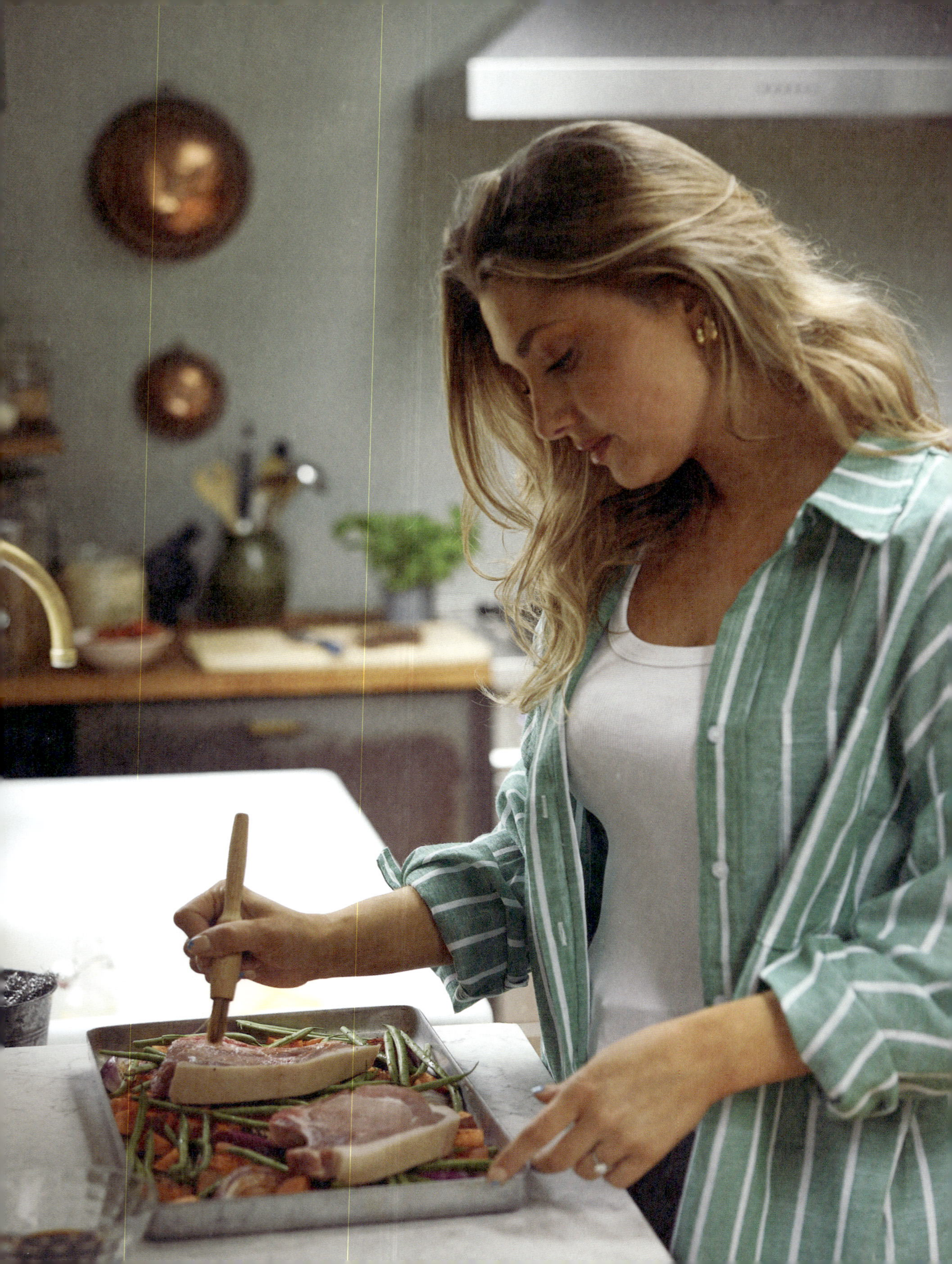

ONE TRAY 97

Teriyaki Pork Chops

SERVES 4
TOTAL TIME: 40 MINUTES

When I was younger, we would always have pork chops in the freezer – often a gift from some of the local farmers for Christmas. Mum found them versatile, but I never really cooked with them too much. However, when I met my fiancé, Jake, he was obsessed with teriyaki so I thought, why don't we use some stuff from the freezer! We also used up some sweet potatoes and other veggies that needed eating and made this delicious dish that was put together with very little effort.

1 large sweet potato, diced
125g (4¼oz) green beans
1 red onion, sliced
3 tbsp olive oil
1 tsp garlic granules
½ tsp ground ginger
½ tsp paprika
2 large pork chops or 4 smaller ones
3 tbsp teriyaki sauce
2 pineapple rings
fine sea salt
freshly ground black pepper
chopped spring onions (scallions), to serve
a handful of chopped coriander (cilantro), to serve

EQUIPMENT
chopping board)—knife—baking tray (pan) pastry brush

1 Preheat the oven to 200°C (180°C fan/400°F/gas mark 6).

2 Put the sweet potato, green beans and red onion into a baking tray (pan). Drizzle the olive oil over everything and then sprinkle over the garlic granules, ground ginger, paprika and some salt and pepper. Get your hands in there and massage everything together so the veggies are coated in all the seasoning.

3 Place the pork chops on top of the vegetables and brush half of the teriyaki sauce over the top. Roast in the oven for 15 minutes, then remove the tray from the oven and flip the pork chops over, brushing the remaining teriyaki sauce on the other side.

4 Tear up the pineapple rings and scatter over the tray bake. Cook for a further 15 minutes, then remove from the oven. I like to serve mine with lots of chopped spring onions and coriander on top.

ONE TRAY 99

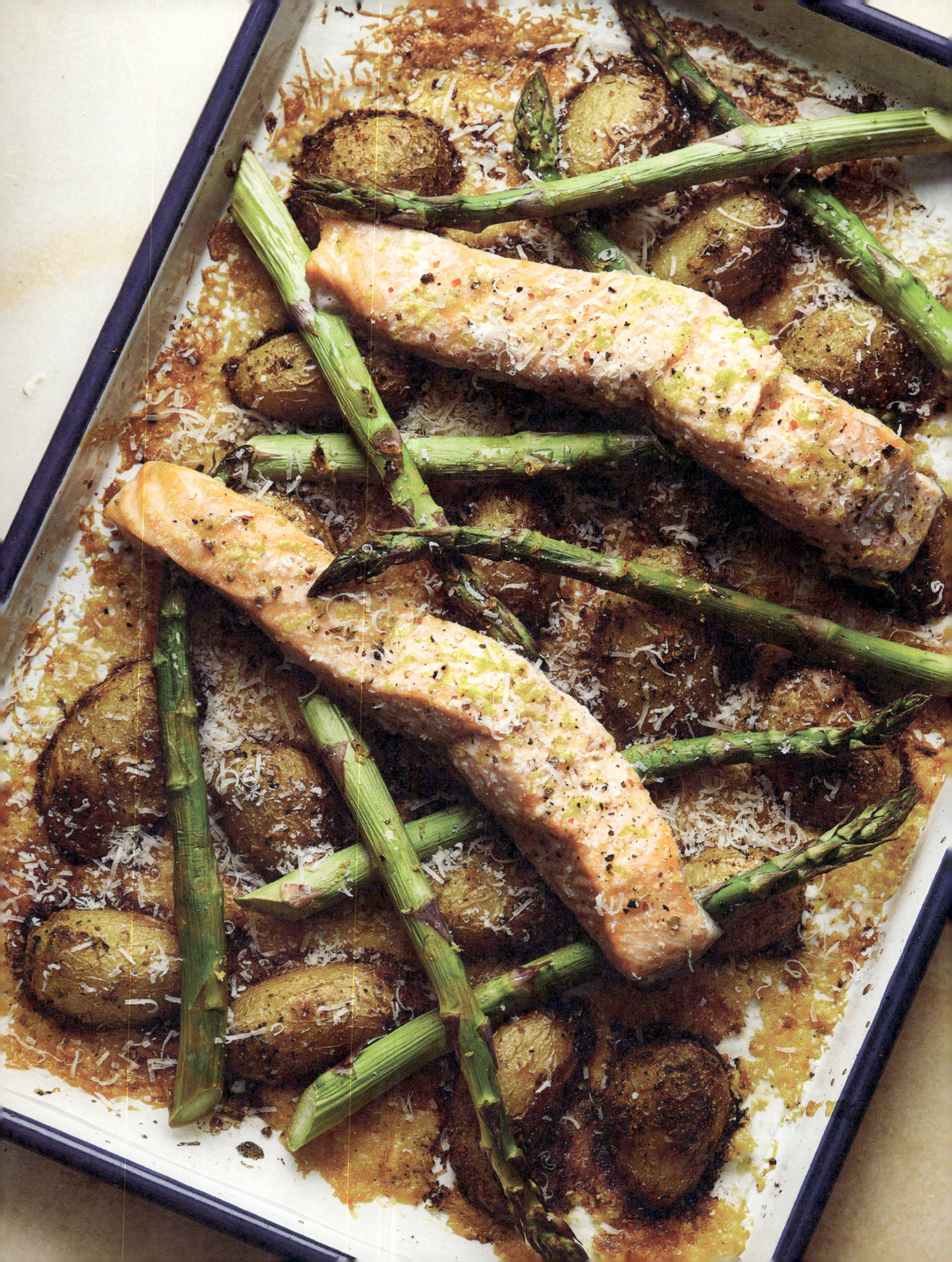

Garlic & Parmesan Crispy Potatoes & Trout

SERVES 2
TOTAL TIME: 50 MINUTES

My Nana gets us fresh fish each week. She has done it every Tuesday since I was a little girl. She often asks me what kind of fish I would like that week, especially when I started experimenting with my own recipes. She knew I would like to try cooking new things. However, I always went back to salmon and trout – I think they have some of the most beautiful meaty flavours and, to me, it's comfort food. These garlic and parmesan potatoes are one of the best things you'll ever have so pairing it with a wholesome fish is the perfect kind of comfort food dinner. I am aware a lot of people don't like pairing cheese with fish as it's against a few 'rules', but to me, cooking is creating beautiful flavours, and these just go so well together.

80g (2¾oz) parmesan
8–12 new (baby) potatoes, halved
4 tbsp olive oil
2 tsp garlic granules
1 tsp onion granules
1 tsp dried mixed herbs
8–12 asparagus, woody stems trimmed
2 trout fillets
zest and juice of 2 lemons
fine sea salt
freshly ground black pepper

EQUIPMENT
baking tray (pan)—grater—zester

1. Preheat the oven to 200°C (180°C fan/400°F/gas mark 6).

2. Line a baking tray with baking parchment or a silicone baking mat (this is going to ensure that the parmesan adheres to the potatoes rather than the tray rather). Grate fine shavings of three quarters of the parmesan onto the tray. Place the potatoes sliced-side down on top of the parmesan. This ensures there is an even layer on the bottom of the potatoes that will crisp up beautifully.

3. Drizzle the potatoes with the oil, then sprinkle evenly with the garlic and onion granules, mixed herbs and salt and pepper. Roast the potatoes in the oven for 20–25 minutes until they are crispy and golden on the outside tender in the middle.

4. After this time, remove the tray from the oven and add the asparagus and trout fillets. Sprinkle with the lemon zest and squeeze over the juice. Place back in the oven for 15–20 minutes until the trout is cooked through and the potatoes are tender.

5. Remove from the oven and finish off by grating the remaining parmesan over the top.

Blue Cheese Steak & Potatoes

SERVES 2
TOTAL TIME: 45–50 MINUTES

I love everything about blue cheese. It's my favourite cheese: it's rich, salty, tangy and is so delicious when paired with the rich flavours of steak. There is a reason why it's a classic flavour combination! I wanted to make this a beautiful date night or special occasion meal, so I have added some beautifully seasoned potatoes.
If you're not a blue cheese fan, you can use garlic butter instead.

2–3 waxy potatoes, peeled and cubed
4 tbsp olive oil, plus extra for brushing
2 tsp garlic granules
2 tsp onion granules
1 tsp paprika
2 rib-eye steaks
2–3 sprigs of thyme or rosemary
100–150g (3½–5½oz) blue cheese of your choice, crumbled
fine sea salt
freshly ground black pepper
green salad, to serve

EQUIPMENT
chopping board)—knife baking tray (pan) pastry brush

1. Preheat the oven at 200°C (180°C fan/400°F/gas mark 6).

2. Put the potatoes into a baking tray and drizzle over the oil, then sprinkle over the garlic granules, onion granules, paprika and some salt and pepper. Get your hands in there and massage the potatoes so they're fully coated in all the seasoning. Roast the potatoes in the oven for 30 minutes.

3. Meanwhile, season the steaks with salt and pepper.

4. Remove the potatoes from the oven after 30 minutes and make a little space in the tray for the steaks to be placed (you ideally want them to sit directly on the metal tray because that's where it will be hottest – no one wants grey steaks!). Place the rosemary and thyme in the space where the steaks will go (the herbs will infuse the steaks with flavour), then brush both sides of the steaks with oil and place them on top of the rosemary and thyme. Return the tray to the oven for 8 minutes (for medium-rare steak – if you want yours cooked more, leave it for another 2–4 minutes).

5. Once cooked, remove the steak and potatoes from the oven and add the blue cheese straight away on top of the steaks (the residual heat should help it melt). Serve immediately with a green salad.

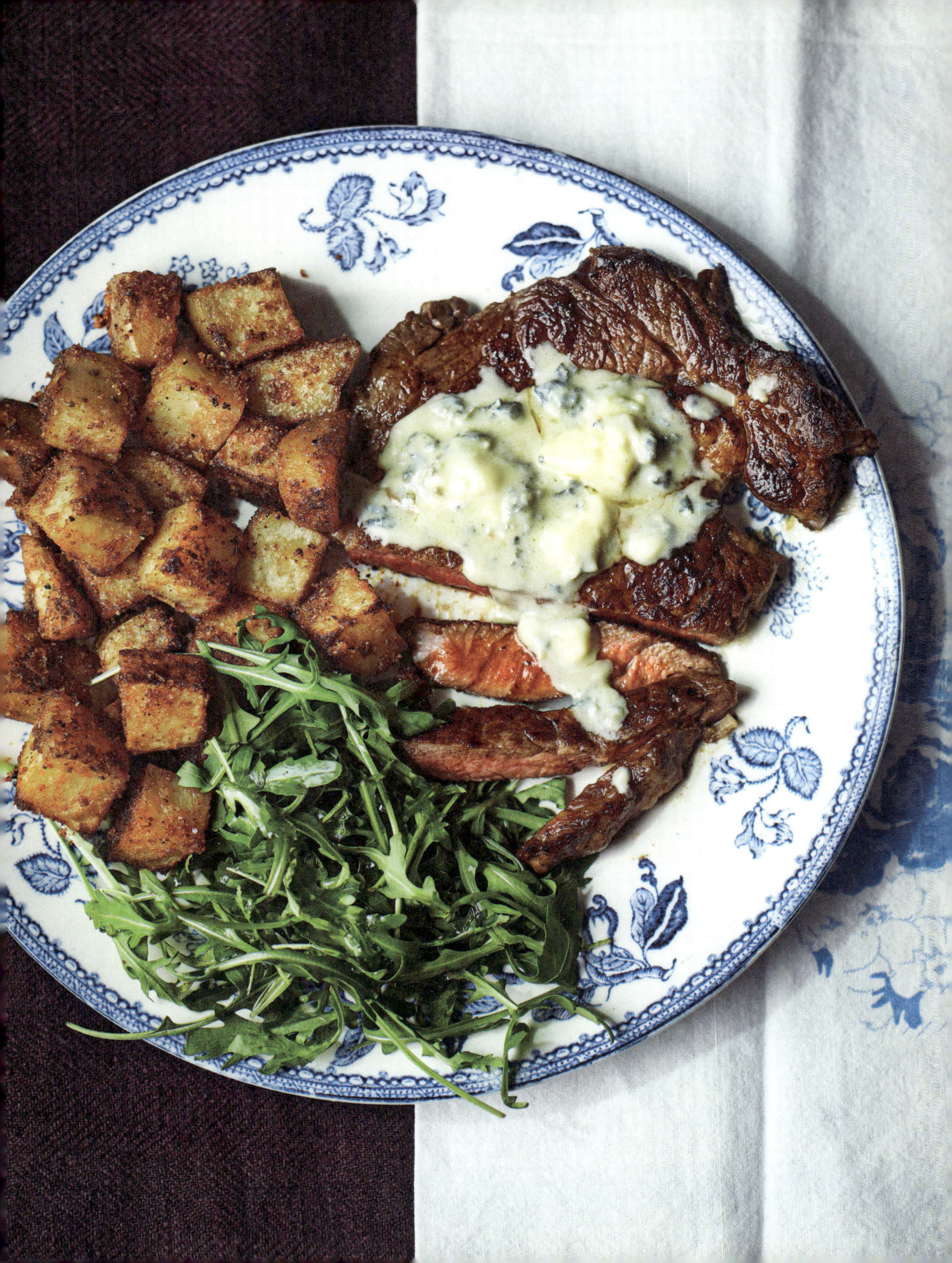

ONE POT

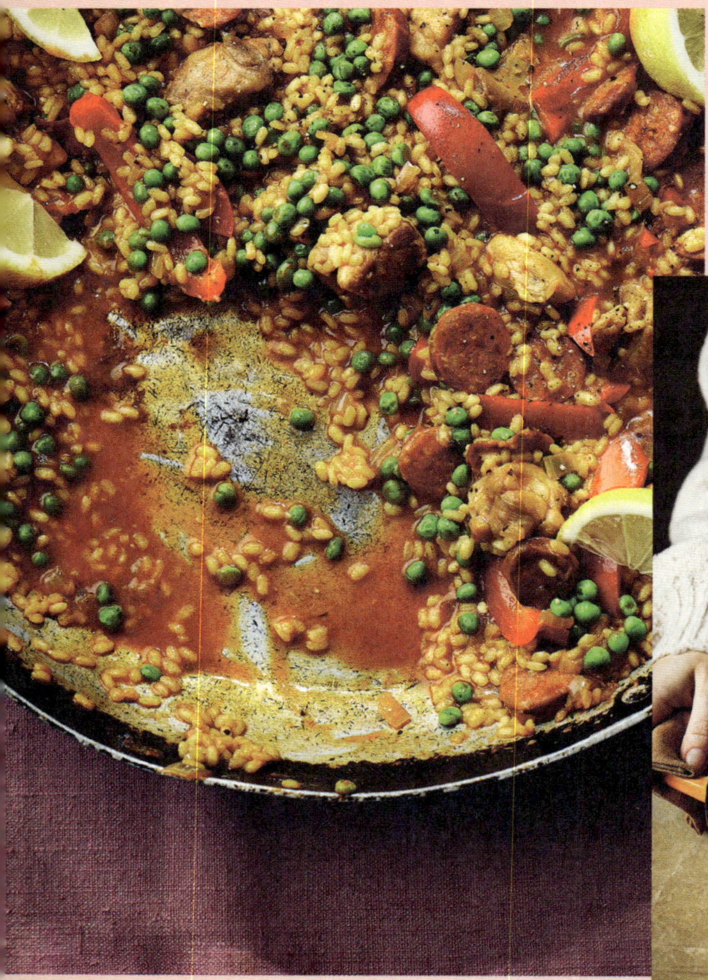
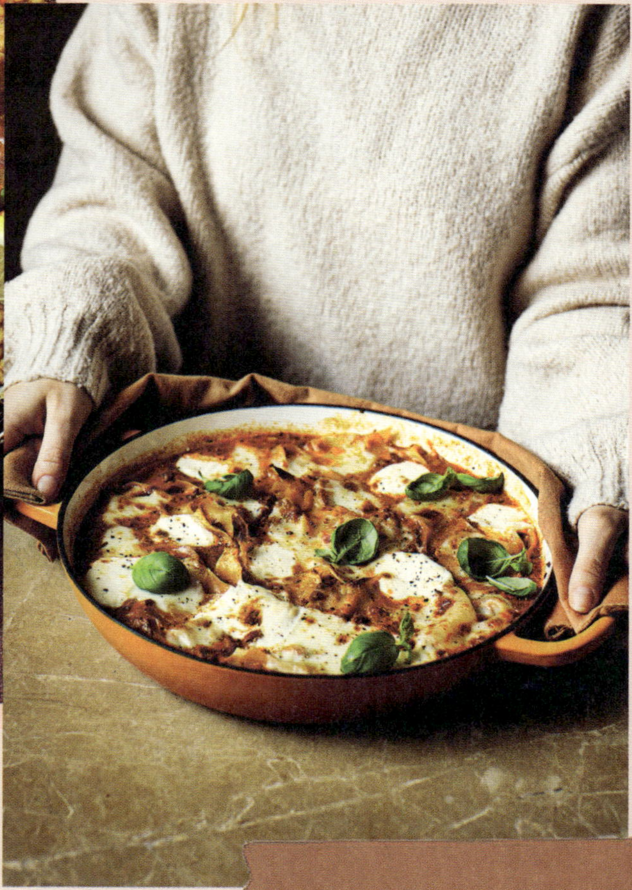
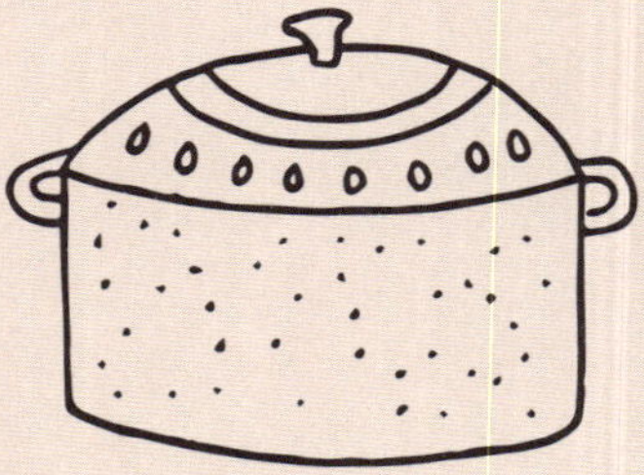
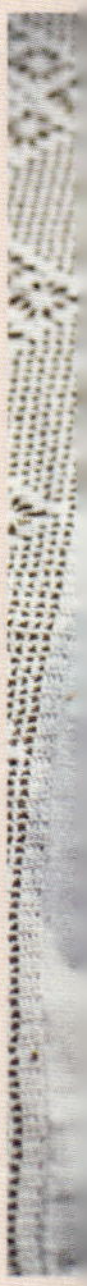

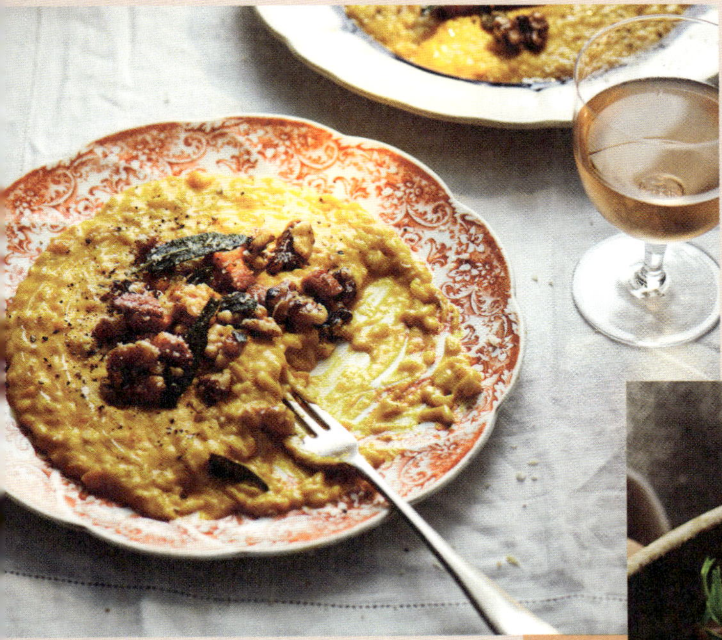
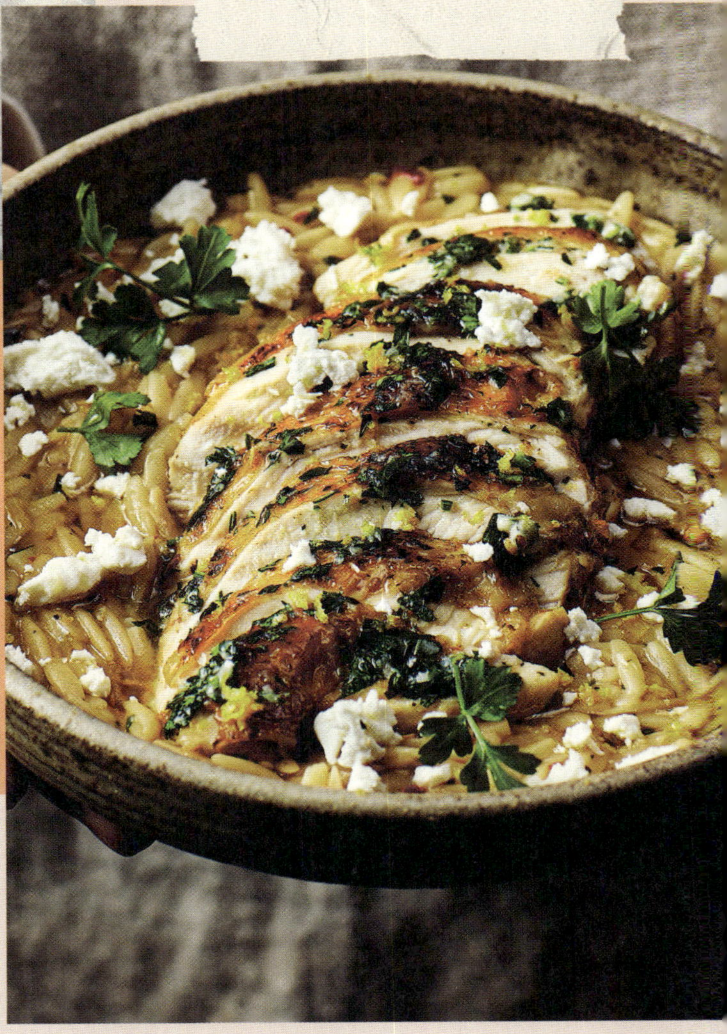

Creamy 'Marry Me' Chicken

SERVES 4
TOTAL TIME: 40 MINUTES

This recipe is an absolute winner, and yes, the person you make this for will propose to you soon after! It can be made in a slow cooker, after which you can shred the chicken, but this is a simple 40-minute one-pot version that you can serve over pasta, rice or, my personal favourite, mashed potatoes. This is going to be one of the best chicken recipes you've ever made, trust me.

My favourite way of serving this is to toss cooked pasta through the sauce and then shred the chicken. With extra parmesan on top, it's delicious.

1 tbsp salted butter
1 tbsp olive oil
1 onion, diced
1 tbsp finely chopped garlic
2 tbsp tomato purée (paste)
1 tbsp dried mixed herbs
1 tsp paprika
500ml (17fl oz/2¼ cups) double (heavy) cream
200g (7oz) parmesan, grated, plus extra to serve
8 skinless, boneless chicken thighs
1 tsp fine sea salt
1 tsp freshly ground black pepper
a few handfuls of basil leaves, to serve
pasta, rice or mashed potatoes, to serve

EQUIPMENT
chopping board—knife—deep frying pan with a lid—wooden spoon—grater—whisk

1. Heat the butter and oil in a deep frying pan with a lid over a medium heat, then add the onion and garlic for 4–6 minutes until softened. Stir in the tomato purée, mixed herbs and paprika, then pour in the cream and add the parmesan, whisking until everything is combined.

2. Nestle the chicken thighs into the sauce and cover with a lid, then cook for 25 minutes until the chicken is cooked through. Sprinkle over the basil then taste and season with the salt and pepper, if you need. Serve over the cosy carb of your choice, with extra parmesan.

SLOW COOKER
Throw everything in together and cook for 4 hours on medium. The chicken should be tender and falling apart after.

ALTERNATIVE INGREDIENTS
Double (heavy) cream: you can use cream cheese here
Chicken thighs: chicken breast is a good substitute

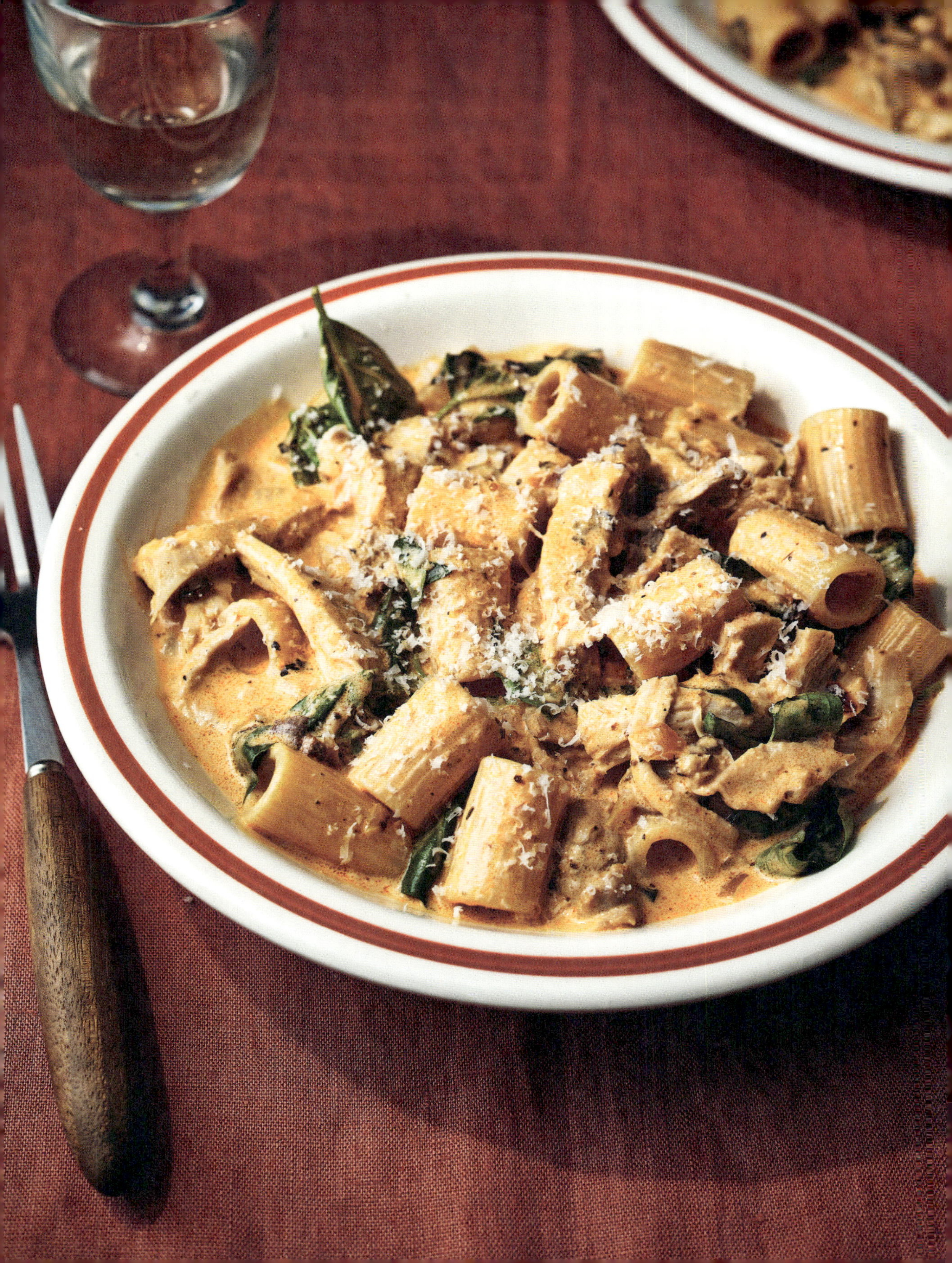

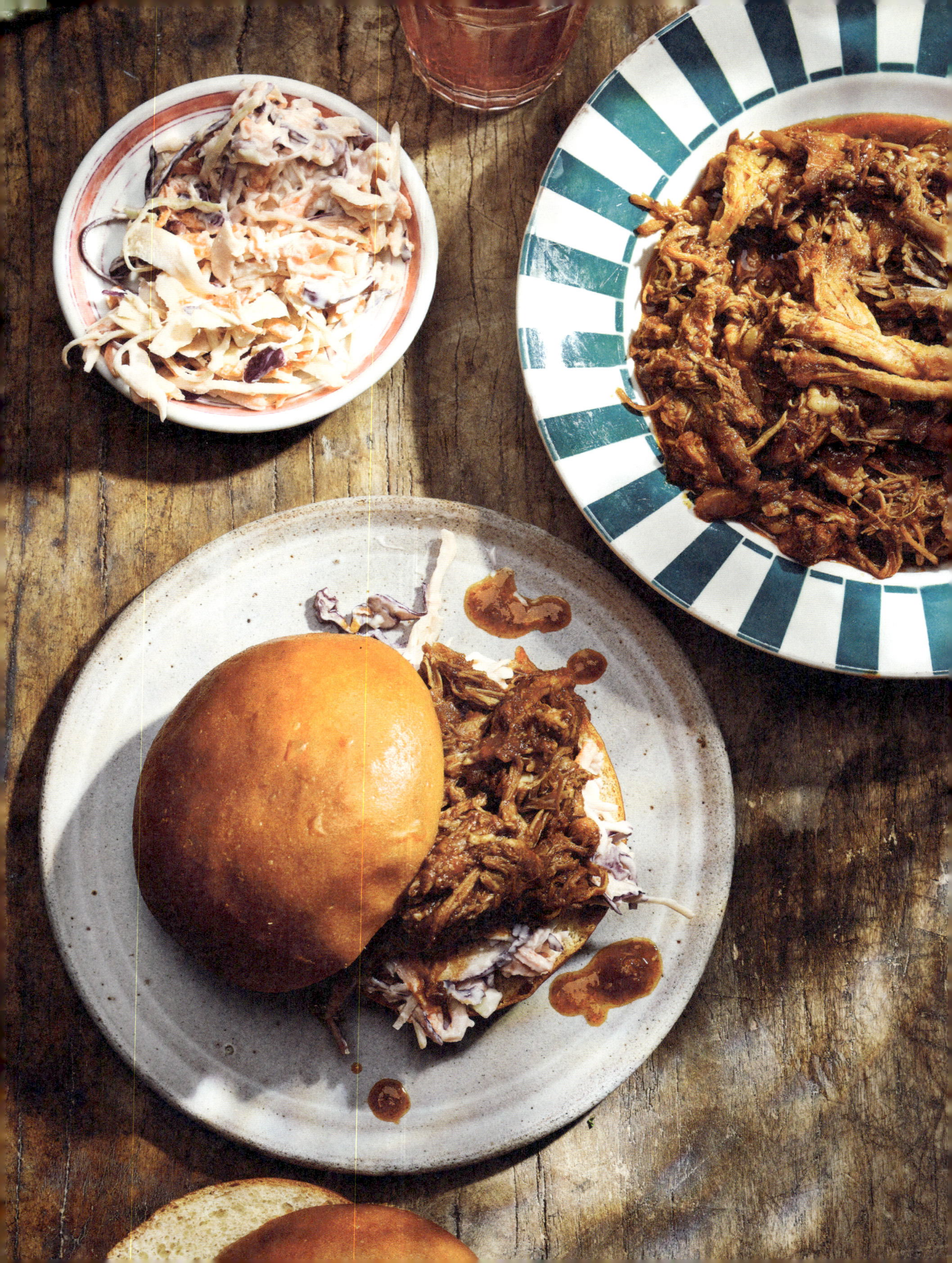

Slow-cooked BBQ Pulled Pork

SERVES 6–8
TOTAL TIME: 8 HOURS

Next time you have friends or family over, get this on in the morning and by the time they arrive there will be gorgeous pulled pork ready for baps and nachos. This is great for barbecue season but the way I love to eat this the most is to sit outside on a cold winter's day with coats on and fire pits lit and have it in a bread bun.

1.5kg (3lb 5oz) pork shoulder
1 onion, diced
1 tsp paprika
1 tsp garlic granules
1 tsp ground cumin
1 tsp ground coriander
2 tbsp tomato purée (paste)
1 tbsp dark brown sugar
4 tbsp BBQ sauce
1 tsp fine sea salt
1 tsp freshly ground black pepper
6–8 buns, to serve
coleslaw, to serve

EQUIPMENT
chopping board—knife—casserole dish or slow cooker

1. If you're using the oven, preheat it to 160°C (140°C fan/320°F/gas mark 3).

2. Combine everything in a casserole dish, cover and cook in the oven for 8 hours. Alternatively, combine everything in a slow cooker and cook on low for 8 hours.

3. Remove from the oven or slow cooker, discard the fat and stir the falling-apart pork through the sauce in the dish. Fill the buns with plenty of pork and the coleslaw.

Garlic Butter & Lemon Chicken Orzo

SERVES 2
TOTAL TIME: 40 MINUTES

In the summertime I always crave citrus flavours and popping this lemon chicken orzo dish on the table for the family to dig into is always a guarantee to make everyone smile. Silky smooth garlic butter orzo with lemon chicken bites works like a dream.

For extra lemon flavour add the squeezed lemon carcasses to the orzo and stock when that goes in and remove after everything is cooked. This really helps infuse the orzo with lemon flavour.

- 4–6 skin-on boneless chicken thighs or breasts
- zest and juice of 2 lemons, plus extra zest to serve
- 1 tsp garlic granules
- 1 tsp lemon salt
- 1 tsp freshly ground black pepper
- ½ tsp chilli (hot pepper) flakes
- 50g (1¾oz) garlic butter (to make your own see page 65)
- 2 tbsp olive oil
- 6 garlic cloves, finely chopped
- 150g (5½oz/¾ cup) orzo
- 400ml (14fl oz/generous 1½ cups) chicken stock
- 60g (2oz) feta
- handful of parsley, roughly chopped

EQUIPMENT
bowl—zester—deep frying pan with a lid wooden spoon

1. Put the chicken thighs or breast, lemon zest and juice, garlic granules, lemon salt, pepper and chilli flakes into a bowl. Mix well so the chicken is coated in the seasonings.

2. Heat the garlic butter, oil and chopped garlic in a deep frying pan over a medium heat. Once the butter has melted, add the chicken skin-side down. Cook for 5 minutes until the skin is crisp, then flip and cook for a further 8 minutes until the chicken is almost cooked through. Remove the chicken from the pan.

3. Add the orzo to the pan and mix it through the oil and seasonings (you can also add any leftover juices or seasoning from the bowl the chicken was seasoned in). Now pour in the chicken stock and return the chicken to the pan. Cover and simmer over a low-medium heat for 8 minutes until the orzo is fluffy and the chicken is cooked through. Sprinkle with the feta, parsley and more lemon zest, then serve.

ALTERNATIVE INGREDIENTS
Chicken thighs: chicken breast is a good substitute
Feta: use mozzarella, goat's cheese or parmesan instead

ONE POT

ONE POT 113

Warming Meatballs & Onion Gravy

SERVES 4
TOTAL TIME: 45–50 MINUTES

Inspired by classic English bangers and mash, this dish is pure comfort on a plate, taking you back to your childhood. Juicy meatballs smothered in rich onion gravy is the hearty meal we all look for when those darker days close in. I've used ready-made meatballs but if you want to make your own I have popped some tips below.

Making your own meatballs is a game-changer – you can play around with herbs and seasoning, but I usually keep it simple with garlic granules, onion granules and a shake or two of Worcestershire sauce. I will often batch-freeze a load at the weekend so I can chuck them into a pot when I need something quick and comforting.

2 tbsp olive oil
24 (600g/1lb 5oz) ready-made beef meatballs
50g (1¾oz) salted butter
4 onions or red onions, sliced
5–6 garlic cloves, finely chopped
2 tbsp plain (all-purpose) flour
600ml (20fl oz/2½ cups) beef stock
200ml (7fl oz/generous ¾ cup) red wine
1 tsp Dijon mustard
5 shakes of Worcestershire sauce
1 sprig of thyme
1 sprig of sage
fine sea salt
freshly ground black pepper
mashed potatoes, to serve
crispy sage leaves, to serve (optional)

EQUIPMENT
large saucepan—wooden spoon
chopping board—knife

1. Heat the oil in a large saucepan over a medium heat, then add the meatballs and cook for 10–12 minutes until brown all over. Remove from the pan once they're coloured and slightly crispy on the edges, then add the butter, onions and garlic. Cook for 10 minutes, making sure the pan isn't too hot and that you're not burning the onions.

2. Next, sprinkle in the flour and stir to coat the onions, then, little by little, pour in the beef stock and red wine – the flour will thicken the liquid. After this, add in the mustard, Worcestershire sauce, thyme, sage and salt and pepper to taste. Give it a good mix.

3. Return the meatballs to the pan and let everything simmer away for about 20 minutes until the gravy is a beautiful thick consistency, depending on your preference. Serve over creamy mash sprinkled with crispy sage leaves and tuck in!

ALTERNATIVE INGREDIENTS
If you're really pressed for time and don't want to make the gravy, use instant gravy, seasoning it with Worcestershire sauce and herbs for more of a homemade flavour.

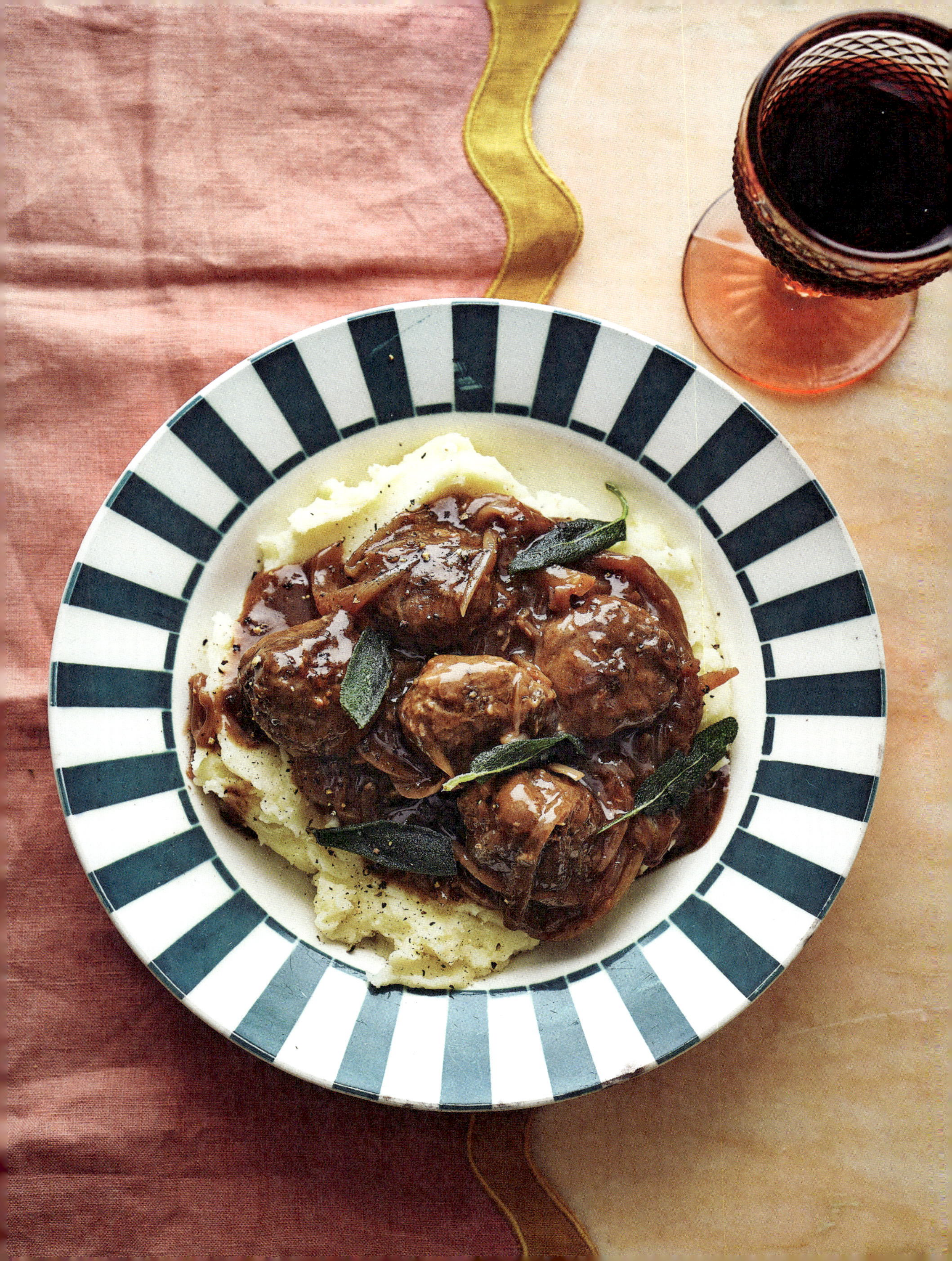

School Night Chicken & Broccoli Pasta Bake

SERVES 4
TOTAL TIME: 40 MINUTES

A pasta bake was always a go-to school night dinner for us when we were kids, and now that I am an adult, if I get to eat pasta during the week I am very happy. All you need to do is throw in some vegetables to make something that has goodness, flavour and comfort in one pot – basically what easy cooking is about, it shouldn't be stressful!

3–4 tbsp olive oil
1 onion, diced
6 garlic cloves, finely chopped
3–4 chicken breasts, diced
½ tsp chilli (hot pepper) flakes
1 tsp garlic granules
1 tsp dried Italian seasoning (or dried mixed herbs)
pinch of paprika
300–350g (10½–12oz) pasta of your choice (shapes I love for bakes are rigatoni, conchiglie or penne)
knob of salted butter
600ml (20fl oz/2½ cups) single (light) cream
200g (7oz) parmesan, grated
200g (7oz) mozzarella, sliced
350g (12oz) broccoli, finely chopped
100g (3½oz) green pesto

EQUIPMENT
chopping board—knife
ovenproof frying pan—wooden spoon
saucepan—grater

1. Preheat the oven to 220°C (200°C fan/425°F/gas mark 7).

2. Heat the oil in an ovenproof frying pan, then add the onion and garlic and cook for 4–6 minutes until softened before throwing in the chicken, chilli flakes, garlic granules, Italian seasoning and paprika. Cook the chicken for 8–10 minutes until browned.

3. Meanwhile, bring a large saucepan of water to the boil and cook the pasta according to the packed instructions, then drain.

4. Once the chicken is cooked, add the butter to the pan and scrape the bottom of the pan to lift off all the flavour that's stuck to it. Pour in the cream, then add the cheeses and broccoli. Cook for 3–5 minutes until the broccoli is cooked through.

5. Spoon in the cooked pasta and pesto and mix everything together. Transfer the pan to the oven and bake for 10 minutes until bubbling and the top has turned golden brown.

ALTERNATIVE INGREDIENTS
If you don't fancy pasta, throw some butter (lima) beans, or, for extra goodness, add both pasta and beans.

Slow-cooked Brisket Tacos

SERVES 8
TOTAL TIME: 4–8 HOURS

This can be thrown in the slow cooker and left to cook during the day, but I have also made it on the hob countless times. I love the way it makes the kitchen smell, so if you have a big saucepan with a lid and want to impress guests, this is the recipe to choose. I add all my favourite toppings to the soft tortillas at the end, and you can make them super personal for loved ones, including whatever they like best.

3–4 tbsp olive oil
1.8–2kg (4–4lb 6½oz) beef brisket
2 onions, finely chopped
1 red chilli, finely chopped
8 garlic cloves, finely chopped
200g (7oz) tomato purée (paste)
2 tsp garlic granules
2 tsp paprika
2 tsp ground cumin
2 tsp ground coriander
2–3 bay leaves
3 litres (5¼ pints/12½ cups) beef stock
fine sea salt
freshly ground black pepper

TO SERVE
small tortillas, toasted
guacamole
jalapeños, sliced
cheese of your choice, grated
coriander (cilantro), roughly chopped
lime wedges

EQUIPMENT
slow cooker or large saucepan with a lid
chopping board—knife—wooden spoon

1. If you're going to use a slow cooker, I recommend searing the meat first. Heat the oil in a frying pan over a medium-high heat and sear the beef for 2 minutes on each side until browned all over. While you're searing the beef, put all the other ingredients together into a slow cooker and give it a mix. Add the seared beef, cover and cook on low for 6–8 hours. When it's ready, the beef will be falling apart and then you're ready to load it into your tacos with all the fillings.

2. If you're cooking on the hob (stovetop), heat the oil in a large saucepan over a medium-high heat and sear the beef for 2 minutes on each side until browned all over. Remove the beef from the pan, then add the onion, chilli and garlic and cook for 4–5 minutes before stirring in the tomato purée. Next, add the garlic granules, paprika, cumin, coriander and bay leaves. Give everything a stir and then pour in the beef stock. Return the meat to the pan, pop the lid on and let this simmer over a high heat for 3–4 hours until the beef is starting to fall apart. Taste and season with salt and pepper as needed.

3. When you're ready to serve, stir the pulled meat into a few ladlefuls of the juice then pile into a tortilla with all your favourite fillings, serve and enjoy! Dunk the tortillas in the beef juices, then place in a hot frying pan. Add your chosen fillings, fold the taco over and flip until crispy and golden brown on both sides. Any remaining juice is lovely as a broth or freeze into cubes and add to meals.

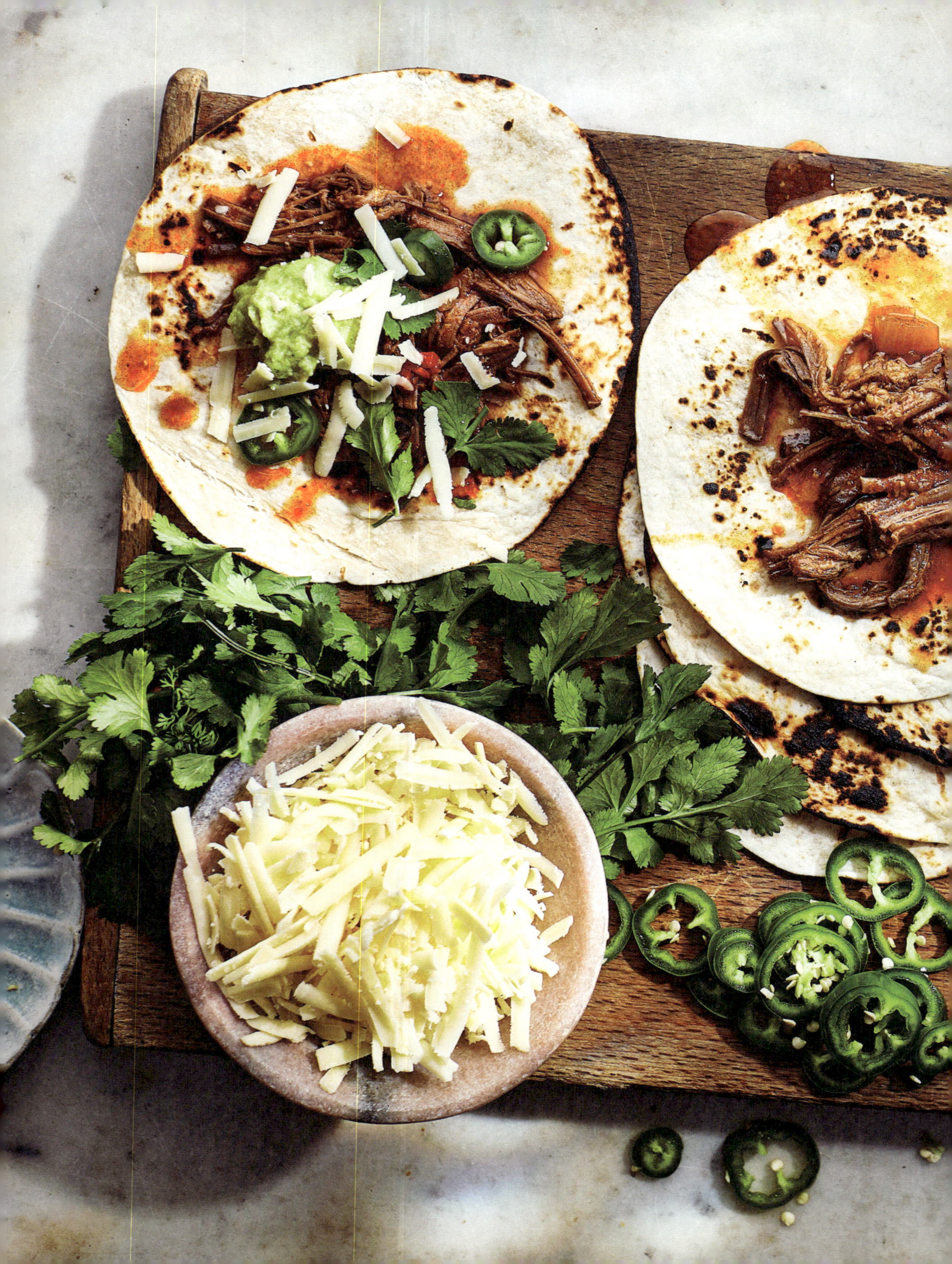

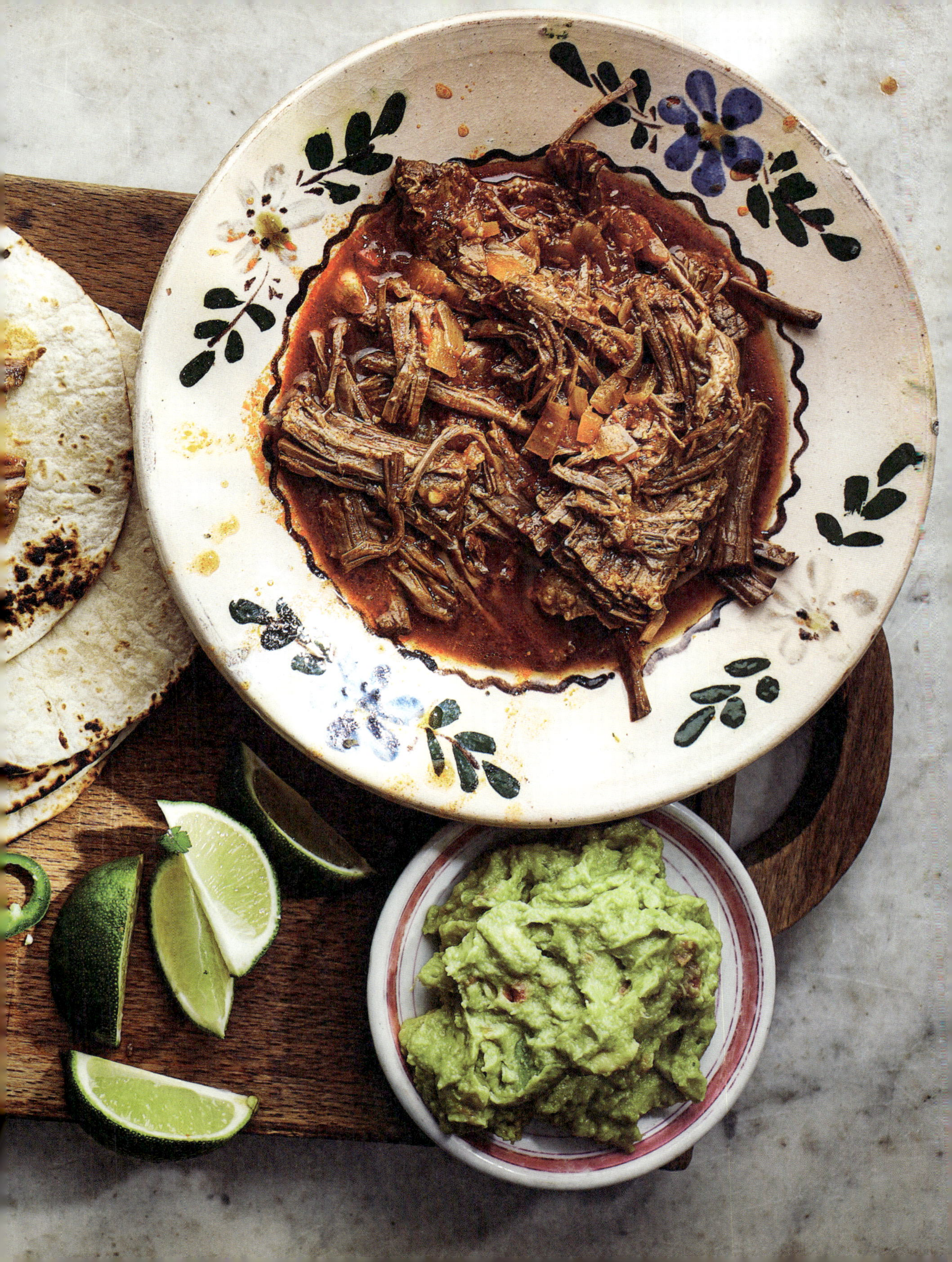

ONE POT

Summertime Tomato Stew

SERVES 4
TOTAL TIME: 20 MINUTES

This recipe it a light stew that comes together in just 20 minutes and uses lots of fresh, salty flavours that complement one another beautifully. It reminds me of puttanesca sauce, which I always enjoy in the warmer months, but you could serve over rice or toss through some pasta for a winter warmer.

2 tbsp olive oil
1 onion, diced
5 garlic cloves, finely chopped
1 tsp chilli (hot pepper) flakes
800g (1lb 12oz) mixed tomatoes (red, orange, yellow, green), quartered
300ml (10fl oz/1¼ cups) chicken stock
40g (1½oz) capers, chopped
240g (8½oz) kalamata olives
4 anchovy fillets, finely chopped
fine sea salt
freshly ground black pepper
a few handfuls of basil leaves, chopped
fresh bread and butter or rice

EQUIPMENT
chopping board—knife—saucepan
wooden spoon

1. Heat the oil in a saucepan over a medium heat, then add the onion, garlic and chilli flakes and fry for 5 minutes until the onion begins to soften.

2. Next, throw in the tomatoes and let them cook for 5–10 minutes, breaking them up with a spoon and letting those sweet, summery tomato juices release. Now stir in the stock, capers, olives and anchovies and let this bubble together for a further 5 minutes. Taste and season with salt and pepper if needed.

3. Serve with lots of buttered fresh bread or over rice, sprinkled with a big handful of chopped basil.

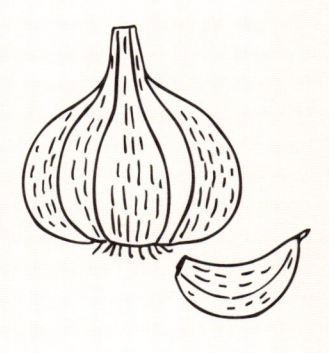

On the Coast 'Rock' Mussels

SERVES 4
TOTAL TIME: 30 MINUTES

My family and I used to go down to Rock in Cornwall every summer with my godparents and other loved ones. If you've been to Rock or Padstow, you will know that mussels are usually on every menu, so I wanted to create a quick, one-pot recipe based around those holidays. When in Cornwall, we take it in turns to cook when we have nights in, and this is something that I love to share with everyone.

If any mussels are open before being cooked, it usually means they are dead and shouldn't be eaten. If you tap them on the work surface and they don't close, throw them away.

100g (3½oz) salted butter, plus extra to serve
1 banana shallot, finely diced
1 bulb of garlic, cloves finely chopped
600ml (20 fl oz/2½ cups) dry white wine
200ml (7 fl oz/scant 1 cup) single (light) cream
1.2 kg (2lb 11oz) mussels, scrubbed
chopped chives, to serve
baguette, to serve

EQUIPMENT
chopping board—knife—deep saucepan with a lid

1. Melt the butter in a deep saucepan over a medium heat, then add the shallot and garlic and fry for a minute or two until fragrant. Now pour in the wine and cream and bring to a gentle simmer. Add the mussels and cover, then cook for 5 minutes until all the mussels have opened – if some haven't, don't force them open, but rather discard them. Sprinkle over the chives and serve with lots of buttered baguette for the ultimate Cornish dinner.

ALTERNATIVE INGREDIENTS
Dry white wine: try using prosecco to add a luxurious touch
Chives: parsley complements the other ingredients well

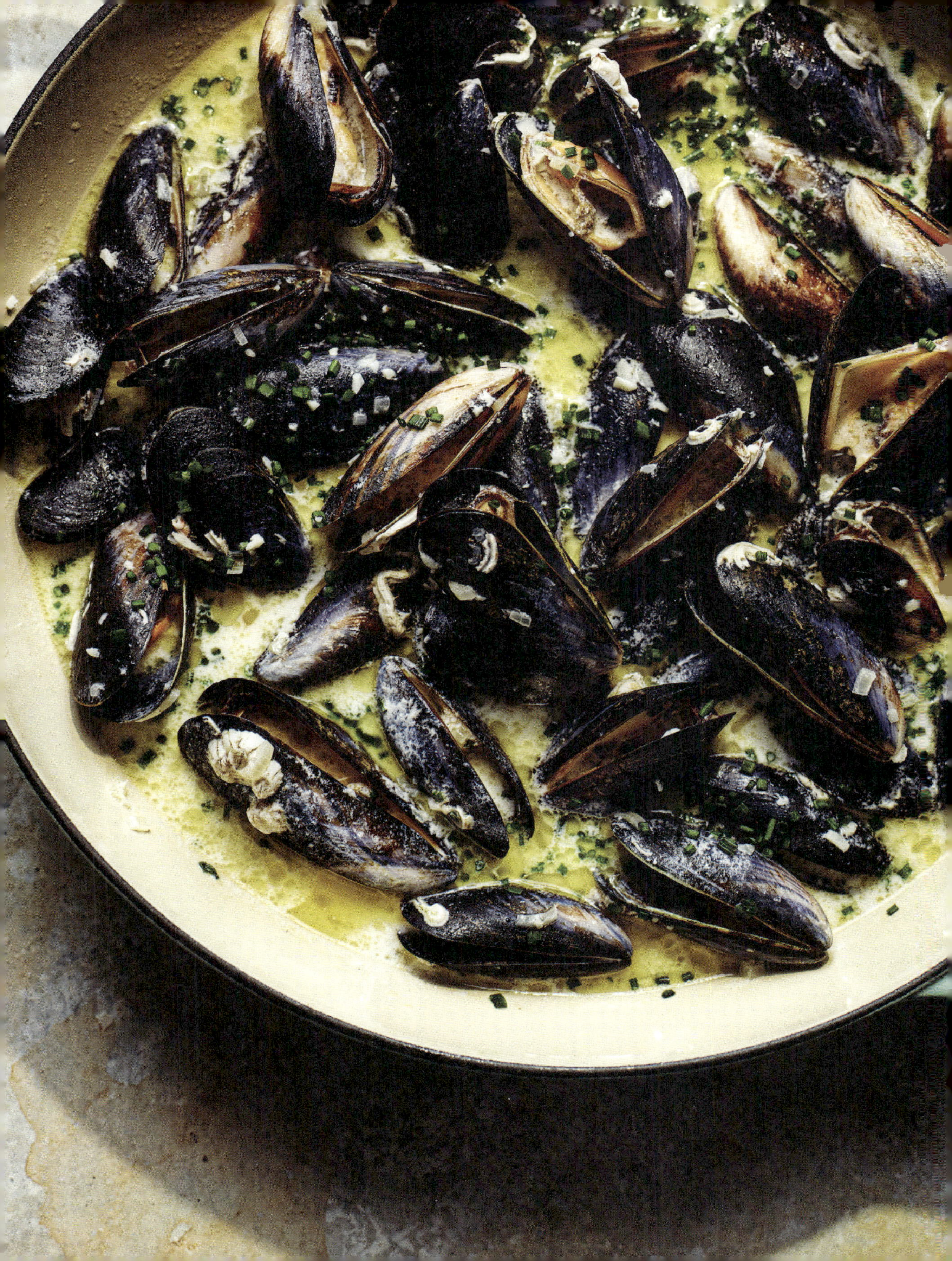

ONE POT

Sausage and Artichoke Pasta

SERVES 2
TOTAL TIME: 30 MINUTES

This sauce can be made in a pan or slow cooker, but either way, it's so easy to make. I love to serve it with small pasta shapes so I can get a big spoon and eat without any effort but also works great with spaghetti. I love using sausages in pasta sauces because they don't require any prep – just chuck them into a pan and crisp them up to add a flavour dimension that you can't find in other sauces.

1 tbsp olive oil
1 onion, diced
4 garlic cloves, finely chopped
1 tsp chilli (hot pepper) flakes
4 pork sausages
2 tbsp tomato purée (paste)
300ml (10fl oz/1¼ cups) double (heavy) cream
150g (5½oz) parmesan, grated, plus extra to serve
280g (10oz) jar of grilled artichoke hearts in oil, drained and chopped
400g (14oz) cooked pasta of your choice
fine sea salt
freshly ground black pepper

EQUIPMENT
chopping board—knife—saucepan
wooden spoon—grater

1 Heat the oil in a saucepan over a medium heat, then add the onion and garlic and fry for 4–6 minutes until softened. Add the chilli flakes and cook for a further minute.

2 Break up the sausages and add them to the pan. Fry for 10–15 minutes.

3 Stir in the tomato purée and cook for a couple of minutes until it turns a darker red. Add the cream, stir well to combine and simmer for 3 minutes then add the parmesan and simmer for a further 2 minutes. Season with salt and pepper.

4 Add the chopped artichokes and stir to combine, then stir in the pasta and serve sprinkled with a extra parmesan.

ALTERNATIVE INGREDIENTS
Pork sausages: you could use chorizo, pancetta or even lamb sausages
Double (heavy) cream: try using cream cheese instead
Artichokes: diced fried aubergine or courgette also work well

ONE POT

Chicken Broth with Mini Meatballs and Pasta

SERVES 4
TOTAL TIME: 30 MINUTES

If someone in your household or a friend is feeling slightly under the weather, whip this up for them and you'll become their new favourite person. This is warming comfort food at its finest. It's light and nourishing with a rich chicken broth dotted with mini meatballs, tiny pasta and mouthfuls upon mouthfuls of goodness. Once you've tried it, it will become a staple as soon as someone gets the sniffles.

Make lots of these meatballs and keep them in the freezer, then when someone in the house is coming down with something you can add them straight to the hot stock from frozen (just make sure to cook them for a bit longer).

250g (9oz) minced (ground) chicken
1 tsp fine sea salt
1 tsp garlic granules
50g (1¾oz) parmesan, grated, plus extra to serve
1 medium egg
1 tsp dried Italian seasoning
1.5 litres (50fl oz/6⅓ cups) chicken stock
300g (10½oz) mini pasta shapes of your choice
chopped parsley, to serve

EQUIPMENT
large bowl—saucepan—grater

1. Put the minced chicken into a large bowl along with the salt, garlic granules, parmesan, egg and Italian seasoning. Give it a good mix until everything is well combined, then use your hands to roll the mixture into mini meatballs, about the size of a 10 pence (1 dollar) coin.

2. Pour the chicken stock into a large saucepan over a medium-high heat and bring to a simmer. Gently plop in the meatballs and cook for 5 minutes, then add the pasta. Cook for a further 8 minutes. Ladle into bowls and serve sprinkled with parmesan and parsley.

ALTERNATIVE INGREDIENTS
Minced (ground) chicken: use another minced meat, although I find they are not as light and delicate as chicken mince
For an extra kick of goodness: throw in some finely chopped carrot and celery

ONE POT

ONE POT 127

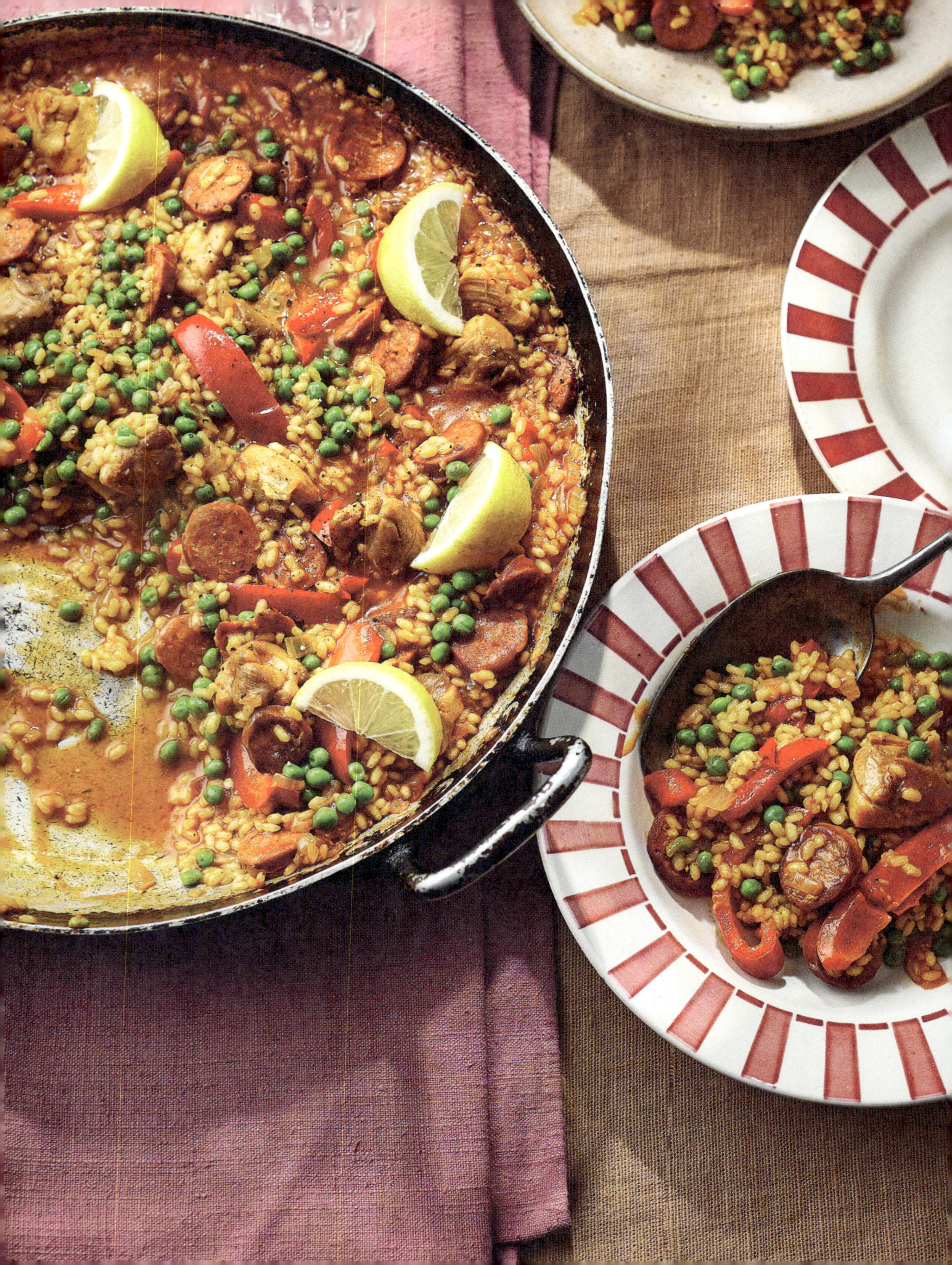

My Kinda One-pot Paella

SERVES 4
TOTAL TIME: 45 MINUTES

If you've got people over during the summer and want to serve something that's delicious, wholesome and keeps a crowd happy, this is your dish! It's so simple, just whack it all in the pot and leave it to cook. Serving this with fresh bread to soak up all those rich flavours is fantastic!

Once the rice has soaked up all the stock, I love to leave it to cook for a little longer so that the bottom crisps up and caramelises.

3–4 tbsp olive oil
225g (8oz) Spanish chorizo, diced or sliced into rounds
1 onion, finely diced
6 garlic cloves, finely chopped
450g (1lb) skinless, boneless chicken thighs, diced
1 tbsp tomato purée (paste)
2 red (bell) peppers, diced or sliced
1 tsp paprika
350g (12½oz/scant 1⅔ cups) risotto rice
1.1 litres (40fl oz/4½ cups) chicken stock
large pinch of saffron threads
large pinch of fine sea salt
large pinch of freshly ground black pepper
150g (5½oz/1 cup) frozen peas
1 lemon, cut into wedges, to serve

EQUIPMENT
chopping board—knife—casserole dish (Dutch oven)—wooden spoon

1. Heat the oil in a casserole dish, over a medium-high heat, then add the chorizo and fry for about 3 minutes until it has crisped up and released its oil. Next, reduce the heat to medium, add the onion and garlic and cook for 3–5 minutes until the onion has softened.

2. Now throw in the chicken and cook for 8–10 minutes until browned, then add the tomato purée and stir so it coats everything. Add the peppers and paprika and cook for 2 minutes, then add the rice and stock along with the saffron and salt and pepper. Cover and simmer gently for about 8 minutes until the rice is cooked but still has a slight bite. Finish this dish by folding through the peas.

3. When serving, place the lemon wedges around the edge of the dish so that when people serve themselves they can squeeze a little lemon over the top.

ALTERNATIVE INGREDIENTS
Chicken: use prawns (shrimp) instead, or just add prawns along with the chicken (that's my mum's favourite)

Pumpkin Risotto with Bacon & Walnut Crunch

SERVES 6
TOTAL TIME: 1½ HOURS

When it gets to pumpkin season, the colours of the trees start changing to reds, oranges, yellows and browns. I wanted to encapsulate that in a seasonal one-pot risotto, both visually and with warming autumnal flavours. Adding walnuts and pancetta brings an essence of autumn to this dish, pairing perfectly with the creamy pumpkin. It's a great dish to cook if you're having friends over when the cosy season approaches.

If you want to save time, you can use tinned pumpkin instead of fresh.

750g–1kg (1lb 10½oz–2lb 4oz) pumpkin, halved and deseeded
3 tbsp olive oil
150g (5½oz) unsmoked pancetta, diced
5 sage leaves
200g (7oz) walnuts, roughly chopped
4 garlic cloves, finely chopped
400ml (14fl oz/1¾ cups) white wine
zest and juice of 1 lemon
350g (12½oz/scant 1⅔ cups) risotto rice
400ml (14fl oz/1¾ cups) chicken or vegetable stock
100g (3½oz) parmesan, grated
100ml (3½fl oz/scant ½ cup) double (heavy) cream
fine sea salt
freshly ground black pepper

EQUIPMENT
chopping board—knife—casserole dish (Dutch oven) or other ovenproof pan small bowl—grater

1. Preheat the oven to 220°C (200°C fan/425°F/gas mark 7).

2. First, we are going to roast the pumpkin. Place the pumpkin in a casserole dish drizzle with the olive oil and season with salt and pepper. Roast in the oven for 1 hour. After this time it will be so easy to pull away from the skin.

3. Remove the pumpkin from the oven and scrape the flesh from the skin with a fork (you can discard the skins – my chickens love them). Put the flesh in a bowl and set aside.

4. Place the casserole dish over a medium-high heat, throw in the pancetta and cook for 6-8 minutes, until golden and crisp. Transfer to another bowl (this is going to be our topping up bowl). Add the sage and walnuts to the pancetta fat in the pan and stir for 2 minutes so they crisp up slightly. Pop these into the bowl with the pancetta.

5. Now put the pumpkin flesh into the pan along with the garlic and white wine, allow the alcohol to cook off for 2 minutes and then throw in the risotto rice. Add the zest and juice of the lemon and stock and let this bubble for 6 minutes or so until the rice is nearly cooked. At this point, add the parmesan and cream and mix through to create a beautifully indulgent pumpkin risotto. Serve sprinkled with the pancetta, walnuts and sage, and more black pepper if you like.

ALTERNATIVE INGREDIENTS
Pumpkin: try butternut squash for a similar flavour
Pancetta: bacon bits or chorizo are both good alternatives
White wine: prosecco or champagne really elevate this dish

ONE POT

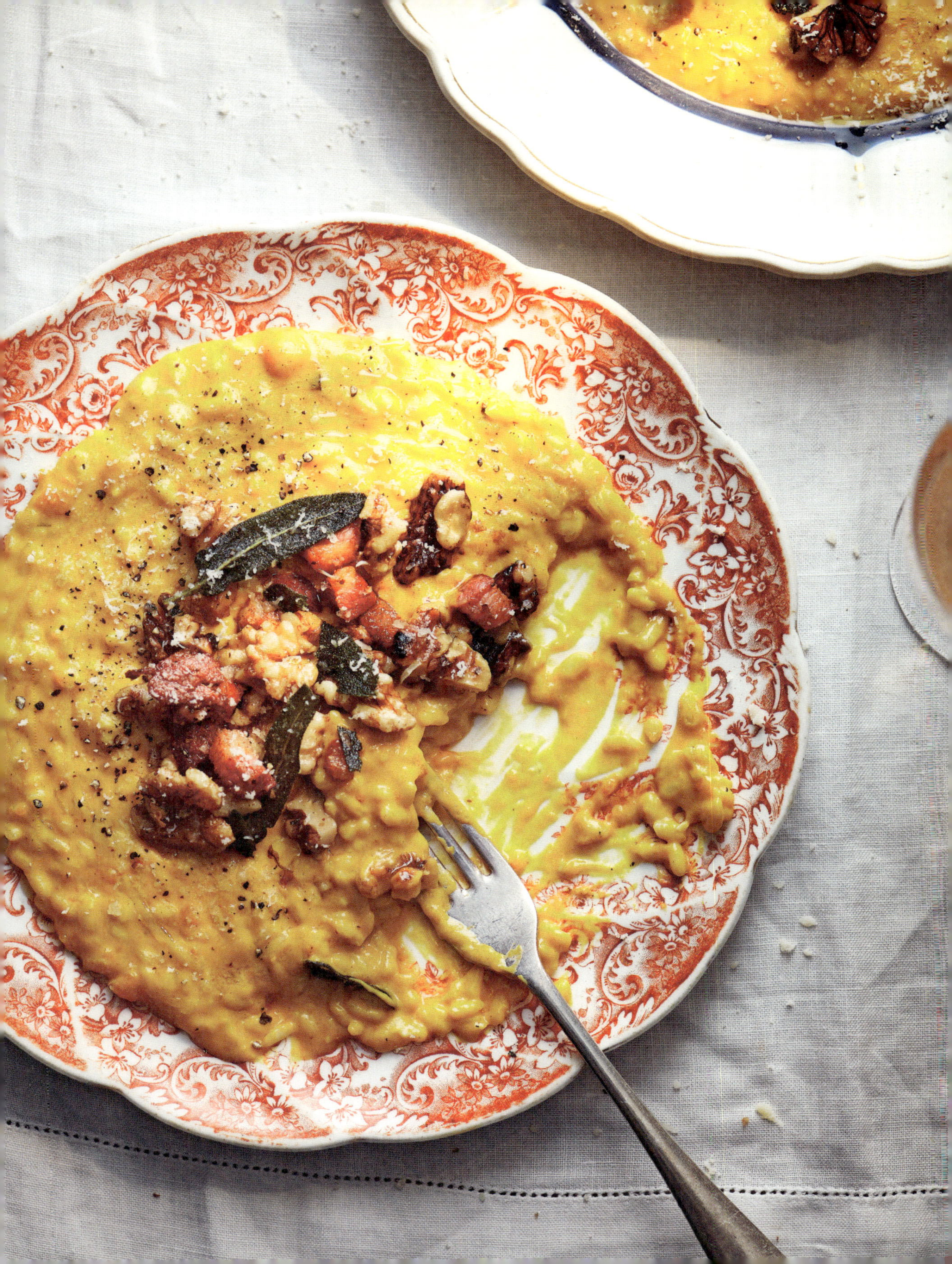

ONE POT

My Version of a Deconstructed Lasagne

SERVES 4
TOTAL TIME: 1¼ HOURS

There was a time when it seemed like everyone on social media was making lasagne soup... I never really got involved with that trend, but I did think that it would be a great way to make lasagne in one pan while throwing in a lot more creamy, cheesy goodness. This is a great recipe to make to use up that half a packet of lasagne sheets that you have hanging around in the back of the cupboard!

3–4 tbsp olive oil
400g (14oz) minced (ground) beef
150g (5½oz) Spanish chorizo, diced
1 onion, diced
5 garlic cloves, finely chopped
large pinch of fine sea salt
large pinch of freshly ground black pepper
1 tsp dried Italian seasoning
1 tsp garlic granules
3 tbsp tomato purée (paste)
150ml (5fl oz/⅔ cup) red wine
400g (14oz) tin of chopped tomatoes
500ml (17fl oz/generous 2 cups) beef stock
50g (1¾oz) parmesan, grated (or a parmesan rind, if you have one in the refrigerator), plus extra to serve
300g (10½oz) lasagne sheets, broken
150ml (5fl oz/⅔ cup) single (light) cream
250g (9oz) ricotta or mascarpone
150g (5½oz) mozzarella, sliced
a handful of basil leaves
garlic bread, to serve

EQUIPMENT
chopping board—knife—large saucepan
grater

1. Heat the oil in a saucepan over a medium-high heat, then add the beef and chorizo and cook for 10–12 minutes until the beef has browned and chorizo releases its oil. Next, throw in the onion and garlic and cook for 4–6 minutes until softened. Season with the salt, pepper, Italian seasoning and garlic granules, then stir through the tomato purée.

2. Next, pour in the red wine, chopped tomatoes and beef stock, then add the parmesan and lasagne sheets. Give this a mix and let the sheets soften for 10–12 minutes as some of this liquid evaporates. Bring to a gentle simmer, then add the cream and stir through. Turn on the grill (broiler).

3. Continue simmering the lasagne for another 25 minutes until the pasta is cooked and the sauce is a consistency you like. Dollop the ricotta or mascarpone on top along with the slices of mozzarella. Stick this under the grill for around 10 minutes until the top is golden and bubbling. Remove from the grill and sprinkle with more parmesan.

4. Get a big spoon and serve (for me, that's always with copious amounts of garlic bread).

ALTERNATIVE INGREDIENTS
Minced ground beef: for a different flavour, you can use lamb or chicken mince
Red Wine: if you'd prefer to avoid alcohol, replace the wine with 150ml (5fl oz/⅔ cup) of beef stock
Mascarpone: you can use dollops of cream cheese here instead

ONE POT

Simple Coconut Curry

SERVES 4
TOTAL TIME: 25 MINUTES

This recipe is jam-packed with flavour, but the best thing is that you can make it veggie or vegan so easily – just swap the chicken for paneer or chickpeas and you have a gorgeous hearty curry perfect for everyone.

4–5 tbsp olive oil (or coconut oil if you like the flavour)
4 banana shallots, sliced
6 garlic cloves, finely chopped
5cm (2in) piece of ginger, finely chopped
1 red chilli, finely chopped
450g (1lb) skinless, boneless chicken thighs, diced
1 tsp caraway seeds
2 tsp garam masala
1 tsp ground cumin
1 tsp garlic granules
½ tsp paprika
400ml (14fl oz/1⅔ cups) coconut milk

TO SERVE
chopped coriander (cilantro),
jasmine rice
naan

EQUIPMENT
chopping board—knife—large saucepan with a lid

1. Heat the oil in a large saucepan over a medium heat, then add the shallots and garlic and fry for 4–6 minutes until softened. Throw in the ginger and chilli and cook for a minute longer.

2. Next, add the chicken and cook for a few minutes until it picks up some colour, then stir in in all of the spices. Cook for 1 minute until the spices are fragrant. Pour in the coconut milk, cover and simmer for 5–10 minutes until all the flavours have infused and the chicken is cooked through.

3. Serve with a sprinkle of coriander over fluffy jasmine rice with lots of naan.

ALTERNATIVE INGREDIENTS
Caraway seeds: cumin seeds add an aromatic warmth

ONE POT

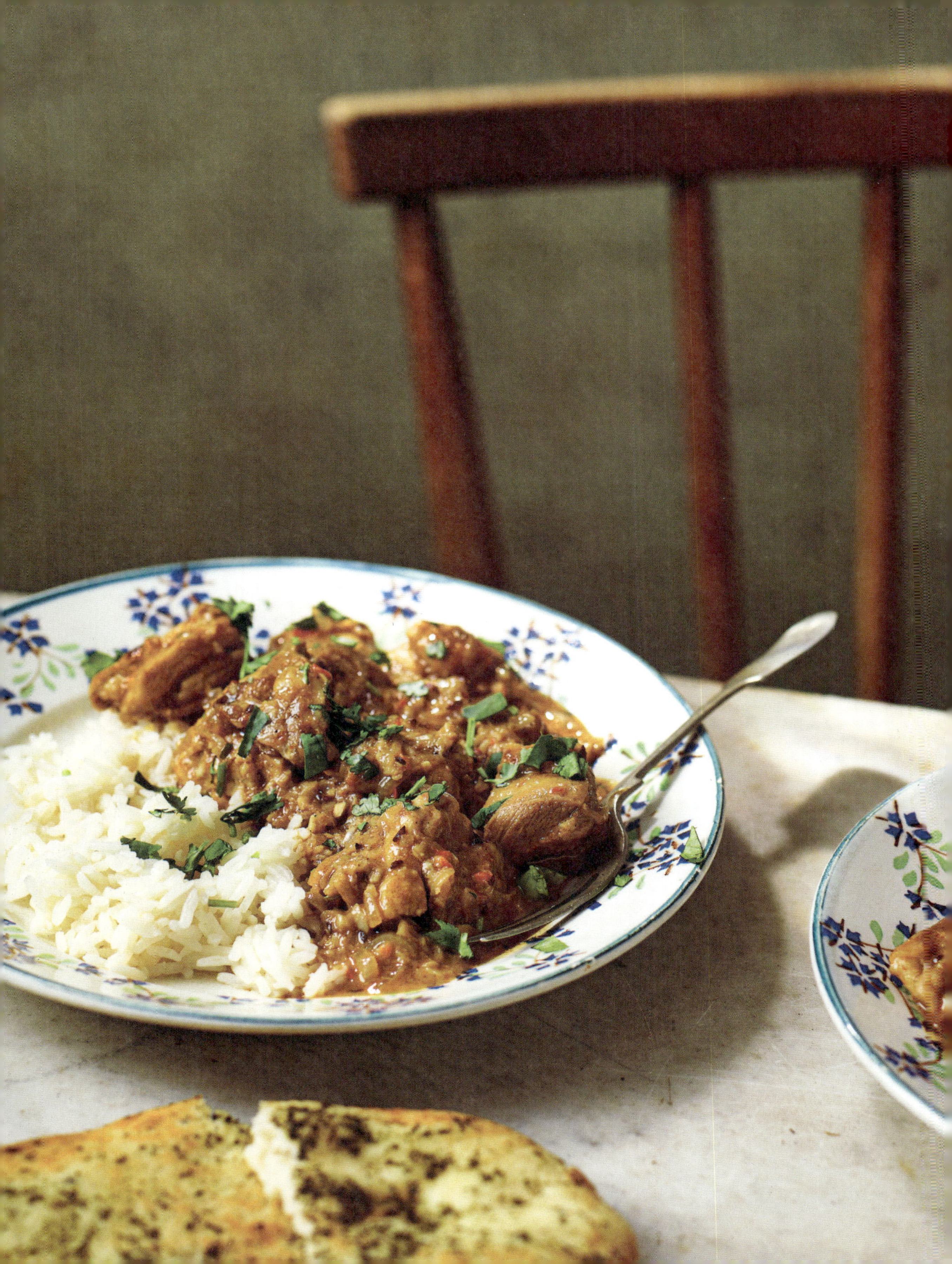

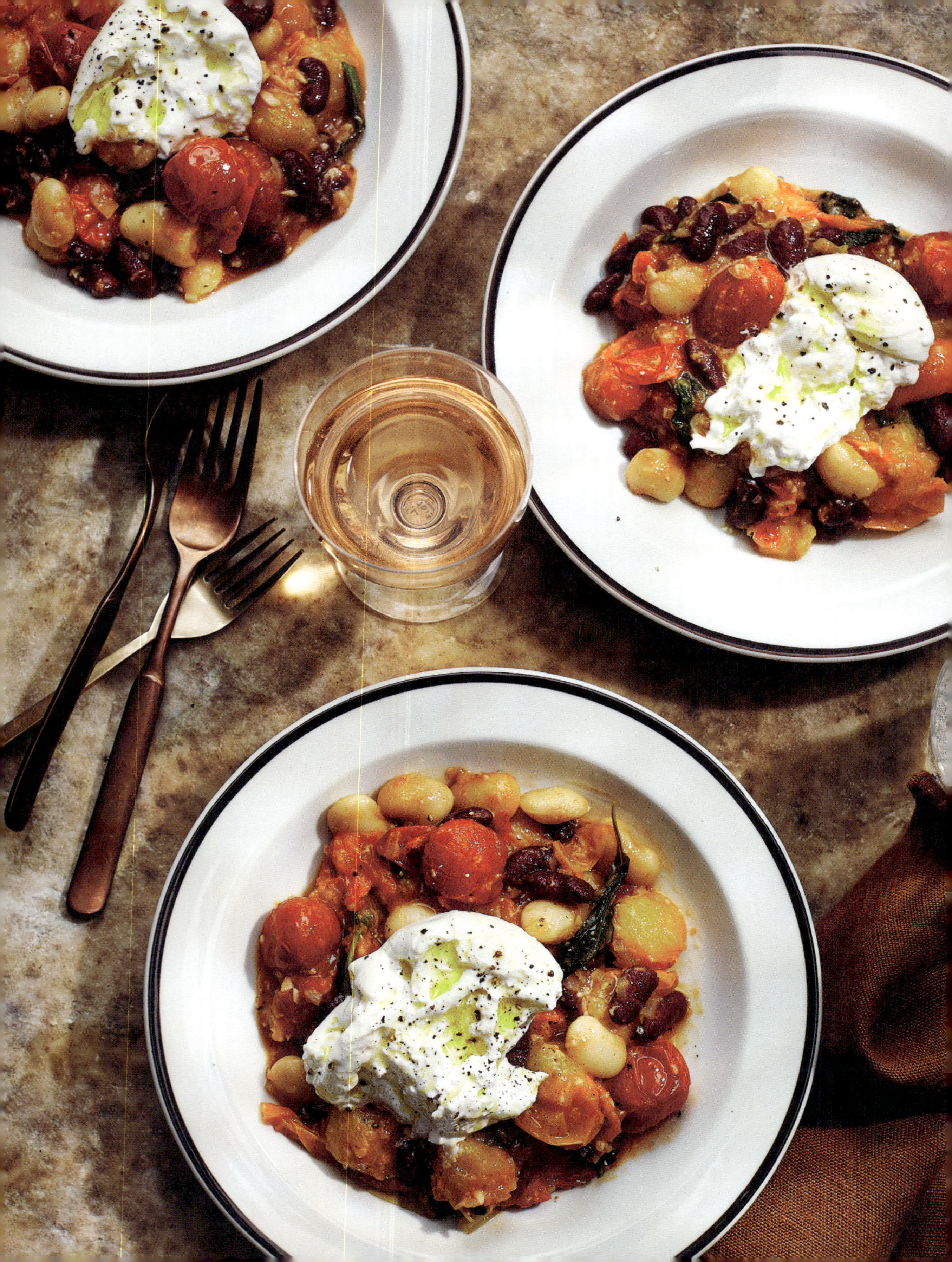

Mixed Tomato & Bean Stew with Burrata

SERVES 4
TOTAL TIME: 30 MINUTES

It's no secret amongst my friends that I am a bean fan, in fact when my girls and I get together each Tuesday for our run club, we all go back to mine for jacket potatoes. We take turns bringing the filling and the joke is that Hari will be happy every week with something bean based! Beans on a jacket potato is so comforting and I wanted to develop something just as satisfying for those warmer days. This stew is light yet filled with all of those flavours, and enjoyed best with buttery sourdough. Perfect for any meal time, weekend breakfasts, lunches or dinners, it's a great way to enjoy beans all year round!

4 tbsp extra virgin olive oil, plus extra to serve
1 bulb of garlic, cloves finely chopped
4 banana shallots, finely diced
800g (1lb 12oz) mixed cherry tomatoes
25g (1oz) basil leaves
400g (14oz) drained, jarred butter (lima) beans
400g (14oz) drained jarred kidney beans
100ml (3½fl oz/scant ½ cup) chicken or vegetable stock
50g (1¾oz) parmesan, grated
150g (5½oz) burrata
freshly ground black pepper, to serve
toasted sourdough bread and salted butter, to serve (optional)

EQUIPMENT
chopping board—knife—large saucepan with a lid—wooden spoon—grater

1. Heat the oil in a saucepan over a medium heat, then add the garlic and shallots and fry for 3 minutes until starting to soften.

2. Next, add the tomatoes. You can slice the tomatoes first or just throw them in whole, but be aware that we will want to break them down in the pan, so halving can make this step easier. Cook the tomatoes for 10 minutes until they are soft and almost creating their own sauce. Once they have totally collapsed, stir in the basil.

3. Now add the butter beans and kidney beans along with the stock and parmesan. Cover and let this simmer for 5–10 minutes until you have a glossy, thick sauce.

4. Serve in bowls with the burrata torn over the top and drizzled with olive oil and sprinkled with black pepper. Eat with copious amounts of toasted sourdough lathered in salted butter.

ALTERNATIVE INGREDIENTS
Cherry tomatoes: feel free to remove a handful of tomatoes and replace with some jarred roasted red peppers
Butterbeans: cannellini (lima) beans or any other large white bean work here
Burrata: grated mozzarella can be used instead

Comfort Mac & Cheese with a Buffalo Twist

SERVES 6
TOTAL TIME: 1 HOUR

I think any chef would tell me off for the way I make this mac and cheese, but I will say to go with your gut on this. The most important thing is that it's delicious, doesn't use multiple pans and keeps the family happy. For me there is no right or wrong way to cook. If you can combine flavours and textures that you enjoy to make a meal, then that's what cooking is all about.

Check your mac and cheese halfway through cooking and if you think it's looking a little dry, add a splash more milk.

100g (3½oz) salted butter
6 tbsp plain (all-purpose) flour
1 tsp garlic granules
1 tsp onion granules
1 tsp paprika
1 tsp fine sea salt
1 tsp freshly ground black pepper
1 litre (34fl oz/4¼ cups) whole milk
400ml (14fl oz/1⅔ cups) chicken stock
500g (1lb 2oz) macaroni
200g (7oz) cheddar, grated
200g (7oz) red Leicester, grated
100g (3½oz) mozzarella, torn
200g (7oz) parmesan, grated
150ml (5fl oz/⅔ cup) buffalo hot sauce
chopped chives, to serve

EQUIPMENT
deep casserole dish (Dutch oven)
wooden spoon—grater

1. Preheat the oven to 200°C (180°C fan/425°F/gas mark 6).

2. Melt the butter in a deep casserole dish over a medium heat, then whisk in the flour, garlic granules, onion granules, paprika, salt and pepper to make a paste. Now, little by little, whisk in the milk and stock (it will be thin, but don't worry). Add the macaroni along with half the cheddar, red Leicester and mozzarella, and all the parmesan. When this is mixed through, stir in the buffalo hot sauce. Cover and bake in the oven for 18–20 minutes until the cheese has formed a golden crust on top.

3. Remove the pan from the oven and give it a mix and taste – if it needs it, add a little more salt and pepper. Top the macaroni with the remaining cheeses and pop it back in the oven, uncovered, for 12–15 minutes until the cheeses have melted and are golden brown and bubbling. That's it! Serve with a sprinkle of chives.

ALTERNATIVE INGREDIENTS
Plain flour: cornflour (cornstarch) is an alternative gluten-free thickener
Whole milk: single (light) cream works here too
Buffalo hot sauce: any hot sauce or bbq sauce can be used in the place of the buffalo hot sauce

ONE POT 139

Nostalgic Mini Pasta Shape Soup

SERVES 2
TOTAL TIME: 35 MINUTES

My Nana would make this for us when we had a cold or if we were generally feeling a bit rubbish, so for me it's so nostalgic and takes me back to being a little girl. It's simple and one of the best things about this recipe is that it's easy to adapt to whatever you have in your refrigerator. Use any little pasta shapes you like – Nana would use is ditalini, which I always thought was like chopped up macaroni!

3 tbsp olive oil
1 onion, diced
4 garlic cloves, finely chopped
1 carrot, finely diced
1 red chilli, finely diced
4 pork sausages, removed from the casing and broken into pieces
1 tbsp tomato purée (paste)
200g (7oz) ditalini or any tiny pasta
1.1 litres (40fl oz/4½ cups) chicken or vegetable stock
100g (3½oz) parmesan, grated, plus extra to serve
fine sea salt
freshly ground black pepper
chopped chives, to serve

EQUIPMENT
chopping board—knife—large saucepan with a lid—wooden spoon—grater

1. Heat the oil in a large saucepan over a medium heat, then add the onion, garlic, carrot, chilli and sausages. Fry for 15 minutes until the sausages have crisped up and turned golden on their rough edges.

2. Once the sausage is crispy, stir through the tomato purée and season with salt and pepper. Add the pasta, stock and parmesan. Cover and cook for about 15 minutes until the pasta is done to your liking.

3. Serve with a sprinkle of fresh chives over the top, more parmesan and black pepper.

ALTERNATIVE INGREDIENTS
Pasta: throw some butter (lima) beans, or, for extra goodness, add both pasta and beans

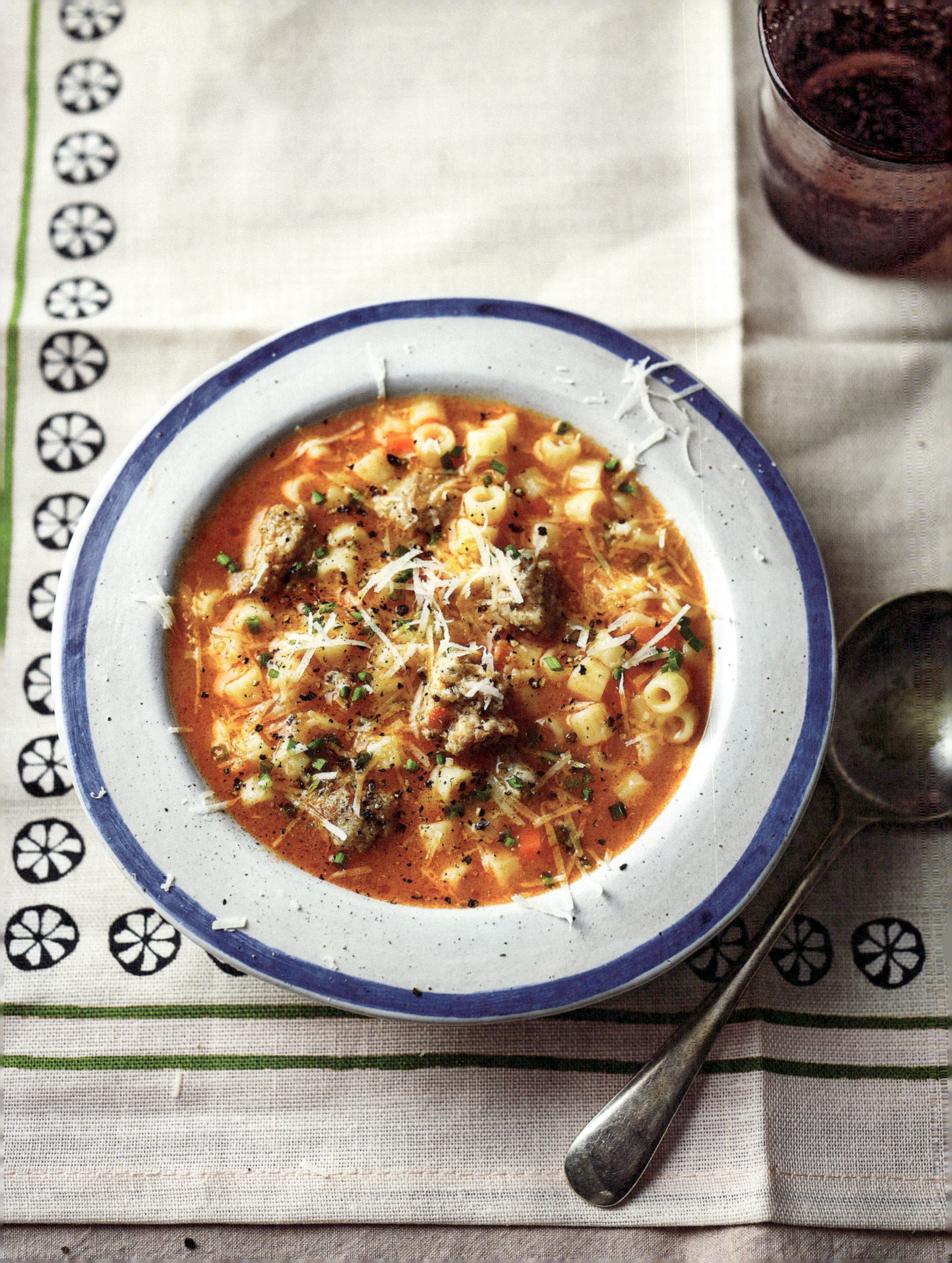

ONE POT

Chorizo & Butter Bean Stew

SERVES 2
TOTAL TIME: 20 MINUTES

This is one of my go to dishes when I am looking for something hearty, vibrant and packed with bold flavours. Getting a warm french baguette or some freshly baked focaccia and dunking it into this chorizo-infused stew, with little pops of creamy butter beans is one of the most comforting and satisfying things you'll do. It's the perfect dish to serve when you're wanting something hot and wholesome.

This is perfect for any meal – if I want to eat it for breakfast or lunch and fancy an added hit of protein, I crack one of our fresh chicken eggs on top while it simmers away to make a kind of shakshuka.

2 tbsp olive oil
1 onion, diced
6 garlic cloves, finely chopped
225g (8oz) Spanish chorizo, diced
1 heaped tbsp tomato purée (paste)
1 tsp dried Italian seasoning
pinch of dried thyme
pinch of fine sea salt
400–500g (14oz–1lb 2oz) drained jarred butter (lima) beans
400g (14oz) tin of good-quality chopped tomatoes (plus half a tin of water, swilled out)
1 bay leaf
chopped parsley, to serve
crusty bread, to serve

EQUIPMENT
chopping board—knife—saucepan with a lid

1. Heat the oil in a saucepan over a medium heat, add the onion and garlic fry for 4–6 minutes until softened. Add the chorizo and let this crisp up for a few minutes and release its oil, which will flavour the stew.

2. When the chorizo has some crispy bits, add the tomato purée, Italian seasoning, thyme and salt. Stir well, then add the butter beans, chopped tomatoes and water, and bay leaf. Cover and simmer for 10 minutes. Serve with a sprinkle of parsley, then get to dunking your bread into this flavourful stew!

ALTERNATIVE INGREDIENTS
Onion: shallots provide a slightly sweeter base
Chorizo: pancetta or bacon are good replacements
Butterbeans: any beans or chickpeas would work well here too

ONE POT

Gyoza Noodle Soup

SERVES 2
TOTAL TIME: 15 MINUTES

Keeping a bag of ready made gyozas in my freezer means that I can whip up something simple and delicious in minutes. This soup feels like a treat, it's warming, satisfying and filled with flavour. If your partner, sister, mum or friend comes over and lets you know they've had a long day, they're cold and all that they want is bed, preparing this for them will make them feel 10 times better!

I like to add prawns (shrimp) or shredded chicken for extra protein, and my partner loves a jammy egg (see page 42) on top! You really can make this your own once you have the creamy curry base.

50g (1¾oz) Thai red curry paste
800ml (27fl oz/3⅓ cups) coconut milk
150ml (5fl oz/⅔ cup) chicken stock
250g (9oz) pak choi (bok choy), roughly chopped
250g (9oz) ramen noodles
240g (8½oz) gyozas
chilli oil, to serve
a handful of roughly chopped coriander (cilantro), to serve

EQUIPMENT
saucepan with a lid—wooden spoon

1. Put the curry paste into a saucepan over a medium heat, add the coconut milk and stock and bring to a gentle simmer. Add the pak choi and noodles, cover and cook for 3–5 minutes (depending on how long your noodles need).

2. I like to cook my gyozas in the oven or air fryer for 5 minutes at 200°C (180°C fan/425°F/gas mark 6) to crisp them up. Alternatively, you can just throw them into the soup at the same time as the noodles (but check the packet in case they need longer).

3. Once everything has cooked, ladle the soup into bowls and garnish with lots of chilli oil and coriander. Serve and enjoy!

ONE POT 145

Beef & Horseradish Stew

SERVES 10
TOTAL TIME: 4–5 HOURS

This recipe is for those of you who you don't want soup when you have a cold but still need something warming. This is my mum's recipe and she makes it once a year – usually when she is having friends over in the run up to Christmas. Slow cooked, rich and deeply comforting, the kick of horseradish cuts through the rich beef flavours and warms you from the inside out. I love this dish ladeled over mountains of creamy mashed potato with a side of garlic bread. It guarantees a full belly and a good nights sleep!

5–6 tbsp olive oil
1.8kg (4lb) diced beef
4 red onions, diced
2 tbsp mild curry powder
1 tsp ground ginger
2 tbsp muscovado sugar
3 tbsp cornflour (cornstarch)
1 litre (34fl oz/4¼ cups) good-quality beef stock
4 tbsp Worcestershire sauce
2 tbsp horseradish sauce, plus extra to serve
fine sea salt
freshly ground black pepper
mash, to serve
seasonal veg of your choice, to serve

EQUIPMENT
chopping board—knife—casserole dish (Dutch oven)—wooden spoon

1. Preheat the oven to 200°C (180°C fan/425°F/gas mark 6).

2. Heat the oil in a casserole dish over a medium heat, then add the beef and sear all over until well coloured. Add the red onions and cook for 5 minutes before adding the curry powder, ginger and muscovado sugar. Mix well so that spices are distributed throughout the dish.

3. Now, add the cornflour a tablespoon at a time, mixing well after each addition (this is going to thicken the stew). Once all the flour has been added, pour in the stock and Worcestershire sauce and season with some salt and pepper. Cover and transfer to the oven. Cook for 4–5 hours until the beef is really tender. Alternatively, you can just throw everything into a slow cooker and do it that way.

4. Just before serving, stir in the horseradish sauce for a bit of kick, then enjoy this very wintery and warming stew! Serve with mash and seasonal veg of your choice.

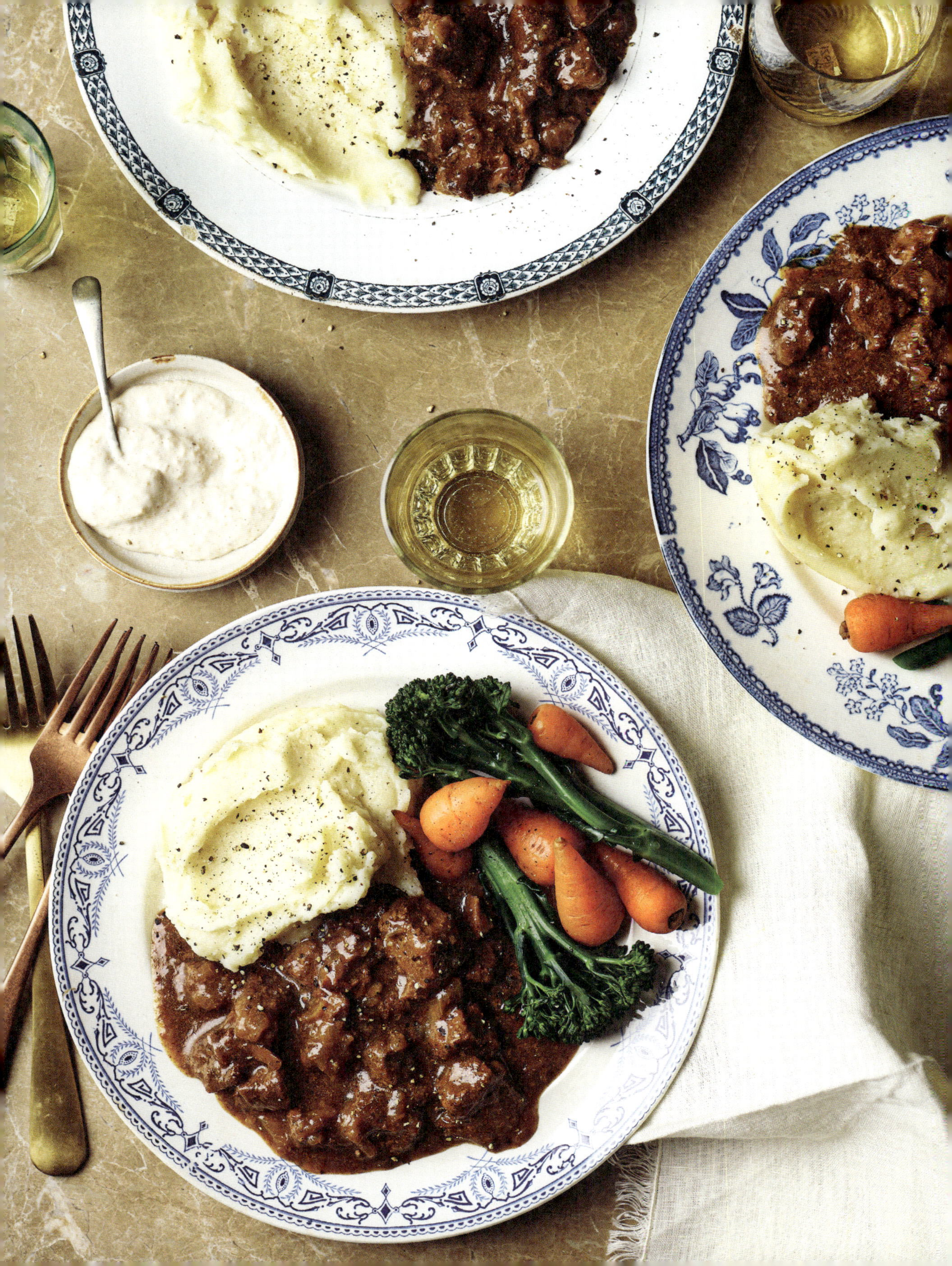

ONE SALAD BOWL

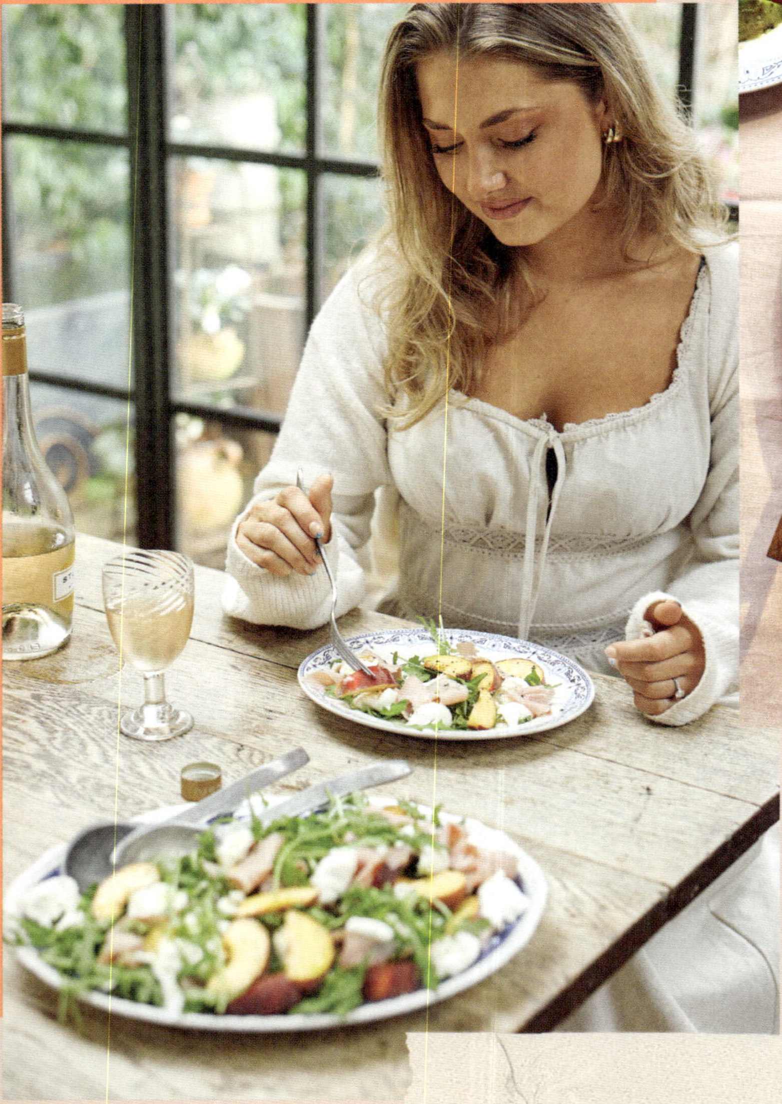

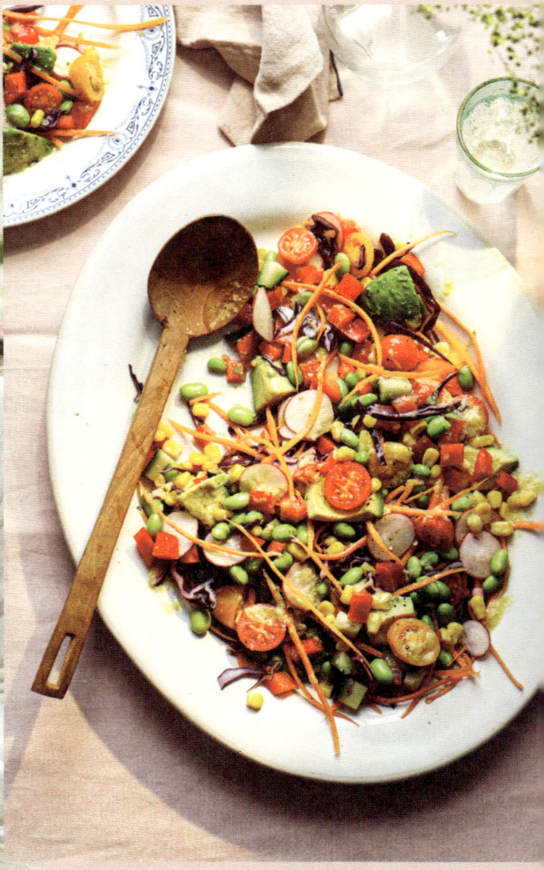

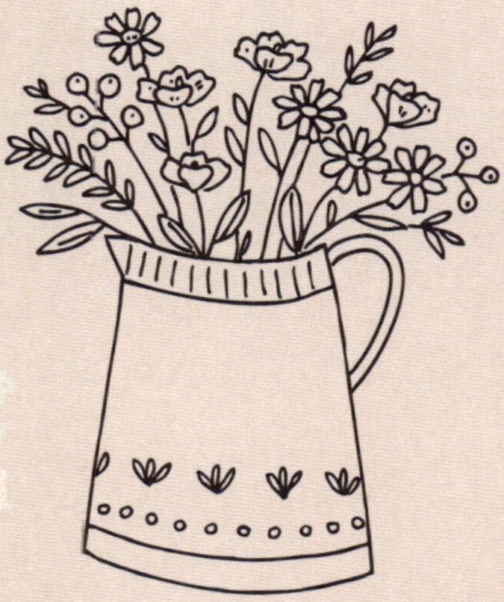

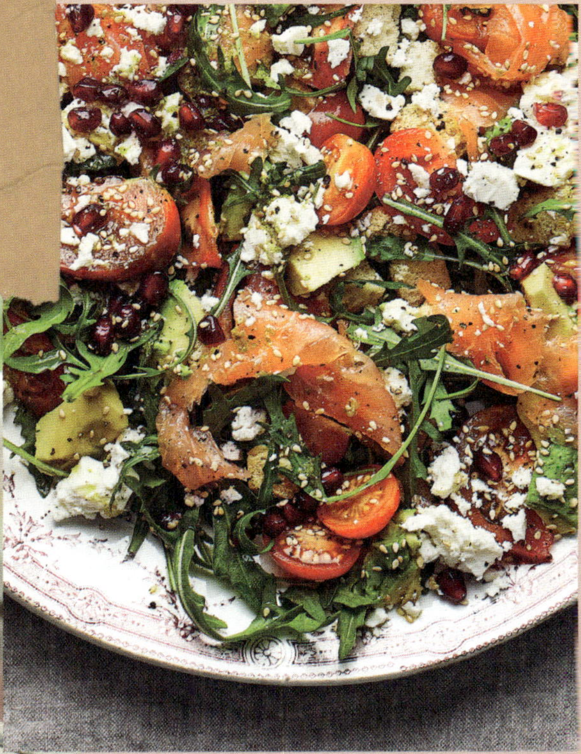

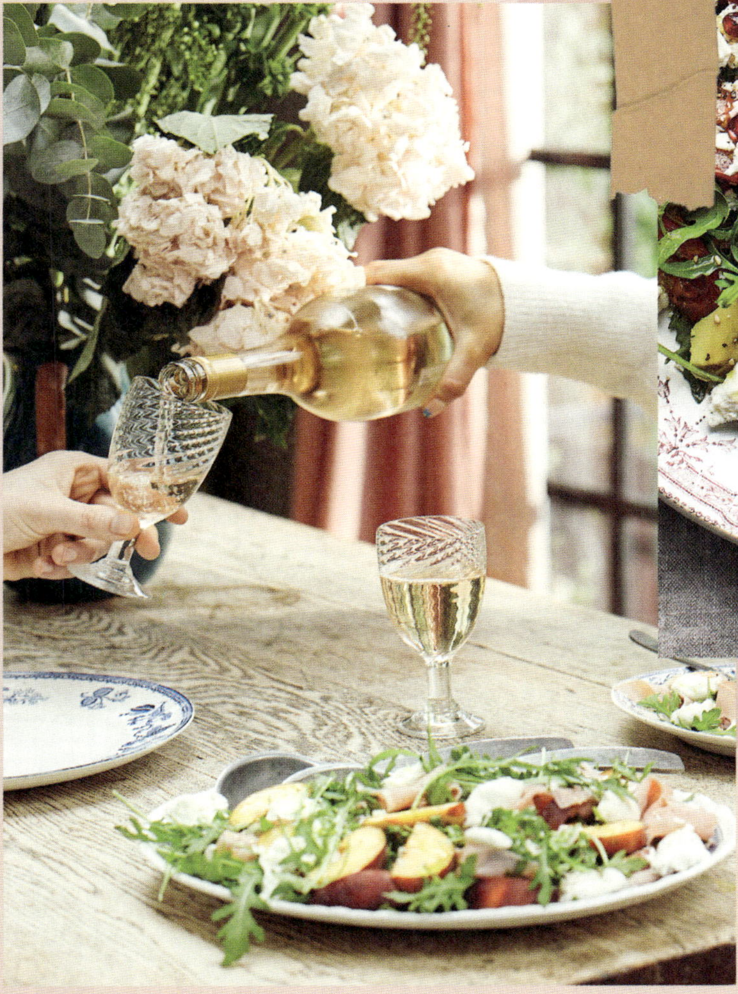

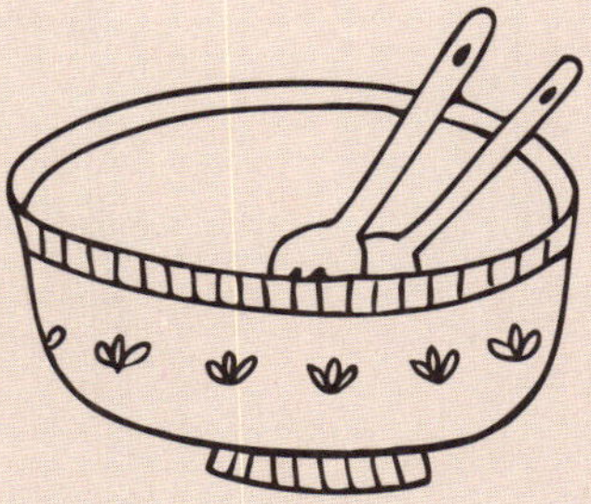

Goat's Cheese, Fig and Parma Ham Salad

SERVES 2
TOTAL TIME: 15 MINUTES

This salad uses a mixture of all the best things that pair with goat's cheese: salty Parma ham, figs or pears for sweetness, crunchy pecans and a hint of honey in the dressing. It really is a lovely light lunch, or equally this makes a gorgeous starter for dinner.

FOR THE DRESSING
3 tbsp olive oil, or as needed
2 tbsp balsamic vinegar, or as needed
1 tsp honey
1 sprig of thyme, leaves picked
fine sea salt
freshly ground black pepper

FOR THE SALAD
a handful of rocket (arugula)
a handful of spinach
100g (3½oz) goat's cheese, crumbled
80g (2¾oz/⅔ cup) chopped pecans
2–3 figs, quartered (or 1 large pear, sliced)
80g (2¾oz) Parma ham, torn

EQUIPMENT
large bowl—whisk—chopping board
knife

1. Start by making the dressing. Combine all the ingredients in a large bowl and whisk together until smooth. Taste and adjust accordingly – it may need slightly more olive oil, balsamic or seasoning.

2. Add all the ingredients for the salad and toss everything together, ensuring all the ingredients are well coated in the dressing. Serve immediately.

ALTERNATIVE INGREDIENTS
Rocket: any salad leaves would work well
Goat's cheese: try other soft cheeses or creamy mozzarella or burrata
Pecans: substitute with walnuts, almonds or cashews
Balsamic vinegar: try a good squeeze of lemon juice for added freshness

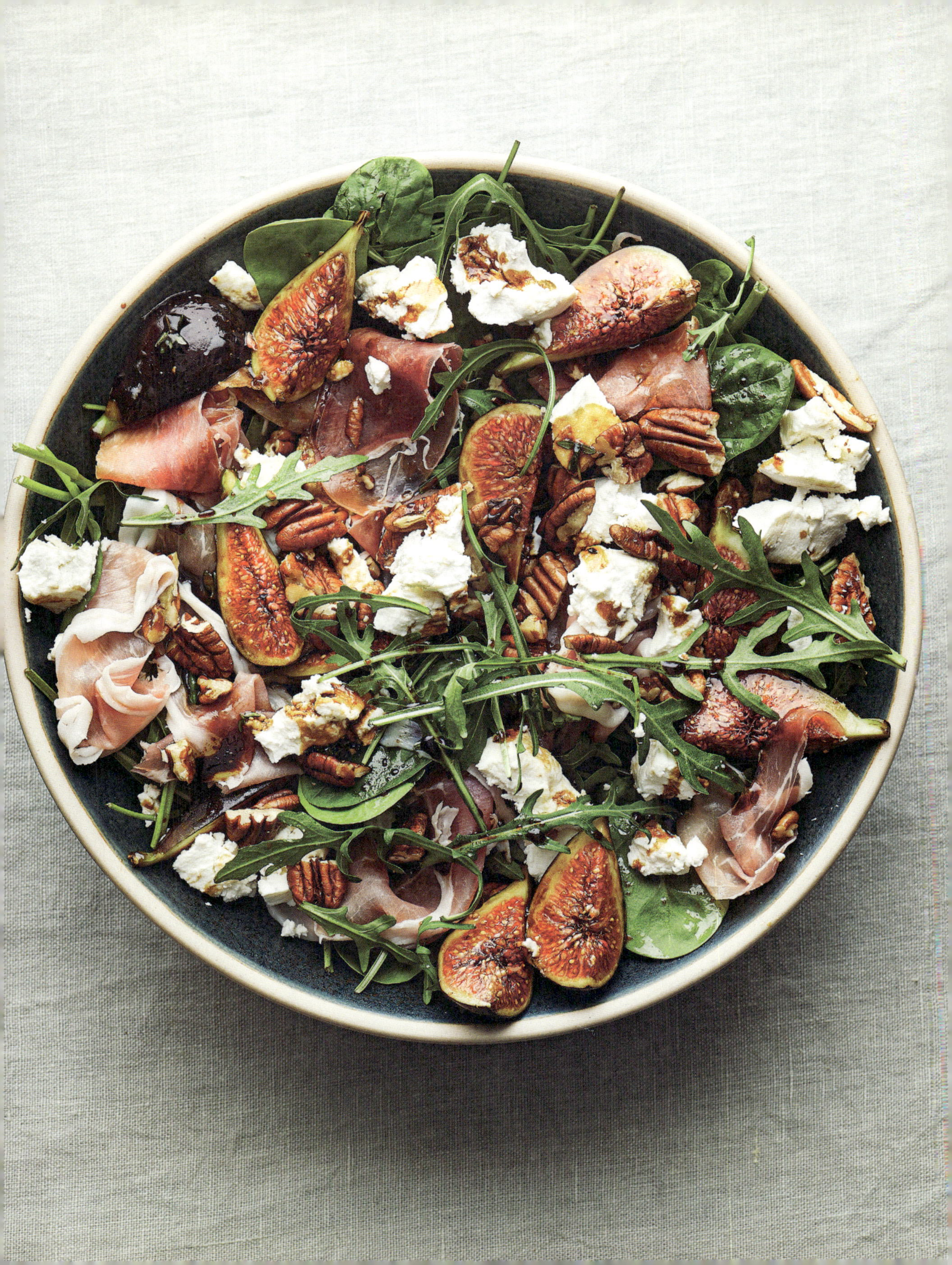

Creamy Salmon Salad with Dill & Chive Dressing

SERVES 4 AS A STARTERS OR 2 AS A MAIN
TOTAL TIME: 15 MINUTES

This is the perfect summer salad – the light dressing has lots of fresh herbs and when combined with flaked salmon it goes brilliantly with a glass of chilled wine out in the garden with loved ones. If more people are coming over, just double up the recipe, as it's a great dish to serve in a big salad bowl for friends.

If you're cooking the salmon fillets yourself, I recommend pan-searing them for 2–3 minutes on all sides with lots of salt and pepper and then flaking them into the salad – this way you'll get crispy edges and a melt in the mouth centre.

FOR THE DRESSING
3 tbsp olive oil
3 tbsp crème fraîche or Greek yoghurt
2 tsp Dijon mustard
1 garlic clove, grated
3 tbsp lemon juice
a handful of dill, finely chopped
a handful of chives, finely chopped

FOR THE SALAD
2 large cooked salmon fillets (or 150–200g/5½–7oz smoked salmon), flaked or chopped
2 tbsp capers
4 tbsp pitted, sliced kalamata olives
150g (5½oz) cucumber, thinly sliced
2 romaine lettuces, roughly chopped
crispy fried onions, to serve (optional)

EQUIPMENT
salad bowl—whisk or wooden spoon
grater—tongs

1. Start by making the dressing. Put the ingredients into a salad bowl. Give it a good mix together so the dressing is well combined. Add all the remaining ingredients, then get your tongs and give everything a really good toss together so it's all coated in dressing. Serve and sprinkled with the crispy onions, if using.

2. Add all the remaining ingredients, then get your salad tongs and give everything a really good toss together so it's all coated in dressing. Serve and sprinkled with the crispy onions, if using.

ALTERNATIVE INGREDIENTS
Lemon juice: replace with 1 tablespoon of white wine vinegar
Dill: chives, basil, parsley and coriander (cilantro) all complement this salad
Salmon fillets: use cooked chicken, cod or trout
Capers: anchovies are a good substitute

ONE SALAD BOWL 155

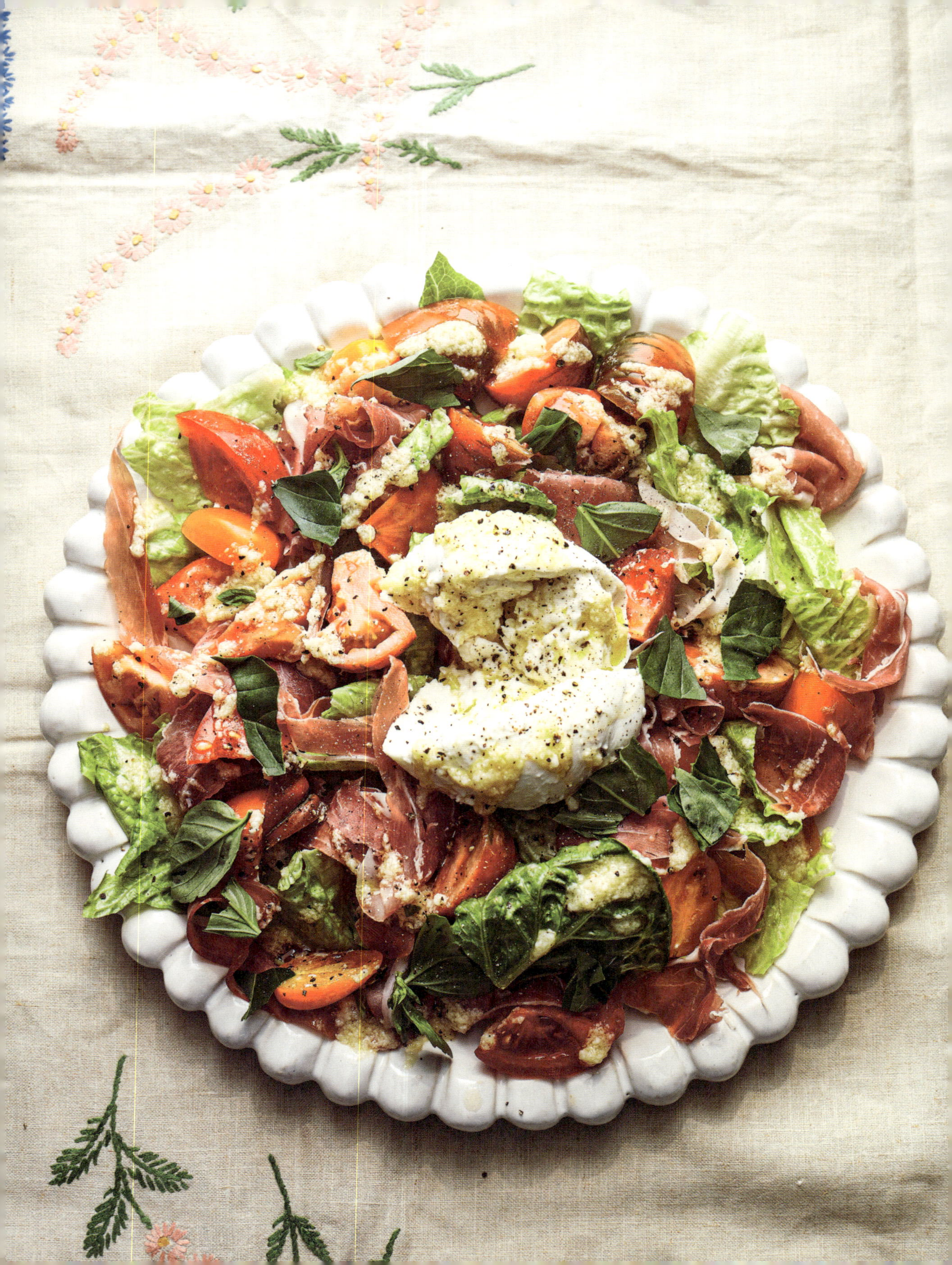

Taste of Italy Salad

SERVES 4 AS A STARTER OR 2 AS A MAIN
TOTAL TIME: 15 MINUTES

Italy is one of my favourite places ever and that probably has a lot to do with the food, so combining all the most quintessential Italian flavours in one bowl together made total sense!

I love to add a few more cured meats to this sometimes, just roughly chop them and throw in for a little extra depth.

FOR THE DRESSING
4 tbsp extra virgin olive oil, plus extra to serve
50g (1¾oz) parmesan, grated
1 tsp white wine vinegar
1 garlic clove, grated
½ tsp fine sea salt
½ tsp freshly ground black pepper, plus extra to serve

FOR THE SALAD
1½ romaine lettuces, roughly chopped
200g (7oz) tomatoes, roughly chopped
200g (7oz) mozzarella
150g (5½oz) Parma ham, torn
handful of basil leaves, torn

EQUIPMENT
chopping board—knife—grater—large bowl—whisk

1. Start by making the dressing. Place all the ingredients in a large bowl and whisk together to make a silky smooth dressing (if you want a thicker dressing, add more parmesan; if you want a thinner dressing, add more olive oil).

2. Add the remaining salad ingredients (except for the burrata) to the bowl and toss them through the dressing. Serve topped with burrata, sliced through its middle, drizzled with more olive oil, salt and black pepper.

ALTERNATIVE INGREDIENTS
White wine vinegar: replace the vinegar with lemon juice
Tomatoes: peppers add a similar sweetness along with a crunch
Mozzarella: add a little luxury by using creamy burrata
Parma ham: crispy bacon is a good substitute

Carnival Salad

SERVES 2
TOTAL TIME: 15 MINUTES

This salad was dreamed up one summer afternoon in our household, after which my Nana came out and told us it looked like a carnival because of all of the colours – thus, 'carnival salad' was made. It's bursting with colourful vegetables, it's vegan and, with the hum of ginger, lemon and garlic in the dressing, it definitely has all the flavour. It's visually pleasing and tantalising to those taste buds. One you need to try when the sun starts shining.

FOR THE DRESSING
4 tbsp olive oil
zest and juice of 1 lemon
1 tbsp tahini
1 tsp ginger paste
1 tsp honey
1 tsp Dijon mustard
1 garlic clove, grated
large pinch of fine sea salt
large pinch of freshly ground black pepper

FOR THE SALAD
100g (3½oz) cherry tomatoes, halved
1 (bell) pepper (colour of your choice), diced
100g (3½oz) cucumber, diced
1 carrot, grated
1 avocado, roughly chopped
100g (3½oz) drained tinned sweetcorn
2-3 radishes, sliced
100g (3½oz) cooked edamame beans
60g (2oz) red cabbage, shredded

EQUIPMENT
chopping board—knife—grater—zester
large bowl—whisk

1. Start by making the dressing. Combine all the ingredients in a large bowl and whisk together until smooth, then taste and adjust the seasoning accordingly.

2. Add all the ingredients for the salad and toss everything together, ensuring all the ingredients are well coated in the silky dressing. Serve and enjoy this vibrant salad with those you love.

ALTERNATIVE INGREDIENTS
The joy of this salad is you can literally swap in any veggies you have for those you don't

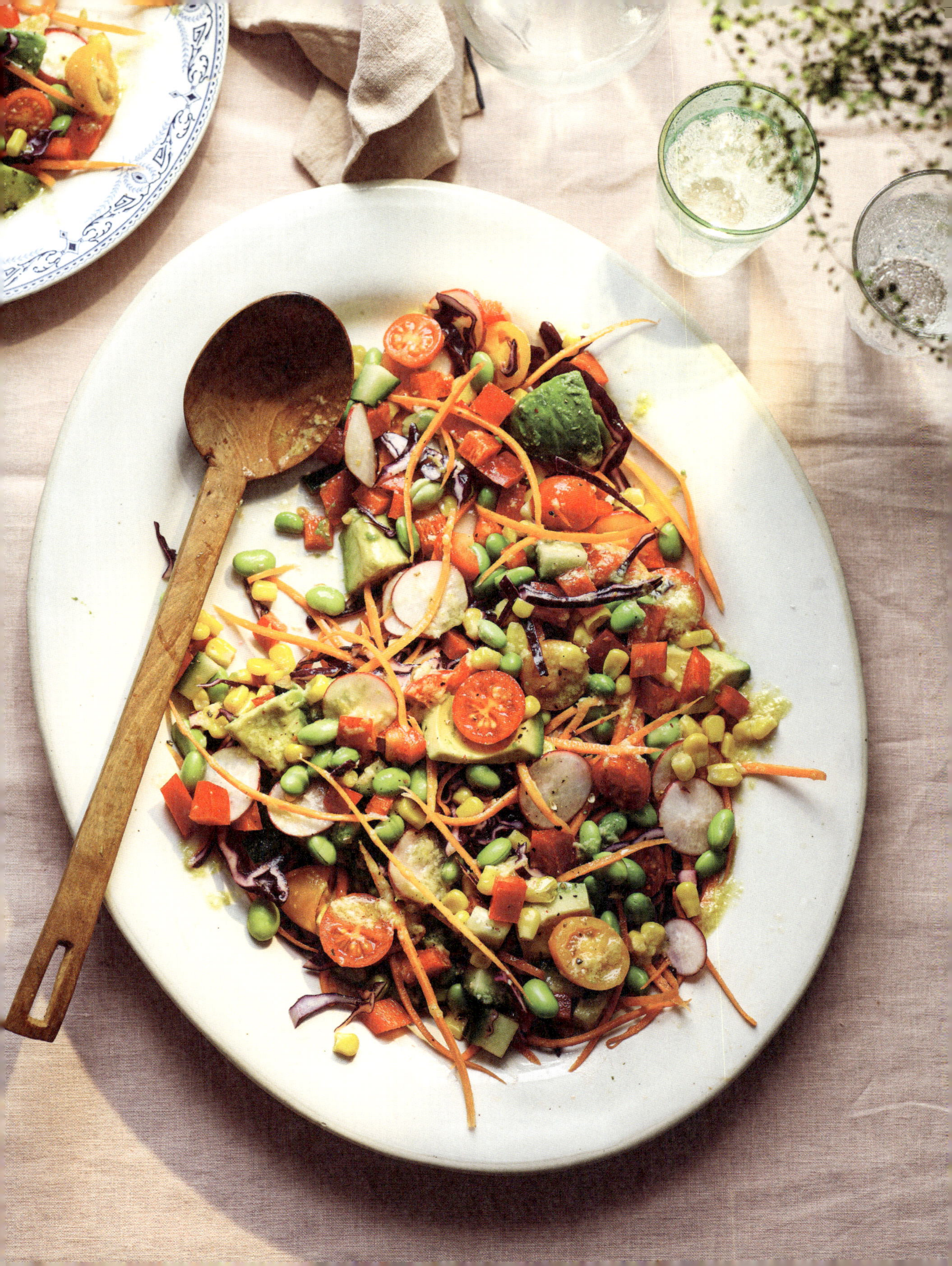

ONE SALAD BOWL

Mango & Kiwi Salad (Just Trust Me) with Basil, Balsamic and Pine Nut Dressing

SERVES 4
TOTAL TIME: 15 MINUTES

This salad is something I used to make a lot for a friend; they loved it, so whenever I suggested dinner, they'd ask for it! I developed the recipe as much as I could after that, but the basics really do work the best for this one. One of my favourite ways of serving this is with king prawns (jumbo shrimp) on the side and lots of baguette to soak up the juices. It's a delicious summer garden salad.

You can save time by using toasted pine nuts which are available from your local supermarket.

FOR THE DRESSING
2 tbsp balsamic vinegar
5 tbsp olive oil
zest and juice of 1 lime
pinch of fine sea salt
pinch of freshly ground black pepper

FOR THE SALAD
50g (1¾oz/³/₈ cup) pine nuts
1 large mango, diced
2 kiwis, diced
1 romaine lettuce, roughly chopped
1 avocado, diced
handful of basil leaves, torn

EQUIPMENT
frying pan—wooden spoon—chopping board—knife—zester—large bowl—whisk

1. First, toast the pine nuts. Put the pine nuts into a small dry frying pan over a medium-low heat and toast for a few minutes until golden brown, stirring regularly so they don't catch. Remove from the pan and set aside.

2. Put all the ingredients for the dressing into a large bowl and whisk together, then throw in the remaining ingredients for the salad along with the toasted pine nuts and toss to coat. Serve immediately.

ALTERNATIVE INGREDIENTS
Pine nuts: cashews, almonds and peanuts all work here
Romaine lettuce: you can use any salad leaves you like
Balsamic vinegar: try using lemon juice for a lighter, fresh dressing

The Best Summer Potato Salad

SERVES: 4–6
TOTAL TIME: 25 MINUTES

You really don't need another potato salad recipe once you have this one. If you want to elevate this for an extra wow factor, use cooked tater tots or hash browns to make a crunchy potato salad. Trust me, this will wow anyone.

750g (1lb 10oz) new (baby) potatoes, diced
150g (5½oz) pancetta, roughly chopped
2 tbsp soured cream
1 tbsp mayonnaise
6 cornichons, finely chopped
3 spring onions (scallions), finely chopped
handful of chopped coriander (cilantro)
1 garlic clove, grated
1 tsp fine sea salt
1 tsp freshly ground black pepper

EQUIPMENT
chopping board—knife—bowl
wooden spoon—saucepan—colander/strainer

1. Bring a medium saucepan of water to the boil and add the potatoes. Boil for 10–12 minutes until cooked through. Remove from the heat and strain. Set aside.

2. Place the saucepan back over a medium heat. Add the pancetta and fry for 5 minutes until crisp.

3. Reserving a little pancetta, cornichons, spring onions and coriander, combine all the ingredients in a large bowl and mix well. Sprinkle the reserved ingredients over the top to serve, to give the finished dish a bit more wow factor.

ALTERNATIVE INGREDIENTS
Soured cream: replace with Greek yoghurt
Pancetta: crispy bacon bits and chorizo provide a similar flavour
Try adding chopped fresh jalapenos for a kick

ONE SALAD BOWL

Just Peachy Summertime Salad

SERVES 4 AS A STARTER OR 2 AS A MAIN
TOTAL TIME: 15 MINUTES

When I have the girls over and there's a bottle of rosé chilling in the refrigerator, this is a salad I like to whip up. I usually serve it with some chicken skewers and fries for the table, and it always puts such a smile on everyone's face!

120g (4oz) rocket (arugula)
2 tbsp olive oil
1 tbsp lemon juice
pinch of fine sea salt
pinch of freshly ground black pepper
150g (5½oz) mini mozzarella balls (or torn mozzarella)
110g (3½oz) Parma ham or prosciutto, torn
2 peaches or nectarines, sliced into half-moons

EQUIPMENT
chopping board—knife
bowl or large plate

1. Put the rocket into a bowl or on a large plate. Add the olive oil, lemon, salt and pepper and toss together so the rocket is fully coated.

2. Over the top, scatter the mozzarella, Parma ham and peaches or nectarines. Just before you're ready to serve, toss the salad so everything has a kiss of olive oil and lemon juice!

ONE SALAD BOWL

164　ONE SALAD BOWL

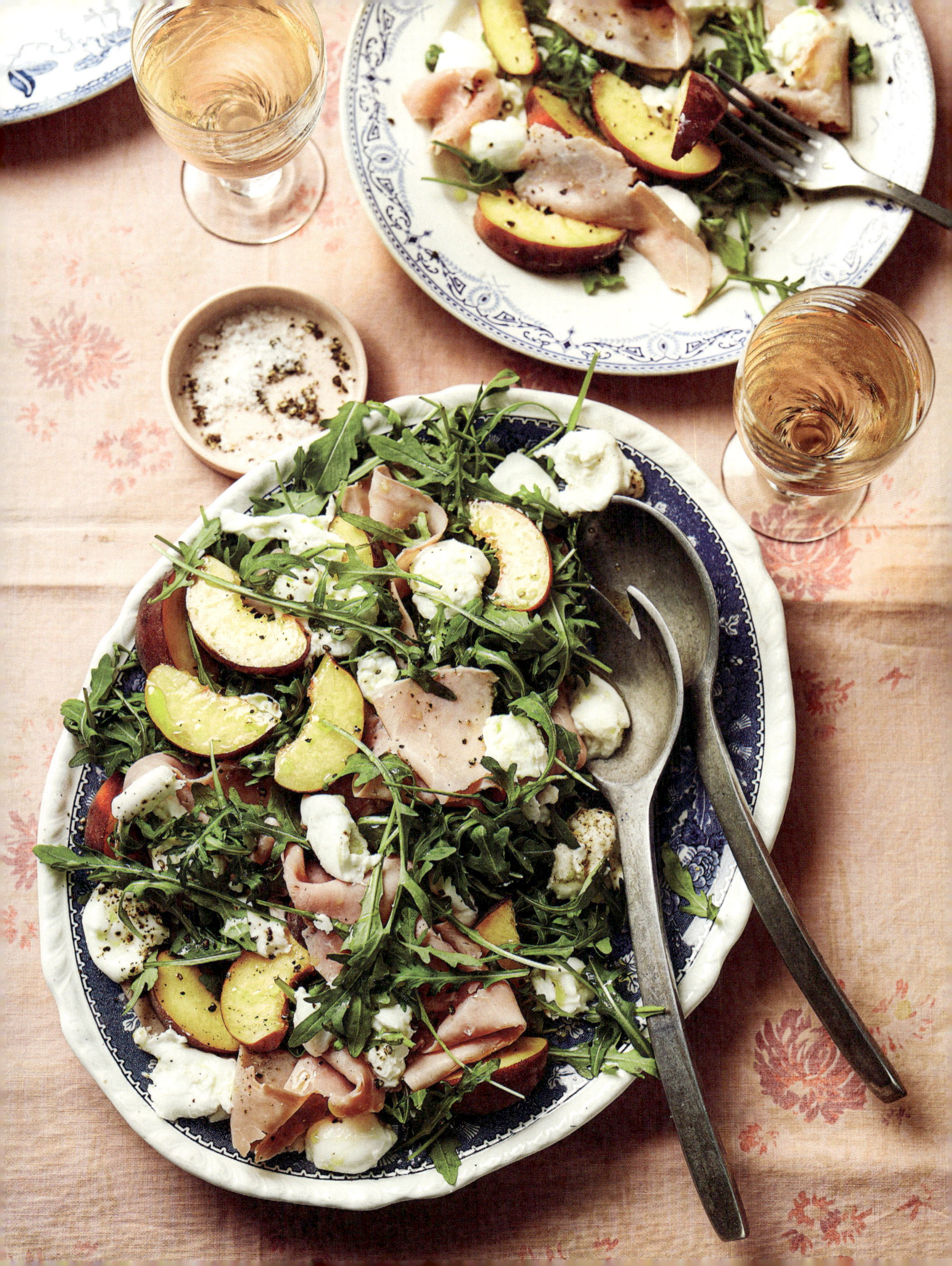

ONE SALAD BOWL

Chimichurri Chicken Salad

SERVES 2
TOTAL TIME: 15 MINUTES

If there is chimichurri on a menu with steak, it is the sauce I will choose every time. It feels fresh and cuts through any fattiness of the steak. So, when I paired chimichurri with chicken thighs, it worked just as well – thus my chimichurri chicken salad was born!

FOR THE DRESSING
large handful of parsley, finely chopped
large handful of coriander (cilantro), finely chopped
2 garlic cloves, grated
½ red chilli, deseeded and finely chopped
1 tbsp red wine vinegar
4 tbsp olive oil
large pinch of fine sea salt
20g (¾oz) parmesan, grated

FOR THE SALAD
4 skin-on precooked chicken thighs, roughly sliced
1 romaine lettuce, roughly chopped
1 avocado, diced
2–4 radishes, sliced
1 mango, diced
2 tbsp olive oil, plus extra for drizzling
juice and zest of 1 lime
fine sea salt
freshly ground black pepper
2 tbsp crispy fried onions, to serve

EQUIPMENT
chopping board—knife—grater—large bowl—zester

1 Make the dressing. Put all the ingredients into a large bowl and mix together. (You can reserve a tablespoon or two to drizzle over the chicken thighs on top of the salad to make the final dish look more impressive.)

2 Now add all the remaining ingredients for the salad (except the crispy onions) to the bowl and toss everything together so it's fully coated. Season to taste. Place the chicken thighs on top and drizzle with the reserved dressing, then sprinkle the salad with crispy onions and serve.

ALTERNATIVE INGREDIENTS
Chicken thighs: skin-on chicken breasts are a great substitute
Romaine: baby gem or any crunchy lettuce works here

Spicy Tuna Salad with Pesto Croutons

SERVES 2
TOTAL TIME: 15 MINUTES

This is a great everyday salad that's packed with flavour and convenient for your purse strings, weekly meals and taste buds. The majority of these ingredients can be kept in the fridge or cupboard for over a week meaning you're not rushing to eat things before they go out of date. This is so delicious with a glass of crisp dry cider on a summer's day or just as meal prep for work lunches! My favourite way of eating this is spooning large helpings onto toasted sourdough.

FOR THE PESTO CROUTONS
1 loaf of ciabatta, diced or torn into bite-size pieces
1 tbsp basil pesto
1 tbsp olive oil
large pinch of fine sea salt
large pinch of garlic granules
large pinch of ground black pepper

FOR THE SALAD
2 x 125g (4¼oz) tins of good-quality tuna, drained
1 tbsp mayonnaise
1 tbsp olive oil
juice of 1 lemon
4 shakes of Tabasco sauce
6–8 pickled jalapeño slices, finely chopped
1 fresh jalapeño, sliced (optional)
2–3 spring onions, finely chopped
1 tsp basil pesto
2 sun-dried tomatoes, diced
1 romaine lettuce, roughly chopped

EQUIPMENT
chopping board—knife—bowl
baking tray—large bowl

1. Make the croutons first so they will be cool by the time you pop them in the salad. Preheat the oven to 180°C (160°C fan/350°F/gas mark 4).

2. Combine all the ingredients for the croutons in a large bowl and mix well. When each crouton is fully coated, transfer them to a baking sheet and toast in the oven for 8 minutes until golden brown and crispy. Remove from the oven and set aside.

3. Put all the ingredients for the salad into the same bowl you coated the croutons in and give it a really good mix together. Add the croutons and mix well again, then serve and enjoy.

ALTERNATIVE INGREDIENTS
Tuna: for a veggie option use good-quality chickpeas
Mayonnaise: replace with Greek yoghurt
Sun dried tomatoes: these are better but if you only have fresh, they will work too

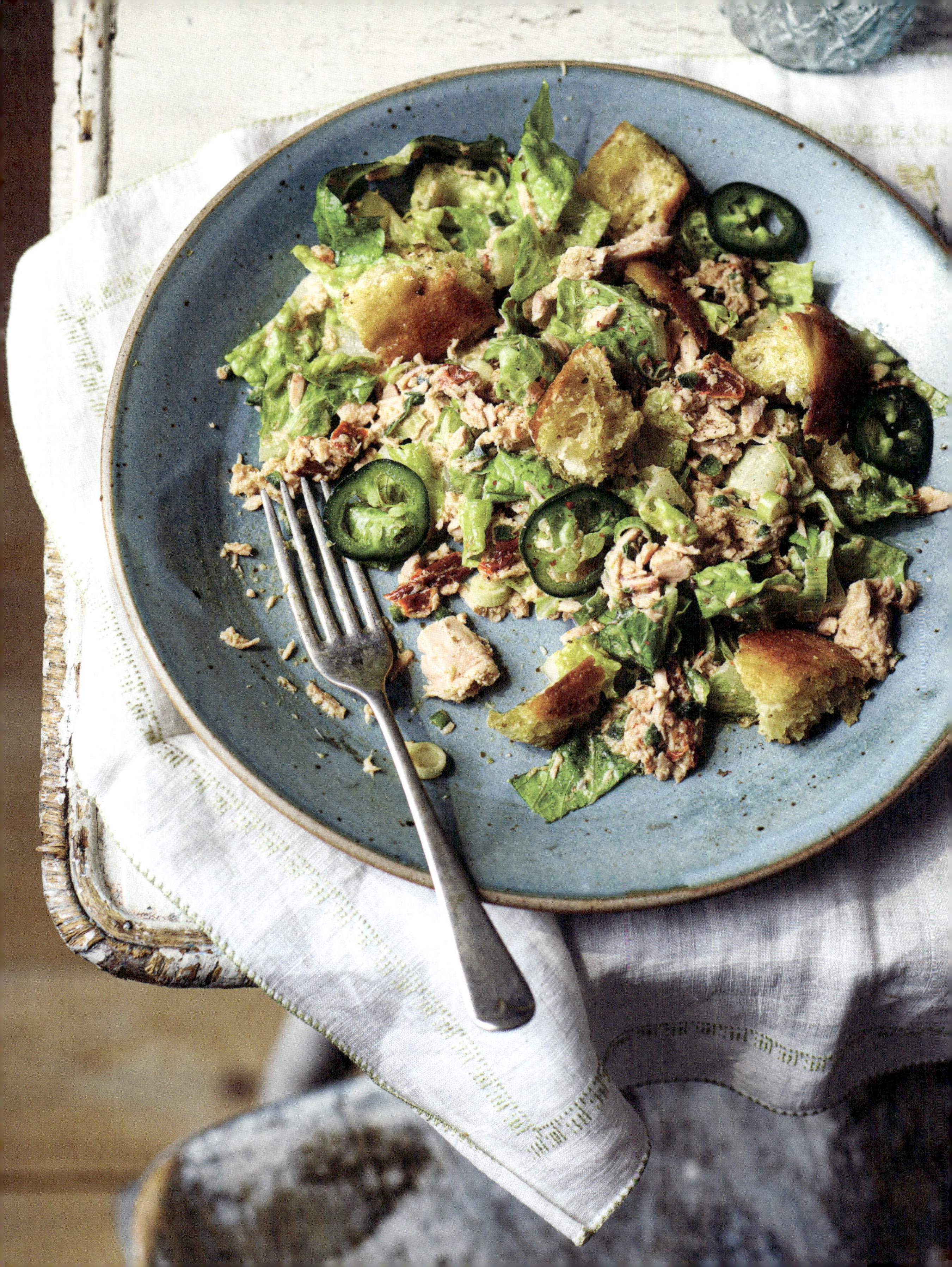

Chickpea and Salami Salad with a Lemon Twist

SERVES 2
TOTAL TIME: 15 MINUTES

This is our go-to 'everything' salad, a kitchen staple in our house. It's one of those meals born out of the moment when you realise you've got a jar of cooked chickpeas (garbanzos) in the cupboard and some salami in the refrigerator that needs using up. What starts as a quick make-do lunch ends up being a surprisingly delicious combination, especially when you toss in a few extra bits and bobs.

FOR THE DRESSING
60ml (2fl oz/¼ cup) olive oil
60ml (2fl oz/¼ cup) lemon juice
1 garlic clove, grated
1 tsp wholegrain mustard
large pinch of fine sea salt, or as needed
1 tsp honey, or as needed

FOR THE SALAD
1 romaine lettuce, roughly chopped
400g (14oz) drained jarred chickpeas (garbanzo beans)
100g (3½oz) salami, thinly sliced and chopped
40g (1½oz) feta or mozzarella, crumbled or torn
50g (1¾oz) cucumber, diced
50g (1¾oz) cherry tomatoes, sliced

EQUIPMENT
large bowl—grater—whisk—chopping board—knife

1. Start by making the dressing. Combine all the ingredients in a large bowl and whisk together until smooth. Taste and adjust the seasoning, adding more salt or honey if needed.

2. Add all the ingredients for the salad and gently toss everything together, ensuring all the ingredients are well coated in the dressing. Serve.

ALTERNATIVE INGREDIENTS
Salami: any dried or cured meats work well here
Feta or mozzarella: creamy goat's cheese provides a lovely balance to the salty meat
Cucumber: peppers provide a similar crunchy freshness
Wholegrain mustard: try Dijon mustard in the dressing

ONE SALAD BOWL 171

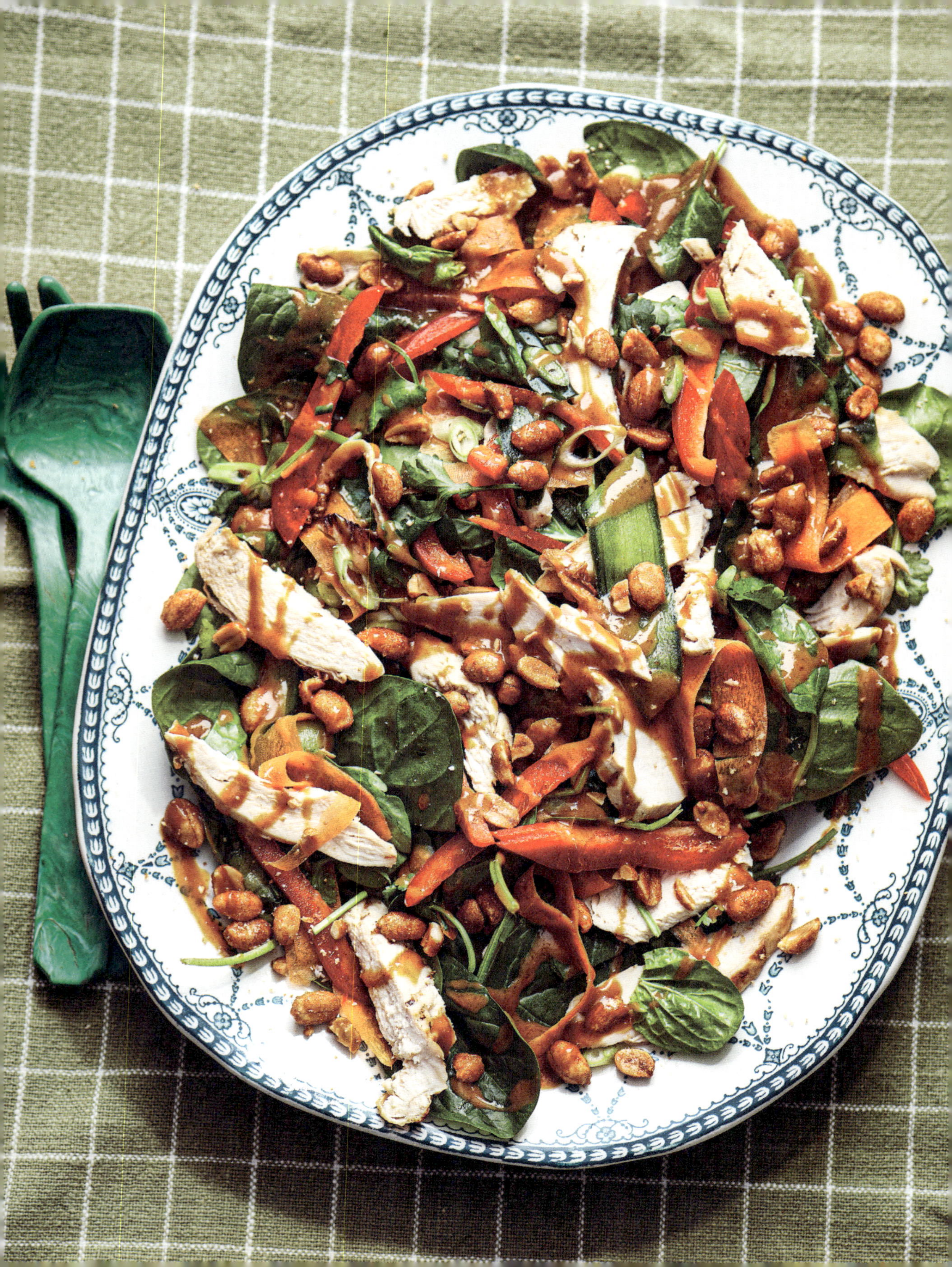

Peanut Crunch Salad

SERVES 2
TOTAL TIME: 15 MINUTES

This recipe is a great one for all seasons, as it pairs lots of colours and crunchy goodness with a rich, creamy peanut dressing. It's so simple to make, whether you're looking for a light lunch, a side dish for your summer barbecue or a comforting dinner to satisfy your taste buds while still getting lots of veggies in. With a few simple cupboard staples, you have a beautiful salad in minutes. Swap the chicken for cooked prawns (shrimp) if you like.

FOR THE DRESSING
1 tbsp light soy sauce
2 tbsp olive oil
1 tbsp smooth peanut butter
1 tbsp white wine vinegar
1 tsp ginger paste
1 tsp honey
pinch of fine sea salt
pinch of freshly ground black pepper

FOR THE SALAD
a large handful of baby spinach
1 large carrot, grated or cut into ribbons
½ cucumber, sliced into ribbons
1 red (bell) pepper, thinly sliced
a large handful of chopped coriander (cilantro)
2–3 spring onions (scallions), finely chopped
60g (2oz/½ cup) honey roasted peanuts
200g (7oz) cooked chicken (slices or shredded, whatever you have)

EQUIPMENT
large bowl—whisk—chopping board knife—grater

1. Start by making the dressing. Combine all the ingredients in a large bowl and whisk together until smooth and the peanut butter is well incorporated. If the dressing is a little too thick, add a little more olive oil or a splash of water.

2. Add all the ingredients for the salad and toss everything together, ensuring all the ingredients are well coated in the dressing. Serve immediately.

ALTERNATIVE INGREDIENTS
Baby spinach: this works well with any salad leaves of your choice
Carrot: courgette ribbons can be used alongside the carrot or in its place
Coriander (cilantro): try parsley or basil

Avocado and Smoked Salmon on Toast Salad

SERVES 2
TOTAL TIME: 15 MINUTES

This recipe brings together everything you love about the smoked salmon and avocado on toast you might have for brunch and combines it into a delicious salad that works for lunch or even a light dinner. The creamy avocado, tangy feta and smoky salmon base is also utterly versatile, so throw in any other ingredients that you love.

FOR THE DRESSING
4 tbsp olive oil, or as needed
zest and juice of 1 lime, or as needed
fine sea salt
freshly ground black pepper

FOR THE SALAD
1 ripe avocado, diced
large handful of rocket (arugula)
60g (2oz) feta, crumbled
60g (2oz) tomatoes, sliced
100g (3½oz) smoked salmon, torn into rough pieces
60g (2oz) pomegranate seeds
sprinkle of sesame seeds
handful of chopped coriander (cilantro)
80g (2¾oz) homemade croutons (see page 168) or crispy chickpea (garbanzo beans) croutons (see right)

EQUIPMENT
large bowl—whisk—chopping board knife—whisk

1. Start by making the dressing. Combine all the ingredients in a large bowl and whisk together until smooth. Give it a taste – if it needs a little more acidity, add some more lime juice; if it's too sharp, add more olive oil.

2. Add all the ingredients for the salad and toss everything together, ensuring they are well coated in the dressing. Serve.

BONUS RECIPE: CRISPY CHICKPEA CROUTONS
If you prefer not to use bread croutons, an absolute favourite of mine is to make crispy chickpea croutons. Pat dry 80g (2¾oz) cooked chickpeas using kitchen towel, throw them on a baking tray, add a drizzle of olive oil and some seasoning of choice (I love paprika, ground cumin, salt and pepper along with some garlic granules). Pop them in an oven preheated to 200°C (180°C fan/400°F/gas mark 6) for 25 minutes, giving them a shake or stir halfway through so they crisp evenly. I finish mine by grating some lemon zest over them. Add these to any salad for a flavourful crunch.

ALTERNATIVE INGREDIENTS
Rocket: spinach really complements the other ingredients
Feta: a creamy cheese like mozzarella or goat's cheese would be nice here too
Smoked salmon: try prosciutto, Parma ham or crispy streaky bacon

ONE SALAD BOWL

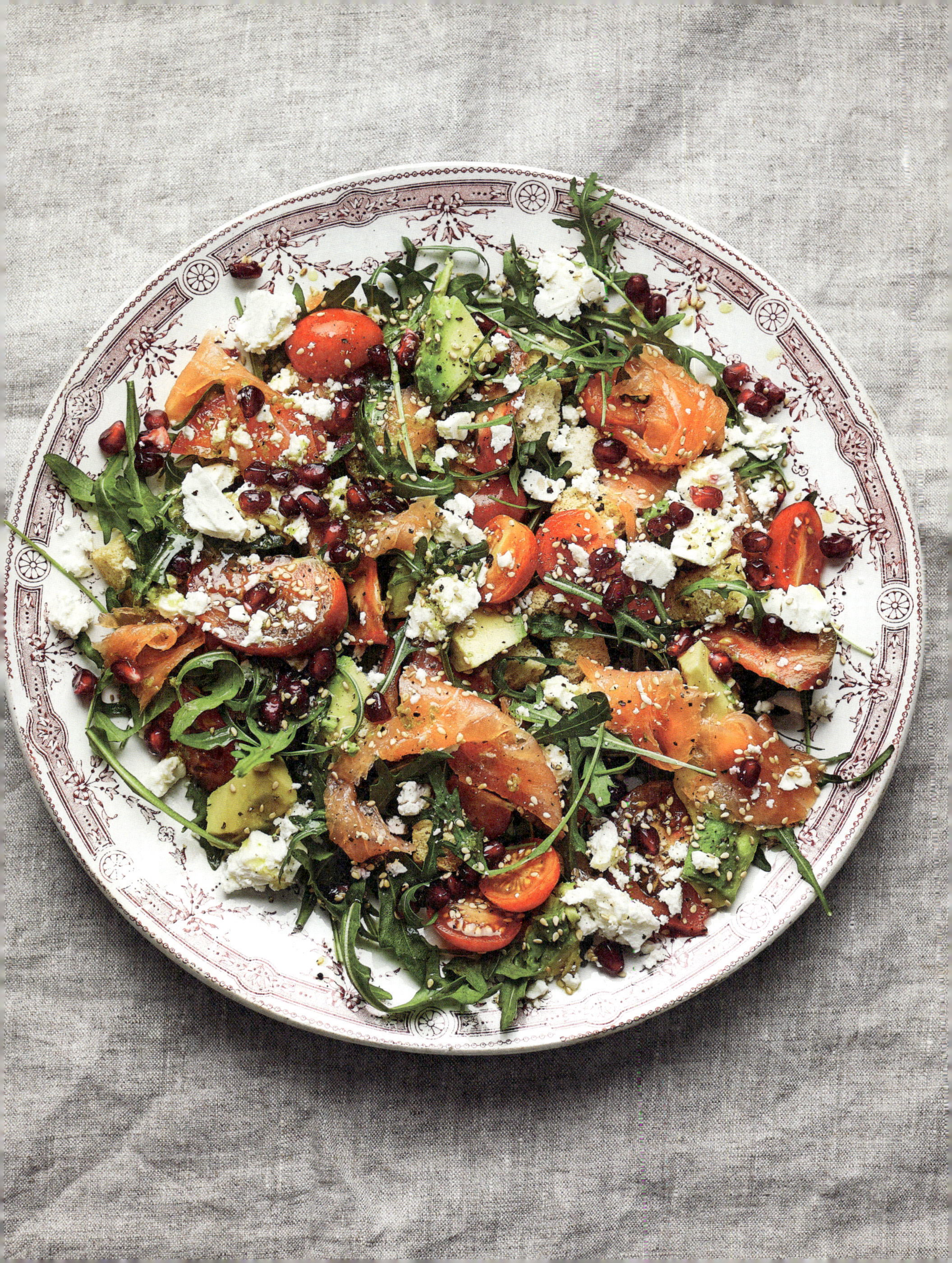

Kale and Chicken Caesar Salad

SERVES 2
TOTAL TIME: 15 MINUTES

This twist on a classic Caesar salad works well in the winter when you're in need of a few more vitamins. Kale is a good source of vitamin K, C and A, so it is a great swap if you're feeling slightly under the weather. In summer, if you love the classic romaine lettuce, use half and half. I also recommend throwing in some of my crispy chickpea (garbanzo bean) croutons (see page 174).

FOR THE DRESSING
2–3 heaped tbsp mayonnaise
40g (1½oz) parmesan, grated
2 anchovy fillets, finely chopped and mashed into a paste with some of the oil from the tin
1 garlic clove, finely chopped
1 tbsp white wine vinegar

FOR THE SALAD
125g (4¼oz) kale, stems removed
olive oil, for drizzling
1–2 tbsp parmesan shavings
80g (2¾oz) garlic and herb croutons (extra points for making your own - see page 168)
4-6 anchovy fillets, chopped (or 1–2 tsp capers)
200g (7oz) shredded or sliced cooked chicken (or grilled or roasted tofu, crispy chickpeas/garbanzos or grilled halloumi)

EQUIPMENT
grater—chopping board—knife—large bowl—whisk

1. Start by making the dressing. Combine all the ingredients in a large bowl and whisk together until smooth.

2. Add the kale leaves to the bowl, give them a little drizzle of oil and, without disturbing the dressing at the bottom of the bowl too much, massage the leaves for 2–3 minutes to soften them. Now throw in the parmesan shavings, croutons, anchovies and chicken. Give everything a really good mix together so it's all coated in the dressing. Serve and enjoy.

ALTERNATIVE INGREDIENTS
Anchovy fillets: a couple of tablespoons of mashed capers provide a similar flavour

Taste of Greece Salad (with all the Good Bits)

SERVES 4
TOTAL TIME: 15 MINUTES

This is a great recipe for summer dinners or even to have as a side with other meals. You can really elevate this dish by making your own croutons, but if you just want to chuck it all in and go, then shop-bought will be fine.

FOR THE CROUTONS
300g (10½oz) ciabatta, roughly torn into bite-size pieces
2 tbsp olive oil
1 tsp fried oregano
1 tsp garlic granules
½ tsp fine sea salt
½ tsp freshly ground black pepper

FOR THE DRESSING
3 tbsp olive oil
3 tbsp Greek yoghurt
1 tbsp chopped capers or 4 chopped anchovies
1 tbsp lemon juice
1 tbsp chopped fresh dill
1 tbsp chopped mint leaves

FOR THE SALAD
2 romaine lettuces, roughly chopped
200g (7oz) feta, crumbled
200g (7oz) cherry tomatoes on the vine
200–300g (7–10½oz) pitted kalamata olives
½ cucumber, diced
1 red onion, sliced
1 green (bell) pepper, diced

EQUIPMENT
large bowl—baking tray—chopping board knife—whisk

1. Make the croutons first so they will be cool by the time you pop them in the salad. Preheat the oven to 180°C (160°C fan/350°F/gas mark 4).

2. Put the torn ciabatta into a large bowl, then drizzle over the olive oil (I have suggested 2 tablespoons but honestly you can't overdo it, they'll just be crispier), sprinkle in the oregano, garlic granules, salt and pepper and mix well. When each crouton is fully coated, transfer them to a baking sheet and toast in the oven for 8 minutes until golden brown and crispy. Remove from the oven and set aside.

3. Put all the dressing ingredients into the same bowl that you mixed the croutons in and whisk together. Throw in the salad ingredients and give these ingredients a toss through the dressing, then finally add the croutons and toss again. Serve.

ONE SALAD BOWL

Watermelon, Halloumi and Mint Salad

SERVES 2
TOTAL TIME: 15 MINUTES

When we go to visit family in Greece, this is the only thing my sister and I want to eat. My aunt and uncle grow their own olives, so they really are just the most fresh and beautiful tangy olives ever. If we want dinner, we throw this salad together with some of their homemade olive oil, fresh mint and a squeeze of lemon juice and it just works so beautifully. The next hot day you have at home or on holiday, you have to try this – even just a piece of sweet watermelon, a cube of salty halloumi and a kalamata olive. Pop that into your mouth and it'll be a flavour explosion. It's refreshing, tasty and makes for a very happy Hari.

FOR THE DRESSING
2 tbsp olive oil
juice of 1 lemon
6–8 mint leaves, sliced
a pinch of freshly ground black pepper

FOR THE SALAD
650g (1lb 7oz) watermelon, diced
225g (8oz) halloumi, diced
60g (2oz) pitted kalamata olives, sliced
60g (2oz) cucumber, diced
a handful of rocket (arugula)
balsamic glaze, to finish (optional)

EQUIPMENT
chopping board—knife—large bowl
whisk

1. Start by making the dressing. Combine all the ingredients in a large bowl and whisk together until smooth. Set aside to let the mint infuse the dressing (if you can, do this overnight, if not just make sure you do it first before prepping the watermelon – even 5 minutes will enhance the dressing).

2. Once infused, add all the ingredients for the salad (except for the balsamic glaze) and toss everything together, ensuring all the ingredients are well coated in the dressing. Serve with a drizzle of balsamic glaze, if using, for a little tart sweetness.

ALTERNATIVE INGREDIENTS
Rocket: this can be replaced with any salad leaves of your choice
Mint: basil works really well in this salad

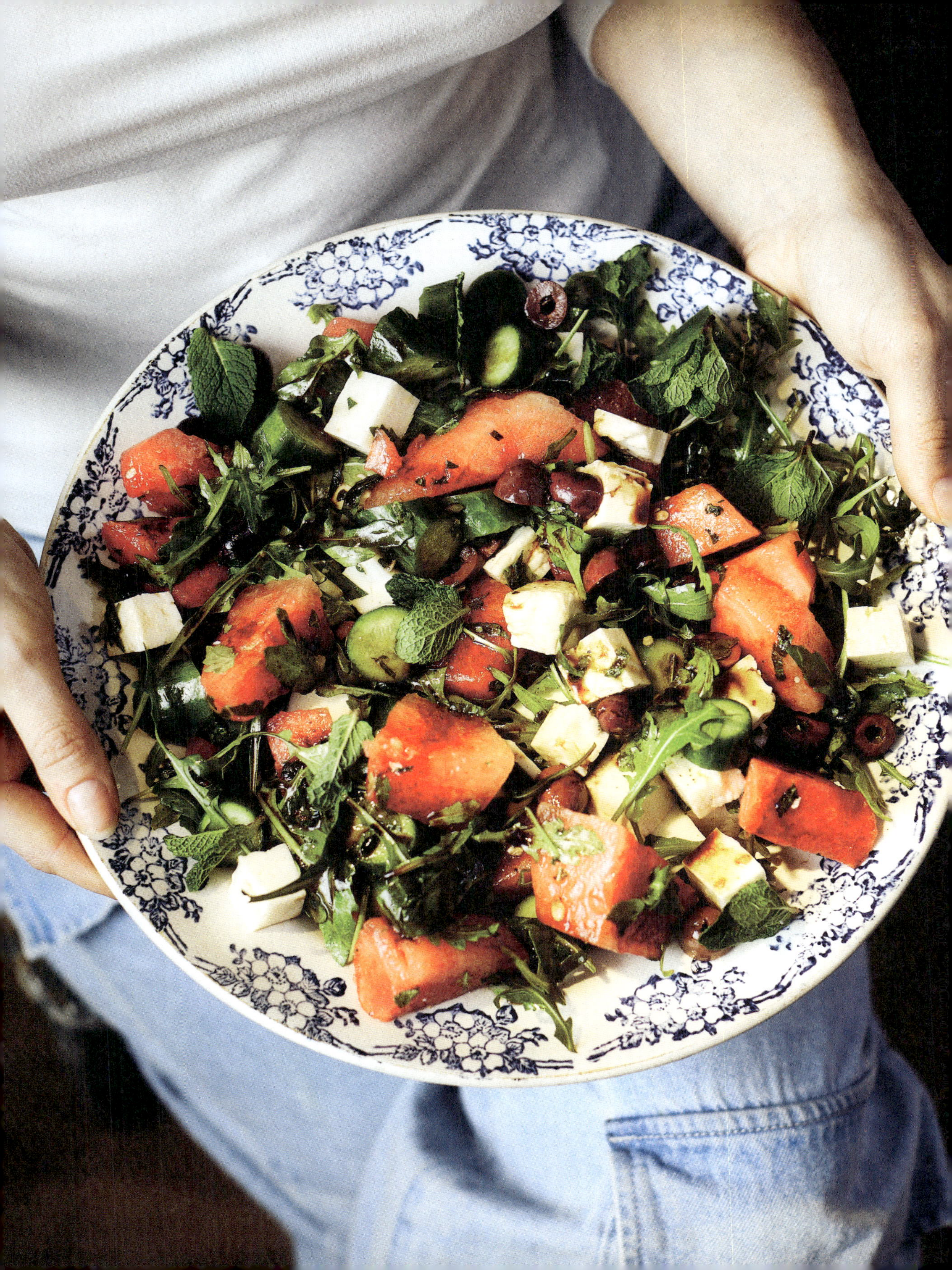

ONE TIN

Baking Using Just One Bowl

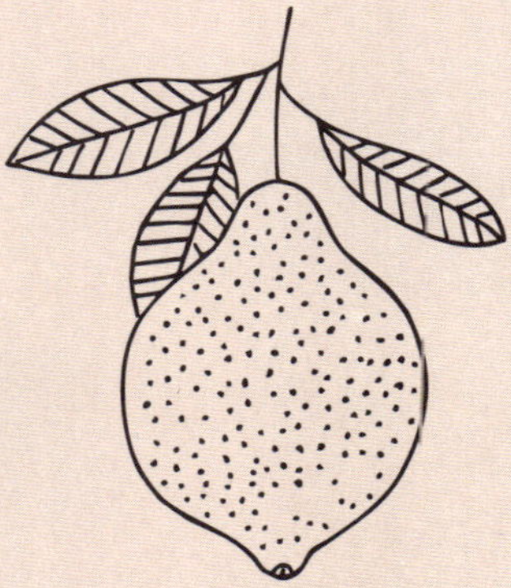

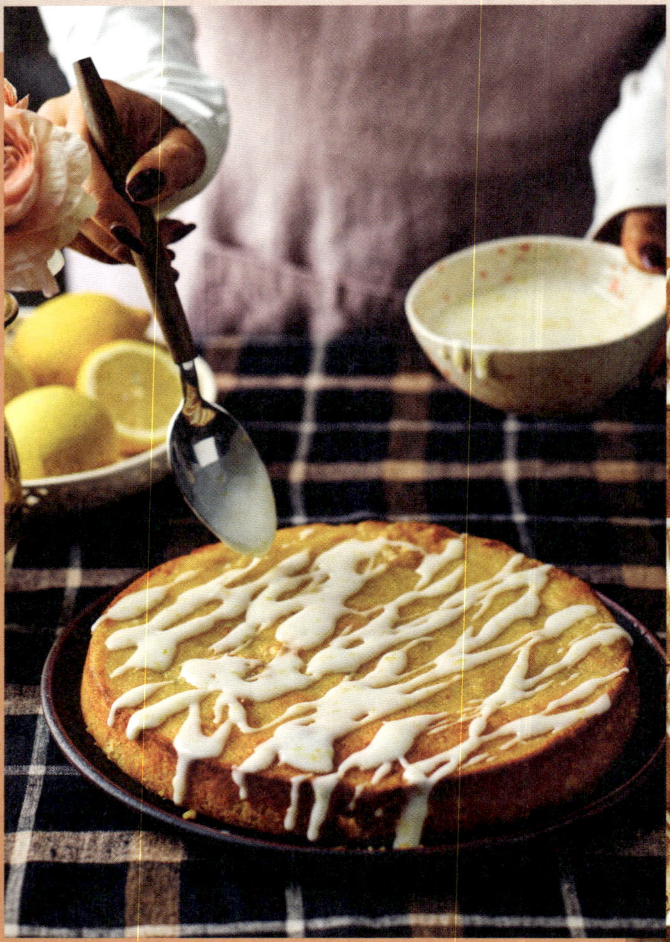

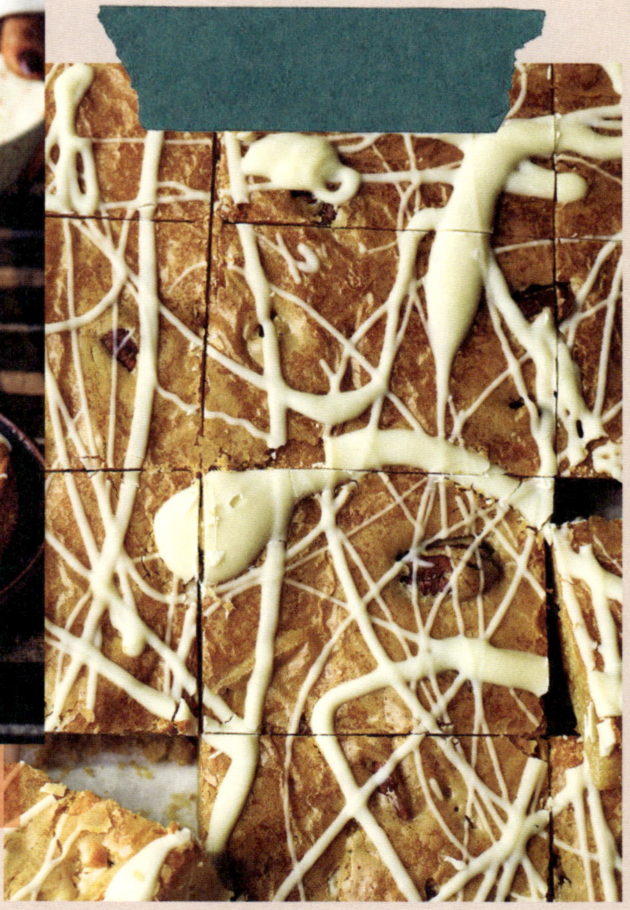

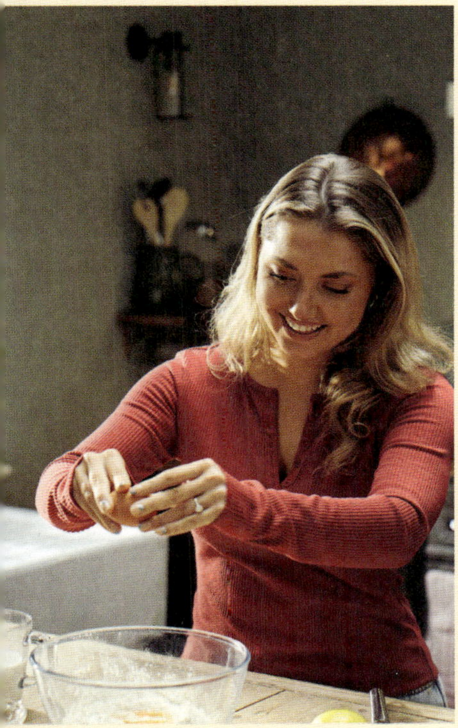

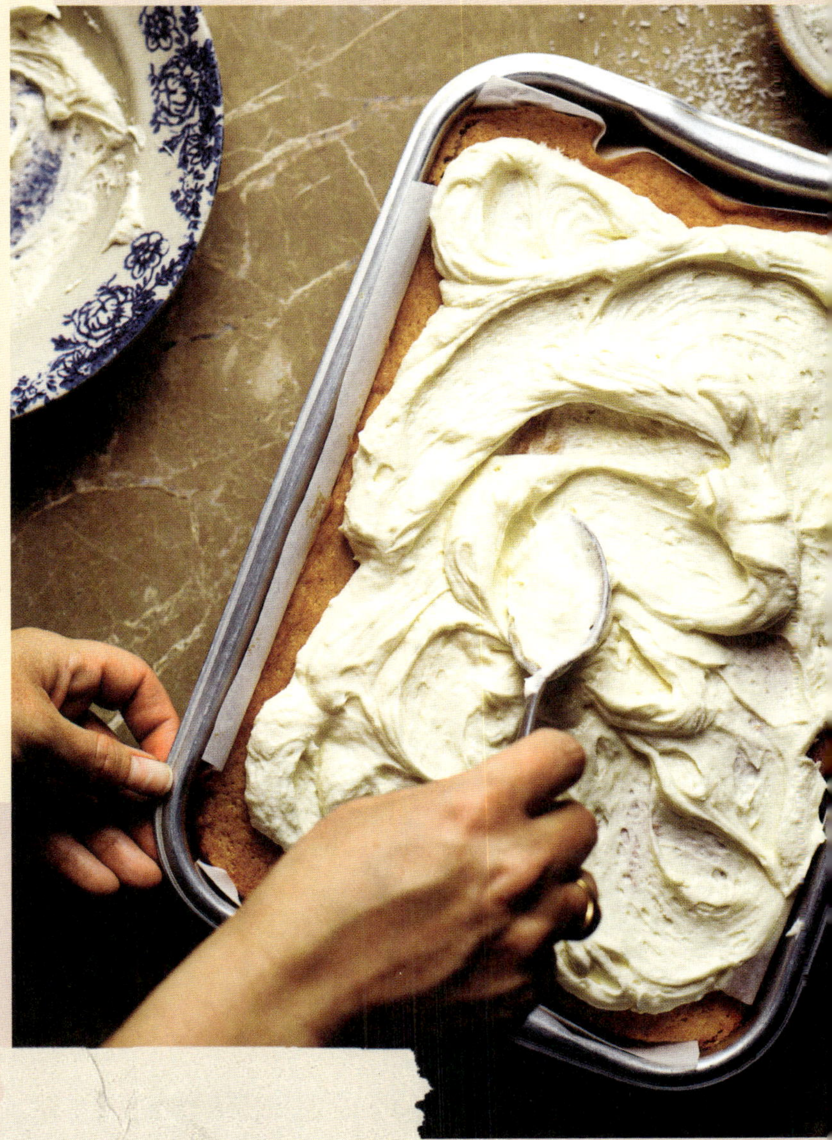

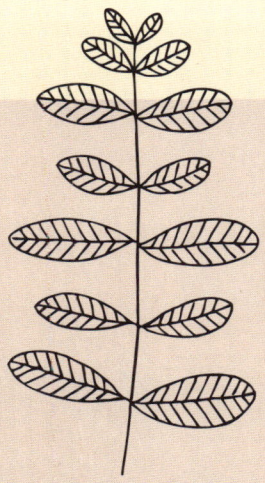

Lemon, Olive Oil & Thyme Cake

SERVES 12
TOTAL TIME: 45 MINUTES

The perfect cake recipe for every occasion – whether you're taking it round to a friend's barbecue or making it for an autumnal dinner party, the compliments you'll receive will be endless! When I was solo chalet hosting on my ski season at the age of 18, I made cakes once a day for guests as their elevenses. Because of the altitude, there are a few ingredients you can use to stop cakes from imploding or exploding and yoghurt and oils are the best. They also result in the moistest cakes, so using them in my recipes when I got back home was a must.

2 medium eggs
130g (4½oz/generous ½ cup) Greek yoghurt
150ml (5fl oz/⅔ cup) extra virgin olive oil
75ml (2½fl oz/⅓ cup) honey
zest of 3 lemons, plus the juice of 2
70g (2½oz/generous ⅓ cup) light brown soft sugar
2 sprigs of thyme, leaves picked, plus extra for decorating
225g (8oz/2¼ cups) ground almonds (almond meal)
1 tsp baking powder
large pinch of fine sea salt

EQUIPMENT
25cm (10in) round cake tin (pan)—mixing bowl—whisk—zester

1. Preheat the oven to 200°C (180°C fan/400°F/gas mark 6). Grease and line a 25cm (10in) round baking tin with baking parchment.

2. Put the eggs, yoghurt, olive oil and honey into a mixing bowl and whisk together. Add the lemon zest and juice and give it another mix, then add all the remaining ingredients and whisk together again.

3. Transfer the mixture to a 25cm (10in) round cake tin and bake in the oven for 35 minutes, then remove from the oven. Allow to cool in the tin for 10 minutes then sprinkle with thyme leaves before serving.

OPTIONAL LEMON FROSTING
Combine 275g (9¾oz/2¼ cups) icing (powdered) sugar with the zest of 1 lemon and 4 tablespoons lemon juice to create a thick glaze. Drizzle or spread this over the top of the cake once cooled, before adding the extra thyme leaves. You can also poke holes in the cake with a skewer first so that the glaze soaks into the cake.

ALTERNATIVE INGREDIENTS
Lemon: try orange or grapefruit

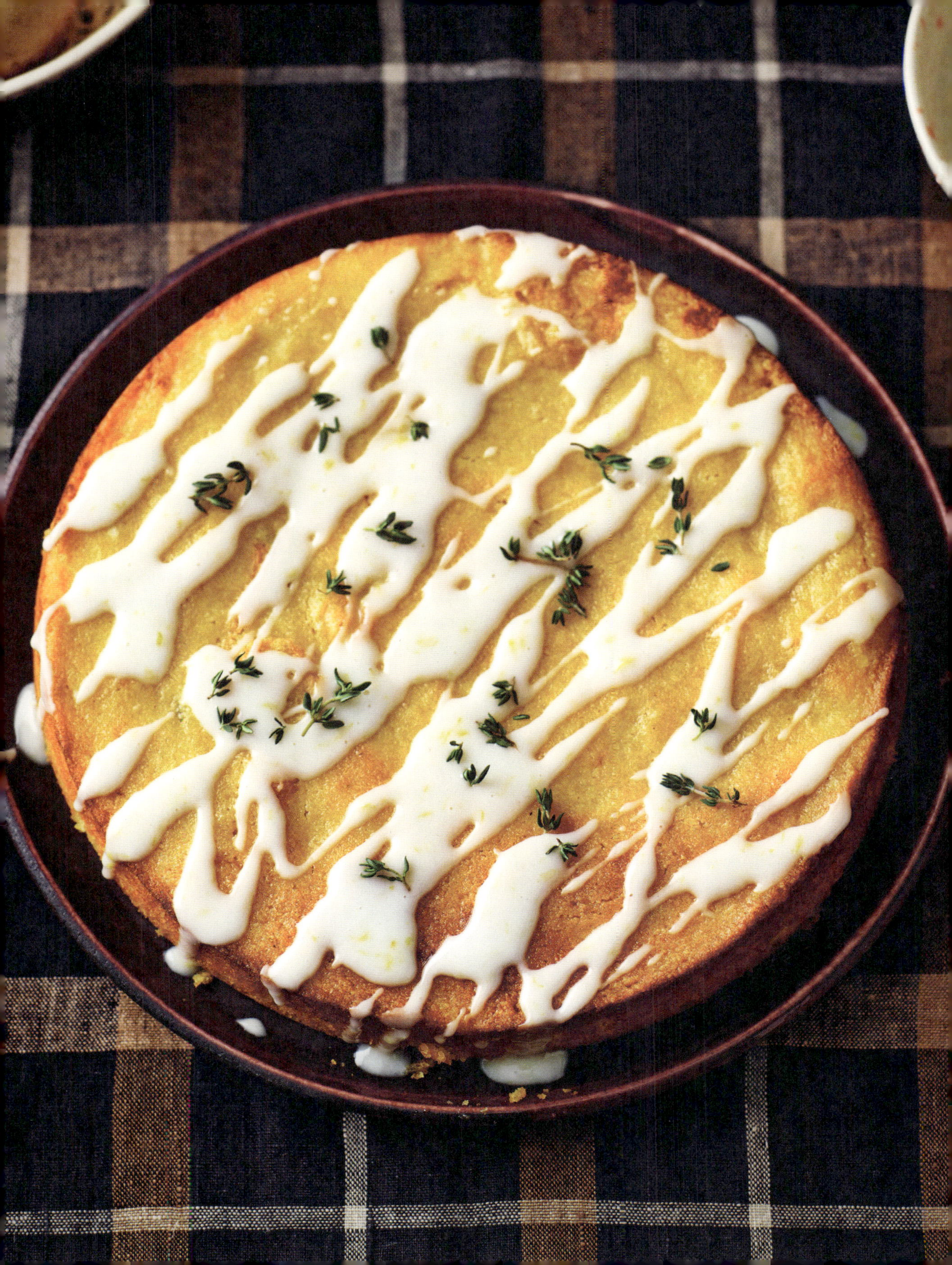

ONE TIN

Orange & Blueberry Loaf Cake

SERVES 12
TOTAL TIME: 45 MINUTES

I made this by accident about four years ago when I was making a lemon drizzle cake and found we had no lemons or lemon juice in the house but a load of oranges, so I thought, why not! It turned out even better than I could have imagined.

150g (5½oz) salted butter, softened
190g (6¾oz/generous ¾ cup) caster (superfine) sugar
zest of 2 oranges, plus 2 tbsp juice
3 medium eggs
90g (3oz/¾ cup) self-raising (self-rising) flour
pinch of fine sea salt
110g (3¾oz/scant 1¼ cups) ground almonds (almond meal)
100g (3½oz/⅔ cup) blueberries
1–2 tbsp demerara sugar

EQUIPMENT
900g (2lb) loaf tin (pan)—baking parchment—mixing bowl—whisk or wooden spoon—zester

1. Preheat the oven to 180°C (160°C fan/350°F/gas mark 4) and line a 900g (2lb) loaf tin with baking parchment.

2. Put the butter and sugar into a mixing bowl and cream together until smooth, then stir in the orange zest and juice. Add the eggs one at a time, beating the mixture after each addition.

3. Next, add the flour, salt and ground almonds and stir to create a smooth cake mixture (it will be quite thick). Fold in the blueberries, making sure you don't overmix them or you'll end up with a purple cake. We are just looking for them to be evenly distributed throughout the cake.

4. Transfer the mixture to the prepared tin and sprinkle over the demerara sugar. Bake in the oven for 35 minutes until springy to the touch. Remove from the oven and leave to cool in the tin before slicing.

ALTERNATIVE INGREDIENTS
Orange: any citrus fruit, such as lemons or limes
Blueberry: raspberries work well here

The Perfect Almond Cake

SERVES 8–10
TOTAL TIME: 45 MINUTES

One of the best things about using ground almonds (almond meal) is that it doesn't dry out, instead creating a moist, soft sponge. If you often find yourself in the position of having friends coming over and realising you only have 10 minutes to throw something together, make sure you have ground almonds in the back of your cupboard because they do all the hard work for you.

300g (10½oz/3 cups) ground almonds (almond meal)
150g (5½oz) butter, softened
200g (7oz/1 cup plus 1 tbsp) light brown soft sugar
100g (3½oz/scant ½ cup) granulated sugar
6 medium eggs
2 tsp vanilla extract
30g (1oz) flaked (slivered) almonds
2 tbsp icing (powdered) sugar
custard, to serve

EQUIPMENT
20cm (8in) cake tin (pan)—baking parchment—mixing bowl—wooden spoon

1. Preheat the oven to 200°C (180°C fan/400°F/gas mark 6) and line a 20cm (8in) cake tin with baking parchment.

2. Combine the ground almonds, butter, sugars, eggs and vanilla extract in a mixing bowl and whisk together until smooth. Pour into the prepared tin and sprinkle the flaked almonds over the top. Bake in the oven for 30 minutes, then remove and leave to cool in the tin.

3. Once cooled, sprinkle with icing sugar, slice and serve with lots of custard.

ALTERNATIVE INGREDIENTS
Flaked almonds: desiccated coconut makes a lovely topping

ONE TIN

Gooey Brownies in One

MAKES 9 BROWNIES
TOTAL TIME: 45 MINUTES

This recipe is just the easiest way to make perfect gooey brownies every time. No extra bowls, spoons or washing up needed, just throw it all together and you're done. They really are the best treat to have on your cake stand throughout the week, or even better to take round to friends who may be feeling blue to cheer them up!

70g (2½oz) salted butter, melted
200g (7oz/scant 1 cup) caster (superfine) sugar
50g (1¾oz/¼ cup) light brown soft sugar
2 medium eggs, plus 1 egg yolk
2 tsp vanilla extract
80ml (2½fl oz/⅓ cup) sunflower or vegetable oil
75g (2¾oz/scant ⅔ cup) cocoa (unsweetened chocolate) powder
½ tsp baking powder
65g (2½oz/⅔ cup) ground almonds (almond meal)
2 tbsp plain (all-purpose) flour
50g (1¾oz) white chocolate chips
50g (1¾oz) milk chocolate chips
50g (1¾oz) dark (bittersweet) chocolate chips

EQUIPMENT
mixing bowl—whisk—sieve—23cm (9in) square baking tin (pan)

1. Preheat the oven to 180°C (160°C fan/350°F/gas mark 4).

2. Combine the melted butter and sugars in a mixing bowl and whisk together until you have a smooth batter and the sugar looks like its dissolving. Add the eggs and egg yolk, vanilla extract and oil and whisk again until fully combined.

3. Next, sift in the cocoa powder, baking powder, ground almonds and flour to create a smooth batter, then fold in all the chocolate chips.

4. Pour the mixture into a 23cm (9in) square baking tin, then bake in the oven for 25–30 minutes until a skewer inserted into the centre comes out coated in moist crumbs, not batter.

5. Remove from the oven and leave to cool before slicing in the tin – ensure it is cool before slicing as these are gooey in the middle, which means it will be molten chocolate inside when first out of the oven!

ALTERNATIVE INGREDIENTS
Chocolate chips: these can be substituted for chopped nuts such as hazelnuts, pecans, walnuts or almonds

Simple Vanilla Cake

SERVES 9
TOTAL TIME: 35 MINUTES

For me, summer always calls for a simple sponge cake that you can tart up with sorbets, ice cream, meringues or jams (preserves). Having a cake in your repertoire that takes under 5 minutes to throw together and which can be the base of a few different desserts is a must – especially if you're a social butterfly like me, and you prefer to be enjoying a glass of something cold and fizzy with your guests rather than working away in the kitchen!

My favourite things to serve with slabs of this in the summer are clotted cream and fresh strawberries, raspberries or passion fruit. In the winter, I love it with hot custard and dollops of strawberry or raspberry jam.

300g (10½oz) salted butter, softened
300g (10½oz/1⅓ cups) caster (superfine) sugar
6 medium eggs
3 tsp vanilla extract
300g (10½oz/scant 1½ cups) self-raising (self-rising) flour
½ tsp ground cinnamon or nutmeg
1 tsp baking powder
icing (powdered) sugar, for dusting

EQUIPMENT
20cm (8in) square cake tin (pan)—baking parchment—mixing bowl—wooden spoon—sieve

1. Preheat the oven to 200°C (180°C fan/400°F/gas mark 6) and line a 20cm (8in) square cake tin with baking parchment.

2. Put the butter and caster sugar into a mixing bowl and cream together until smooth, then add the eggs one at a time, beating after each addition. Stir in the vanilla extract.

3. Sift in the flour, cinnamon or nutmeg and baking powder, folding to create a smooth mixture. Transfer the mixture to the prepared tin and bake in the oven for 25 minutes until golden and a skewer comes out clean.

4. Remove from the oven and leave to cool in the tin, then sprinkle over the icing sugar and serve with whatever you fancy.

Creamy Coconut Cake

SERVES 12
TOTAL TIME: 45 MINUTES

I am obsessed with anything coconutty, so for me this cake is an absolute must. If you know anyone that enjoys coconut or anything that reminds them of a Raffaello chocolate, then you're going to want to give this one a go! I often make this recipe in three cake tins (pans) as a celebration cake but you can just use one rectangular cake tin for a more simple bake.

350g (12½oz) salted butter, softened
350g (12½oz/1½ cups) caster (superfine) sugar
4 large eggs, plus 2 egg whites
8 tbsp coconut cream
2 tsp vanilla extract
350g (12½oz/generous 1¾ cups) self-raising (self-rising) flour
1 tsp baking powder
70g (2½oz/¾ cup) desiccated (dried shredded) coconut, plus extra for decorating

FOR THE BUTTERCREAM (FROSTING)
250g (9oz) salted butter
600g (1lb 5oz/4¾ cups) icing (powdered) sugar
3 tbsp cream cheese
4 tbsp coconut cream

EQUIPMENT
28 x 18cm (11 x 7in) rectangular cake tin (pan)—baking parchment—mixing bowl wooden spoon—sieve

1. Preheat the oven to 200°C (180°C fan/400°F/gas mark 6) and line a 28 x 18cm (11 x 7in) rectangular cake tin with baking parchment.

2. Put the butter and sugar into a mixing bowl and cream together for a few minutes until pale, smooth and fluffy, then one-by-one, mix in the eggs, coconut cream and vanilla extract.

3. Sift in the flour and baking powder then stir in the desiccated coconut and mix until smooth. Transfer to the prepared tin and bake in the oven for 25 minutes until evenly risen with no sinking in the middle, golden brown and springy to the touch. Remove from the oven and leave to cool in the tin.

4. While the cake is cooling, grab the mixing bowl that you used to make the cake batter, give it a quick wash and throw in the butter and beat until pale and fluffy – you can use a stand mixer and beat on high for 5 minutes, or if you're using a spoon, beat for as long as you can before you think your arm will fall off. We are looking for smooth, silky, really pale and fluffy butter. Once the butter is fluffy, beat in the icing sugar, cream cheese and coconut cream (add the icing sugar slowly otherwise your kitchen will be covered in a thin layer of sugar) until combined and smooth.

5. When the cake is cool, spread the buttercream over the top and finish with a sprinkle of desiccated coconut. Slice and enjoy!

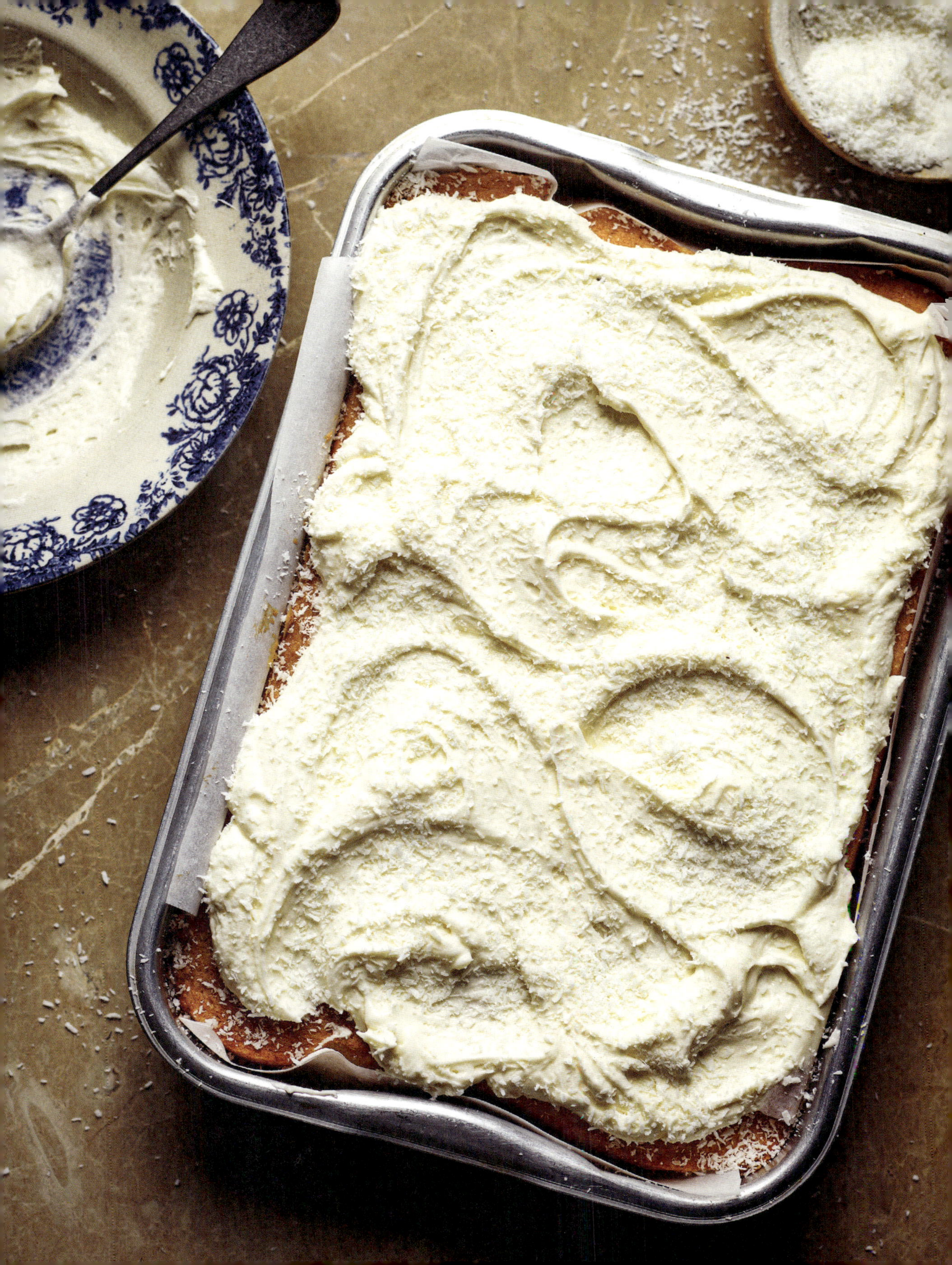

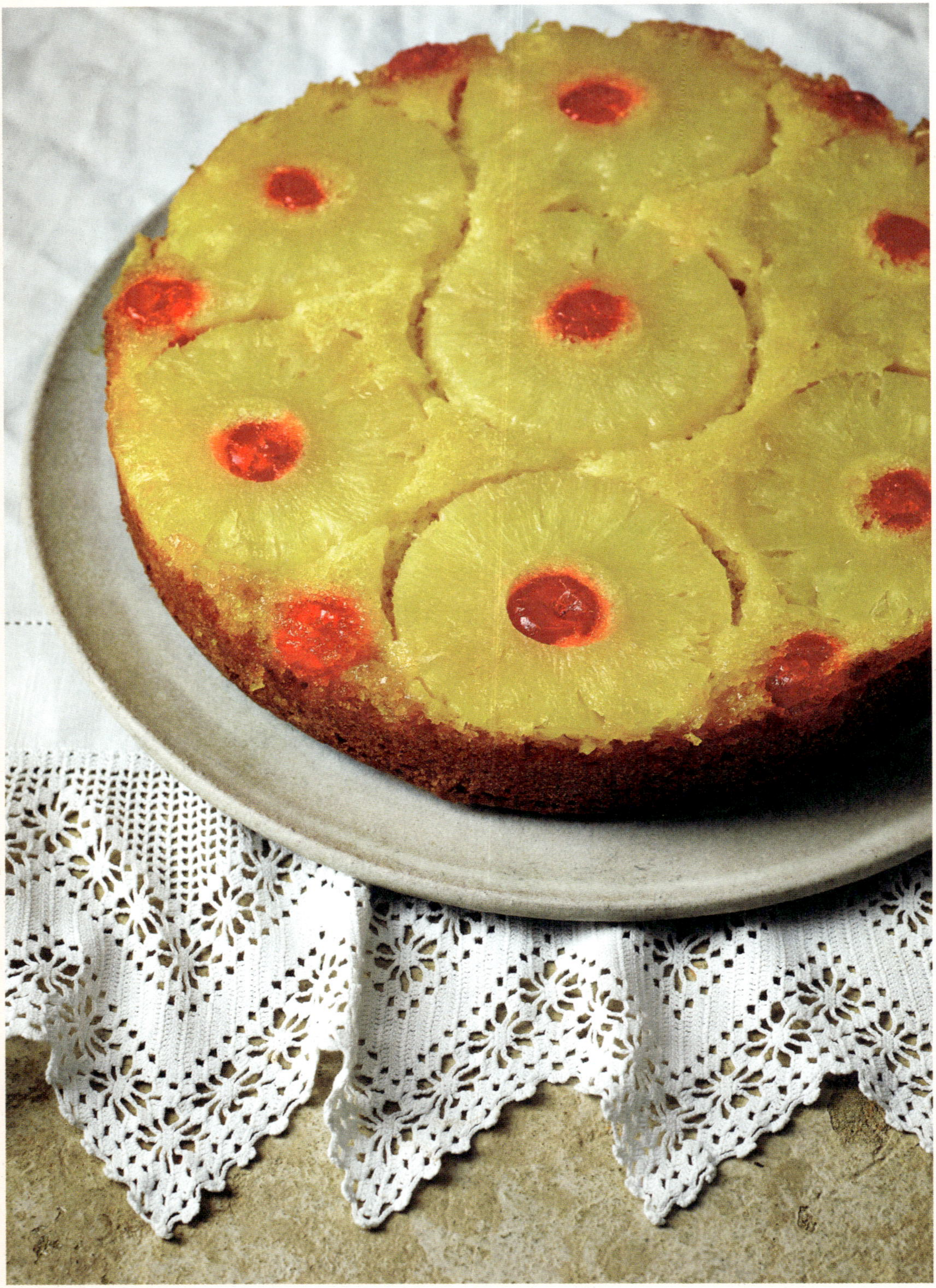

1920s Pineapple Upside Down Cake

SERVES 12
TOTAL TIME: 1¼ HOURS

Pineapple upside down cake always reminds me of my Nana and Gramps. It was invented in the 1920s and is simple and delicious, with tart bites of pineapple and a moist, soft sponge over the top. It looks super effective with maraschino cherries in the middle of the pineapple rounds and is an absolute crowd pleaser when you have the grandparents over!

275g (9¾oz) salted butter, softened
50g (1¾oz/generous ¼ cup) light brown sugar
432g (15oz) tin of pineapple rings in juice
8–10 glacé (maraschino) cherries
225g (8oz/scant 1 cup) caster (superfine) sugar
4 medium eggs
225g (8oz/1¾ cups) self-raising (self-rising) flour

EQUIPMENT
small saucepan—20cm (8in) baking dish
wooden spoon—mixing bowl

1. Preheat the oven to 200°C (180°C fan/400°F/gas mark 6).

2. Melt 50g (1¾oz) of the butter into a small saucepan over a medium heat, then pour it into a 20cm (8in) baking dish, add the brown sugar and mix together to create a thin, even layer on the bottom of the dish. Place the pineapple rings in the dish, reserving the juice in the tin, and place a cherry in the middle of each ring and into any gaps around the edges.

3. Put the remaining butter and caster sugar into a mixing bowl and cream together until fluffy, then add the eggs one by one, beating after each addition. Fold in the flour and then 1 tablespoon pineapple juice from the tin. Pour the batter over the pineapple rings in the dish and bake in the oven for 45 minutes–1 hour until a skewer inserted into the centre of the sponge comes out clean.

4. Remove from the oven and leave to cool, then turn out onto to a wire rack or serving plate.

ALTERNATIVE INGREDIENTS
Glacé cherries: try using fresh cherries or raspberries

My Boozy Carrot Cake

SERVES 12
TOTAL TIME: 1 HOUR

This is such a versatile recipe. It's great for summer dinners, as a lovely surprise dessert, perfect for adult birthday parties or, thanks to all the spices, it even makes a wonderful Christmas cake to share with friends! For this recipe I use a rectangular baking tin (pan) to make a sheet cake, but if you want to elevate your cake game, pop it in three separate round cake tins and make a triple-layered cake.

4 medium eggs
280ml (9½fl oz/generous 1 cup) vegetable oil
50ml (1¾fl oz/scant ¼ cup) rum
390g (13¾oz/2 cups plus 1 tbsp) light brown soft sugar
200g (7oz/1⅔ cups) plain (all-purpose) flour
60g (2oz/½ cup) ground almonds (almond meal)
2 tsp baking powder
1 tsp ground cinnamon
½ tsp ground nutmeg or mixed spice (apple pie spice)
2 big or 3 small carrots, grated and excess water squeezed out
100g (3½oz) chopped pecans, walnuts or flaked (slivered) almonds

EQUIPMENT
32 x 22cm (13 x 9in) baking tin (pan)
baking parchment—mixing bowl—grater
whisk—wooden spoon

1. Preheat the oven to 180°C (160°C fan/350°F/gas mark 4) and line a 32 x 22cm (13 x 9in) baking tin with baking parchment.

2. You're going to want a mixing bowl for this recipe, so nothing escapes! Start by whisking together the eggs, oil and rum. Once well combined, add the sugar, flour, ground almonds, baking powder, cinnamon and nutmeg. Mix together well so that there are no lumps and you have a smooth batter. Now fold in the grated carrots and nuts, then pour the batter into the prepared tin.

3. Bake in the oven for 45 minutes, until springy to the touch and an inserted skewer comes out clean. Remove from the oven and allow to cool in the tin before slicing.

OPTIONAL CREAM CHEESE BUTTERCREAM (FROSTING)
Using an electric whisk, beat 110g (3¾oz) softened salted butter in a bowl for 5 minutes until pale and fluffy, then sift in 270g (9½oz/2¼ cups) icing (powdered) sugar, beat again, and then fold in 150g (5½oz) cream cheese. Add 1 teaspoon vanilla extract if desired. Spread over the cooled cake, then add more chipped pecans and a few pinches of ground cinnamon on top.

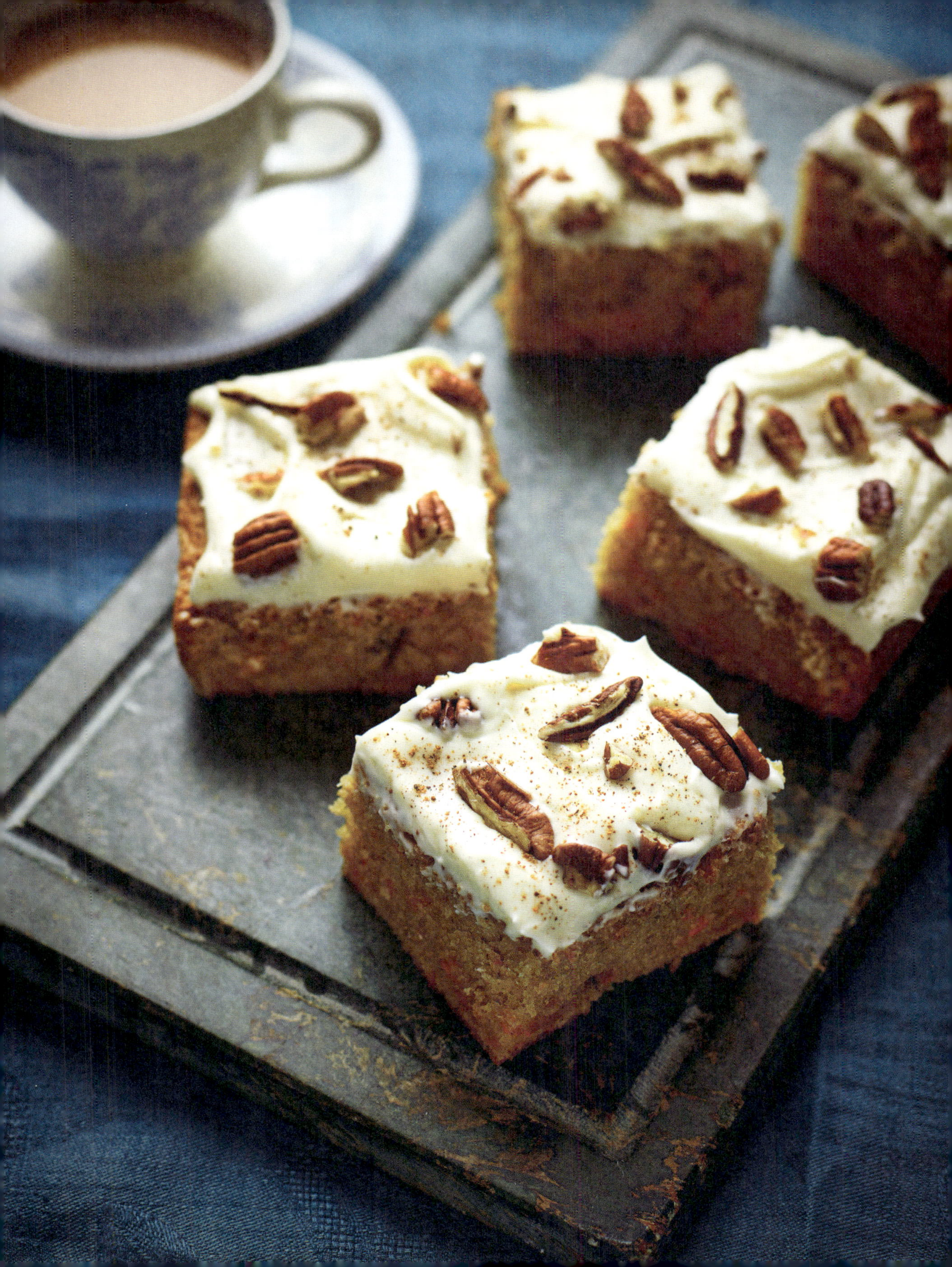

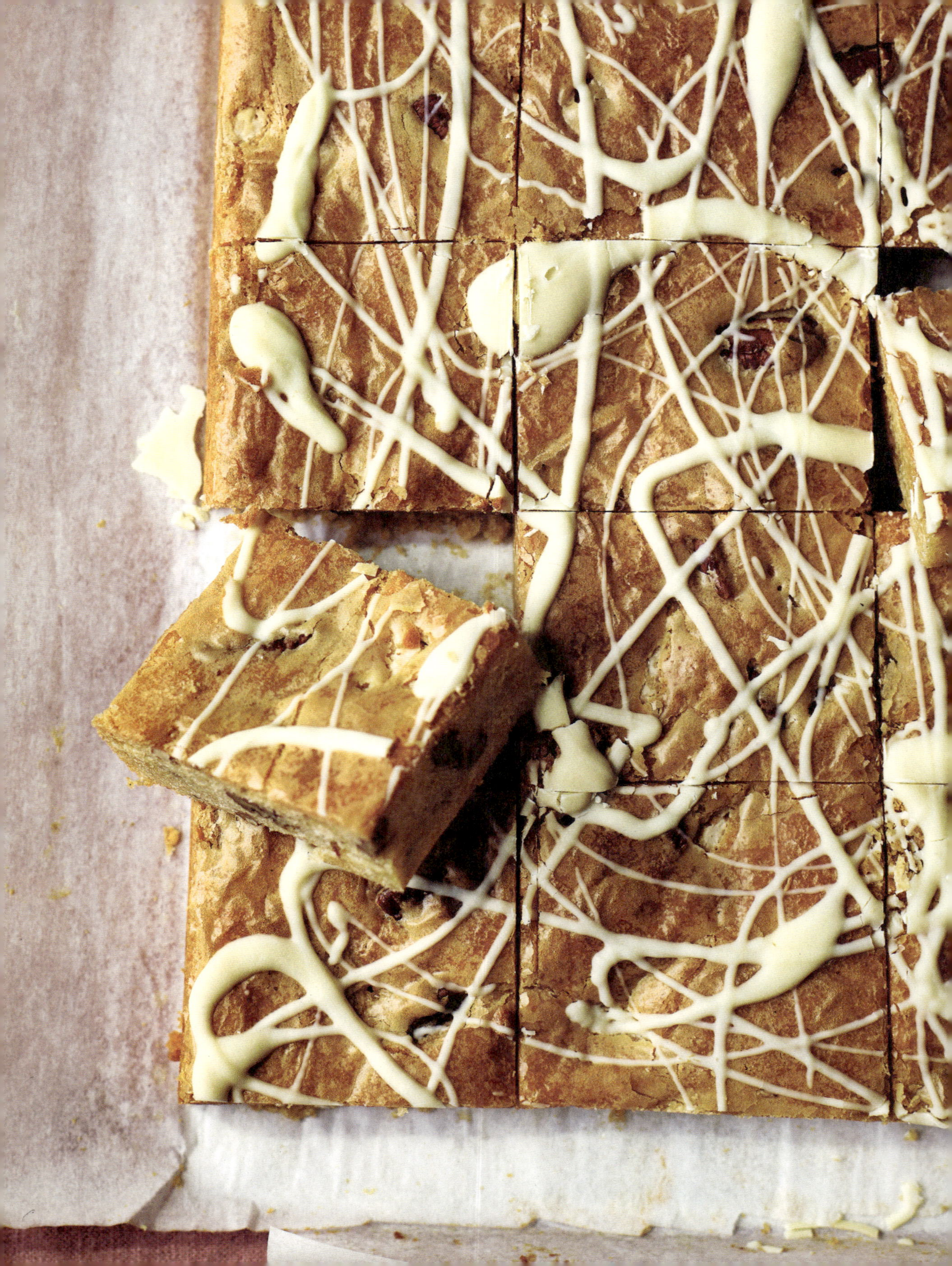

White Chocolate & Nut Blondies

MAKES 9 BLONDIES
TOTAL TIME: 40 MINUTES

These blondies are utter heaven: chewy, buttery and packed with nutty goodness, they are the perfect treat for those moments when you want to curl up and indulge in something truly cosy. The creamy sweetness of white chocolate combines with the crunch of nuts adding just the right amount of texture. Whether you're sharing with a friend or savouring on your own with a cup of tea or coffee, it's the kind of bake that makes you want to put your feet up.

185g (6½oz) salted butter, melted
180g (6¼oz/1 cup) light brown soft sugar
80g (2¾oz/⅓ cup) granulated sugar
2 medium eggs
2 tsp vanilla extract
large pinch of flaked sea salt
265g (9½oz/generous 2 cups) plain (all-purpose) flour
½ tsp bicarbonate of soda (baking soda)
200g (7oz) white chocolate, roughly chopped
75g (2½oz/¾ cup) pecans, roughly chopped
75g (2½oz) flaked (slivered) almonds

EQUIPMENT
mixing bowl—whisk—sieve—23cm (9in) baking tin (pan)—small heatproof bowl

1 Preheat the oven to 190°C (170°C fan/375°F/gas mark 5).

2 Combine the melted butter and sugars in a mixing bowl, then add the eggs, vanilla extract and salt. Whisk together until you have a smooth batter and the sugar looks like its dissolving.

3 Sift in the flour and bicarbonate soda to create a thick batter, then fold in three quarters of the white chocolate and nuts.

4 Pour the mixture into a 23cm (9in) square baking tin and bake in the oven for 25 minutes, then remove from the oven leave to cool in the tin for 10 minutes.

5 Meanwhile, melt the remaining white chocolate by microwaving it in 30 second blasts or in a bain marie, then drizzling it over the cooled blondies. Let cool completely before slicing and serving.

ALTERNATIVE INGREDIENTS
White chocolate: change for any chocolate you like
Pecans: replace with chopped walnuts, hazelnuts or almonds

For the Grown-ups Summertime Brandy & Fig Cake

SERVES 12
TOTAL TIME: 1¼ HOURS

Figs are best later in summer and into the autumn months, so if you can find them during these months this cake will be so sweet and delicious. The dollops of mascarpone really balance out the sweetness and hum of brandy throughout the cake. A beautiful summertime pudding to wow your friends with this year!

- 210g (7½oz) salted butter, softened, plus extra for greasing
- 210g (7½oz/scant 1¼ cups) light brown sugar, plus 1 tbsp for sprinkling
- 3 medium eggs
- 125g (4¼oz/1 cup) self-raising (self-rising) flour
- 75g (2½oz/⅔ cup) ground almonds (almond meal)
- 1 tsp baking powder
- 50ml (1¾fl oz/scant ¼ cup) brandy, plus 1½ tbsp to serve
- 80g (2¾oz/⅔ cup) dark (bittersweet) chocolate chips
- 8 figs, halved lengthways
- 2 tbsp fig jam or compote, to serve
- dollops of mascarpone, to serve

EQUIPMENT
20cm (8in) round cake tin (pan)—baking parchment (optional)—mixing bowl wooden spoon—sieve—pastry brush

1. Preheat the oven to 180°C (160°C fan/350°F/gas mark 4) and grease or line a 20cm (8in) round cake tin (pan).

2. Cream together the butter and sugar in a mixing bowl together until pale and fluffy. Now add the eggs one at a time, beating between each addition. When all the eggs have been added, sift in the flour, ground almonds and baking powder and mix to create a smooth, lump-free batter. Finally, stir through the brandy and chocolate chips. Make sure the chocolate chips are evenly distributed through the batter.

3. Sprinkle the remaining 1 tablespoon of sugar over the bottom of the prepared cake tin, then place the figs cut side down on top of the sugar – this is going to caramelise the figs. Pour over the batter and then bake in the oven for 55–60 minutes until the cake is golden brown and springy.

4. Remove from the oven and allow to cool in the tin for 25–30 minutes (we want it to firm up so that it doesn't fall apart when released from the tin, but we still want it slightly warm to soften the jam or compote).

5. Turn out the cake so that the beautiful golden figs are on the top, then brush the top of the cake with the remaining brandy, then with the fig jam or compote.

6. Slice and serve with dollops of mascarpone for the most beautiful summertime adult pudding.

ALTERNATIVE INGREDIENTS
Figs: instead of figs, use plums or apricots

ONE TIN 201

Thick Chocolate Chip Cookie Bars

MAKES 9 BIG SLABS
TOTAL TIME: 40–45 MINUTES

There is something about gooey, thick cookies that makes me obsessed! These are so thick that they are almost blondies. One of my favourite things to do with this recipe is to make it festive, so at Easter I add Mini Eggs, at Halloween I add whatever leftover chocolate we have and at Christmas I use red and green M&M's – but chocolate chips are year-round!

If the cookie bars seem too soft after baking, place in the fridge to firm up before slicing.

185g (6½oz) salted butter, melted
240g (8½oz/1⅓ cups) light brown soft sugar
2 medium eggs
2 tsp vanilla extract
large pinch of flaked sea salt
265g (9½oz/2 cups plus 2 tbsp) plain (all-purpose) flour
½ tsp bicarbonate of soda (baking soda)
50g (1¾oz/scant ⅓ cup) milk chocolate chips
50g (1¾oz/scant ⅓ cup) dark (bittersweet) chocolate chips
50g (1¾oz/scant ⅓ cup) white chocolate chips

EQUIPMENT
23cm (9in) square baking tin (pan)
baking parchment—mixing bowl—whisk
sieve—wooden spoon

1. Preheat the oven to 190°C (170°C fan/375°F/gas mark 5) and grease and line a 23cm (9in) square baking tin with baking parchment.

2. Add the melted butter and sugar to a mixing bowl and whisk to combine, then add the eggs, vanilla extract and salt and whisk again. Sift in the flour and bicarbonate of soda, then gently mix this together before folding in the chocolate chips.

3. Transfer the mixture to the prepared tin, then bake in the oven for 25–30 minutes until the edge is golden but the centre is still gooey. Remove from the oven and leave to cool in the tin before slicing. A large glass of cold milk is my fiancé's accompaniment to eat these!

ALTERNATIVE INGREDIENTS
Chocolate chips: instead of chocolate you can use chopped nuts of your choice or fudge pieces

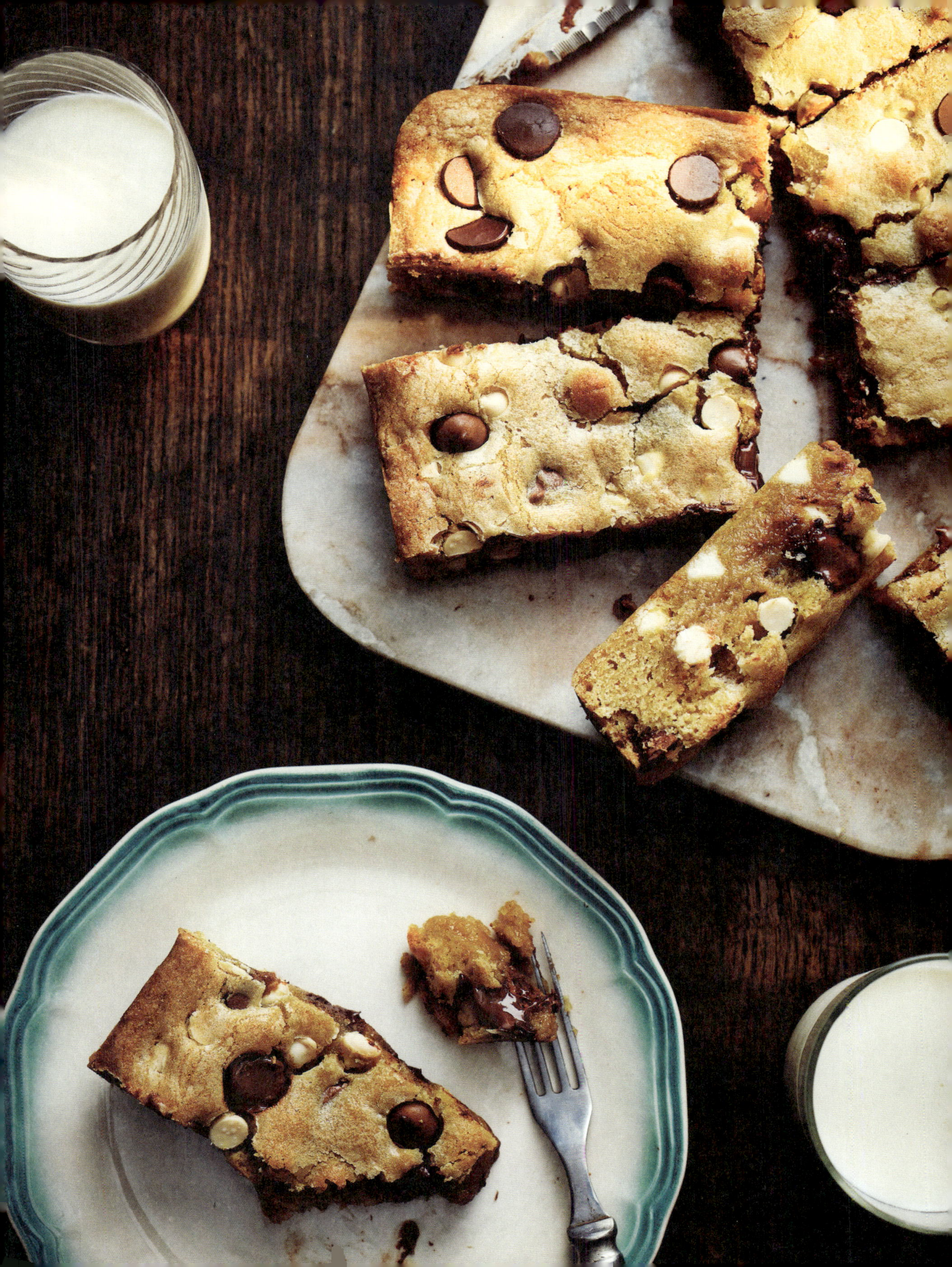

Seasonal Fudgy Apple Cake (with a Dollop of Clotted Cream)

SERVES 12
TOTAL TIME: 1¼ HOURS

This recipe warms mine and my family's hearts when the nights draw in. Coming in from a cold, windy and wet day outside, popping the kettle on and having a slice of this cake with a cup of tea is one of the perks you have to find about darker days. That being said, I've also served this after a beautiful lunch in the garden in the summer – a slice of this with a good dollop of clotted cream makes a beautiful dessert. It really is perfect for every occasion.

200g (7oz) salted butter, softened, plus extra for greasing
200g (7oz/generous 1 cup) light brown soft sugar
4 medium eggs
150g (5½oz/generous 1 cup) self-raising (self-rising) flour
50g (1¾oz/½ cup) ground almonds (almond meal)
½ tsp baking powder
pinch of fine sea salt
150g (5½oz) fudge pieces
2 apples (I use Cox), cored and finely diced
4 tbsp salted caramel sauce
a handful of flaked (slivered) almonds
1 tbsp demerara sugar
clotted cream, to serve

EQUIPMENT
20cm (8in) round cake tin (pan)—baking parchment—mixing bowl—wooden spoon

1. Preheat the oven to 180°C (160°C fan/350°F/gas mark 4) and grease and line a 20cm (8in) round baking tin (pan) with baking parchment.

2. Cream together the butter and sugar in a mixing bowl until pale and fluffy. Now add the eggs one at a time, beating between each addition. When all the eggs have been added, mix in the flour, ground almonds, baking powder and salt. Fold in the fudge pieces and apples until evenly distributed, then pour the batter into a 20cm 8in round cake tin.

3. Drizzle the salted caramel sauce over the top, then use a knife or toothpick to drag the sauce through the cake – this is going to create a caramel marble effect in the cake, so when you slice into it, parts of the cake will be infused with caramel. Finally, sprinkle the flaked almonds and demerara sugar over the top.

4. Bake in the oven for 50–60 minutes until springy and golden brown. Remove from the oven and allow to cool in the tin before slicing and serving with dollops of clotted cream.

ALTERNATIVE INGREDIENTS
Apples: instead of apples, trying using pears

ONE TIN   **205**

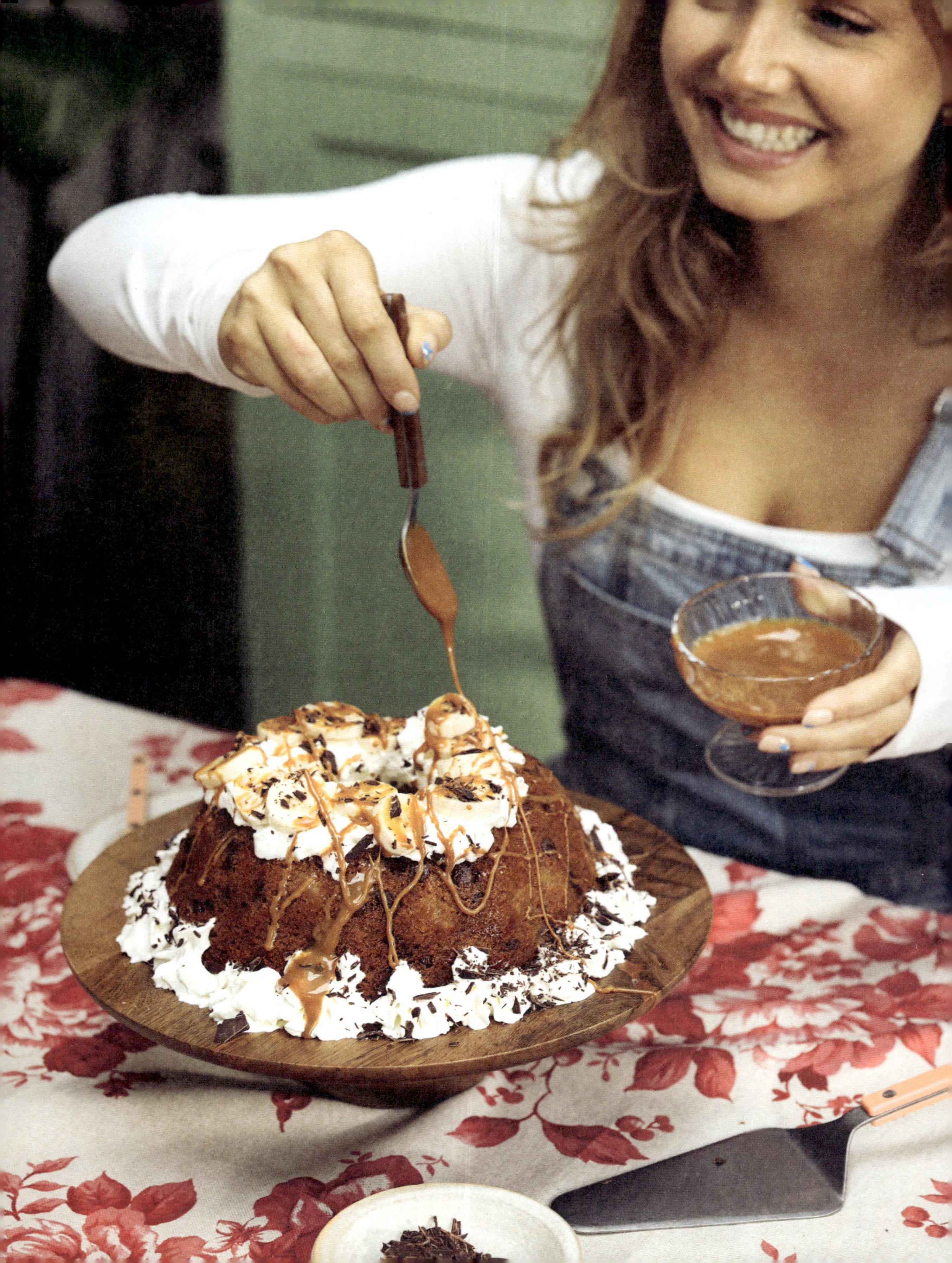

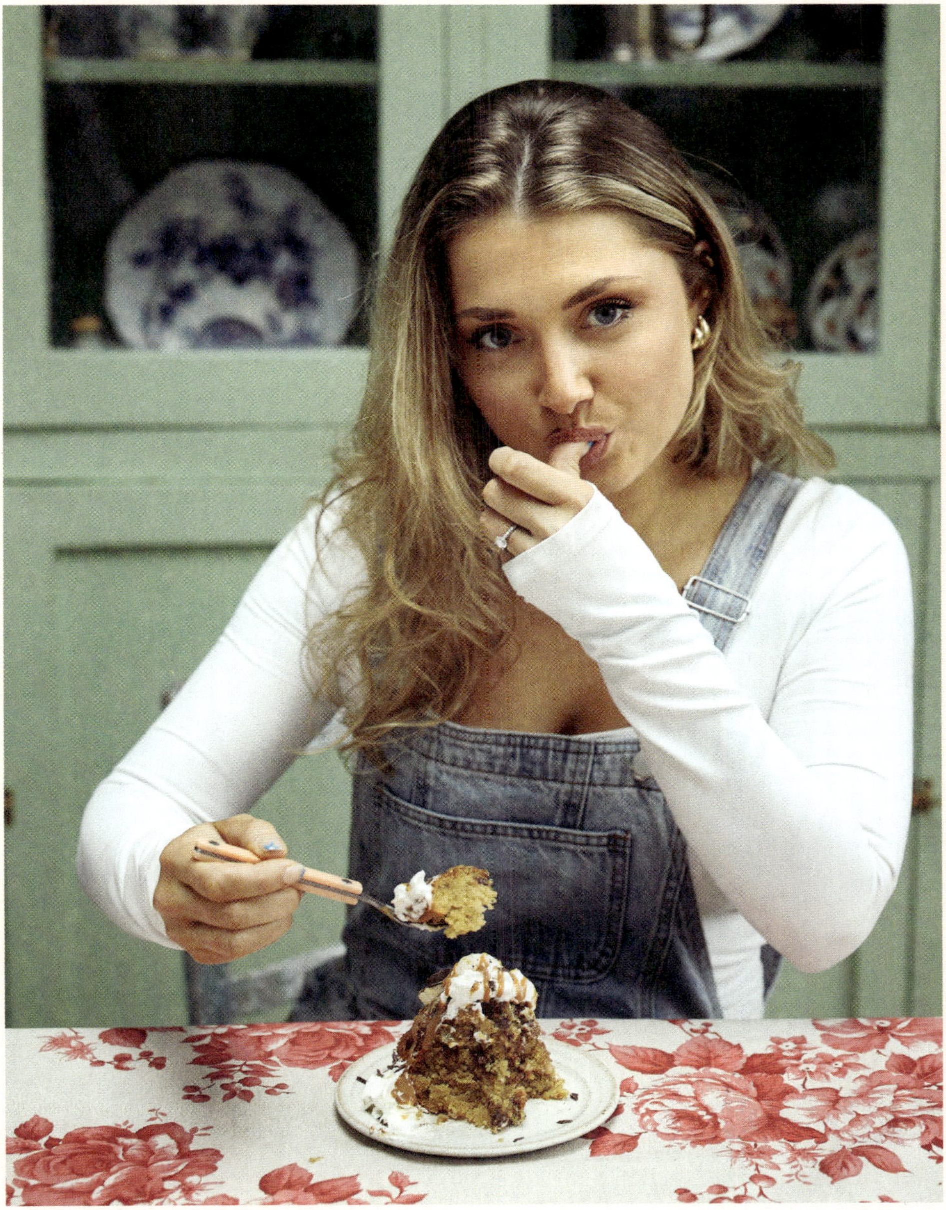

All the Best Bits of Banoffee Pie in a Cake

SERVES 12
TOTAL TIME: 45 MINUTES

My fiancé is obsessed with my banana cake, to the point that he will purposely not eat the bananas in the fruit bowl so that they get too ripe and he can remind me that maybe I should make a banana cake soon! It's a great cake to make because you can use up whatever you have in the cupboards: nuts, dried fruits, chocolate … So, when we had friends over and I was struggling to come up with a pudding, Jake suggested a banana cake. I saw the can of squirty whipped cream in the refrigerator and decided it was time to try banoffee cake!

210g (7½oz) salted butter, softened, plus extra for greasing
210g (7½oz/scant 1¼ cups) light brown soft sugar
3 medium eggs
210g (7½oz/1¾ cups) self-raising (self-rising) flour
1 tsp baking powder
3 ripe bananas, mashed
3 tbsp salted caramel sauce
150g (5½oz/generous ¾ cup) milk chocolate chips

FOR THE TOPPING
1 can of squirty whipped cream
1 banana, sliced
2 tbsp salted caramel sauce
chocolate chips or shavings

EQUIPMENT
20cm (8in) bundt cake tin (pan)
mixing bowl—wooden spoon—sieve

1. Preheat the oven to 180°C (160°C fan/350°F/gas mark 4) and grease a 20cm (8in) bundt cake tin (you can use any similar-sized tin, but I think this looks really effective in a bundt tin).

2. Cream together the butter and sugar in a mixing bowl until pale and fluffy. Now add the eggs one at a time, beating between each addition. When all the eggs have been added, sift in the flour and baking powder and mix, then fold in the bananas and chocolate chips.

3. Pour the batter into the prepared tin and drizzle the salted caramel sauce over the top, then use a knife or toothpick to drag the sauce in swirls through the cake.

4. Bake in the oven for 25–30 minutes until golden brown and springy, then remove from the oven and allow to cool fully in the tin.

5. Once cooled, turn out the cake and squirt the cream in a circle around the cake, then place the slices of banana onto the cream and drizzle over the caramel sauce. Finish with the chocolate chips or shavings.

ALTERNATIVE INGREDIENTS
If you want to add a handful of nuts into the mixture, reduce the quantity of chocolate chips by the same amount

Peanut and Caramel Crispies

MAKES 10 SLICES
TOTAL TIME: 15 MINUTES + CHILLING

A no-bake recipe is always a winner and if you're someone that loves peanut butter, Snickers or anything nutty and chocolatey, I promise these Peanut and Caramel Crispies is one you're going to want to try (and then keep in your snack tin all week).

80g (2¾oz) unsalted butter
50g (1¾oz) smooth peanut butter, plus 1 tablespoon for the topping
6 x 50g (1¾oz) Snickers bars, roughly chopped
350g (12oz) puffed rice cereal
200g (7oz) milk chocolate
handful of salted peanuts, roughly chopped

EQUIPMENT
900g (2lb) loaf tin (pan)—baking parchment saucepan—wooden spoon heatproof bowl

1. Line a 900g (2lb) loaf tin with baking parchment.

2. Put the butter, peanut butter and 5 of the Snickers bars into a saucepan over a low heat and melt it all together until a smooth mixture forms (there will obviously still be lumps from the Snickers, but on the whole you want everything melted!). Remove from the heat and mix in the puffed rice cereal, then add the remaining Snickers and fold through the mix.

3. Scrape the mixture into the prepared loaf tin and firmly pack it down. Melt the chocolate and 1 tablespoon of peanut butter by microwaving it in 30 second blasts or in a bain marie, then drizzle over the top of the mixture in the tin. Sprinkle with the salted peanuts.

4. Pop it in the refrigerator to set for 2 hours, then slice and enjoy!

ALTERNATIVE INGREDIENTS
Snickers: experiment with other chocolate bars such as Mars or Double Decker
Puffed rice cereal: replace with cornflakes or puffed quinoa

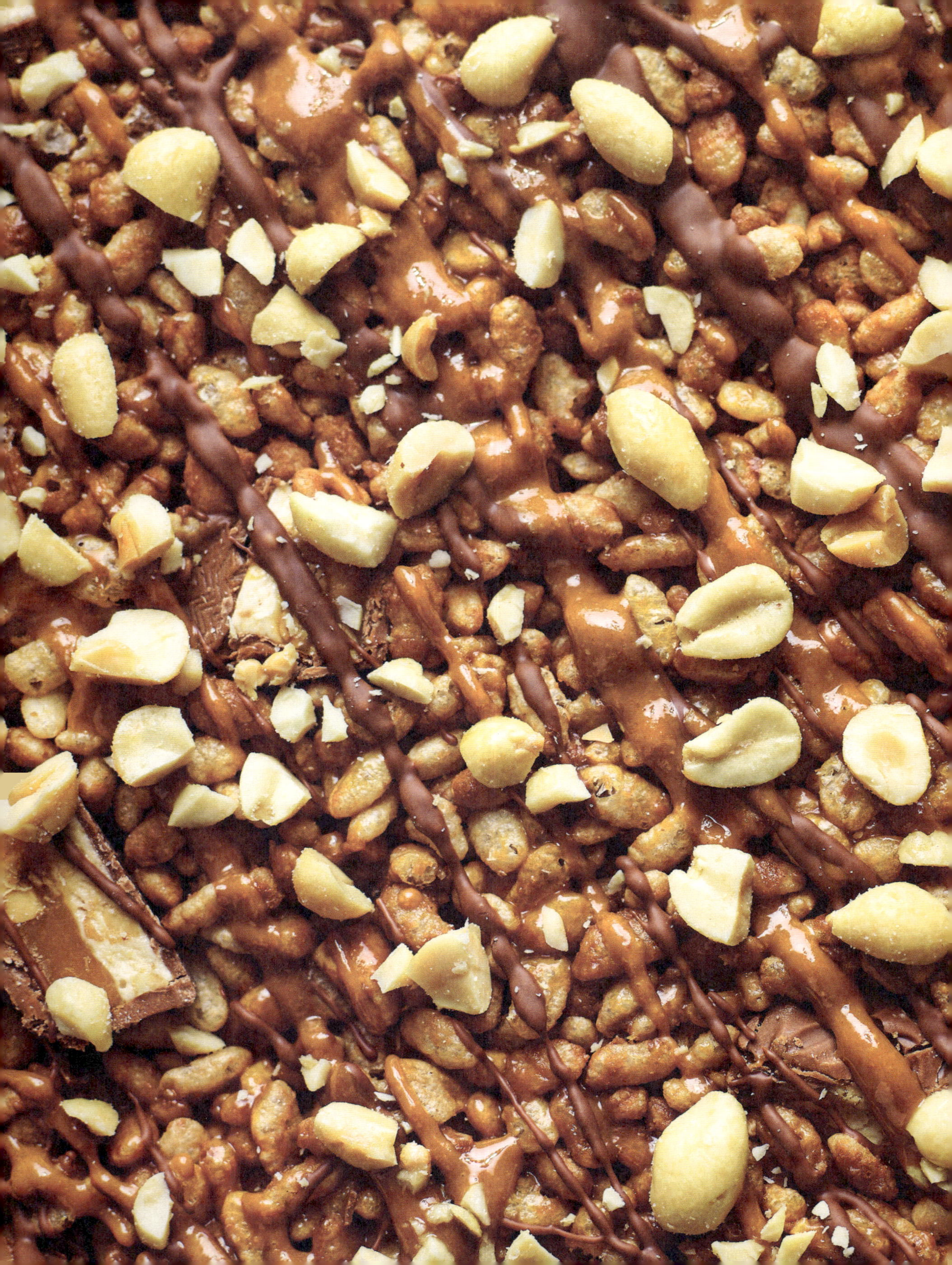

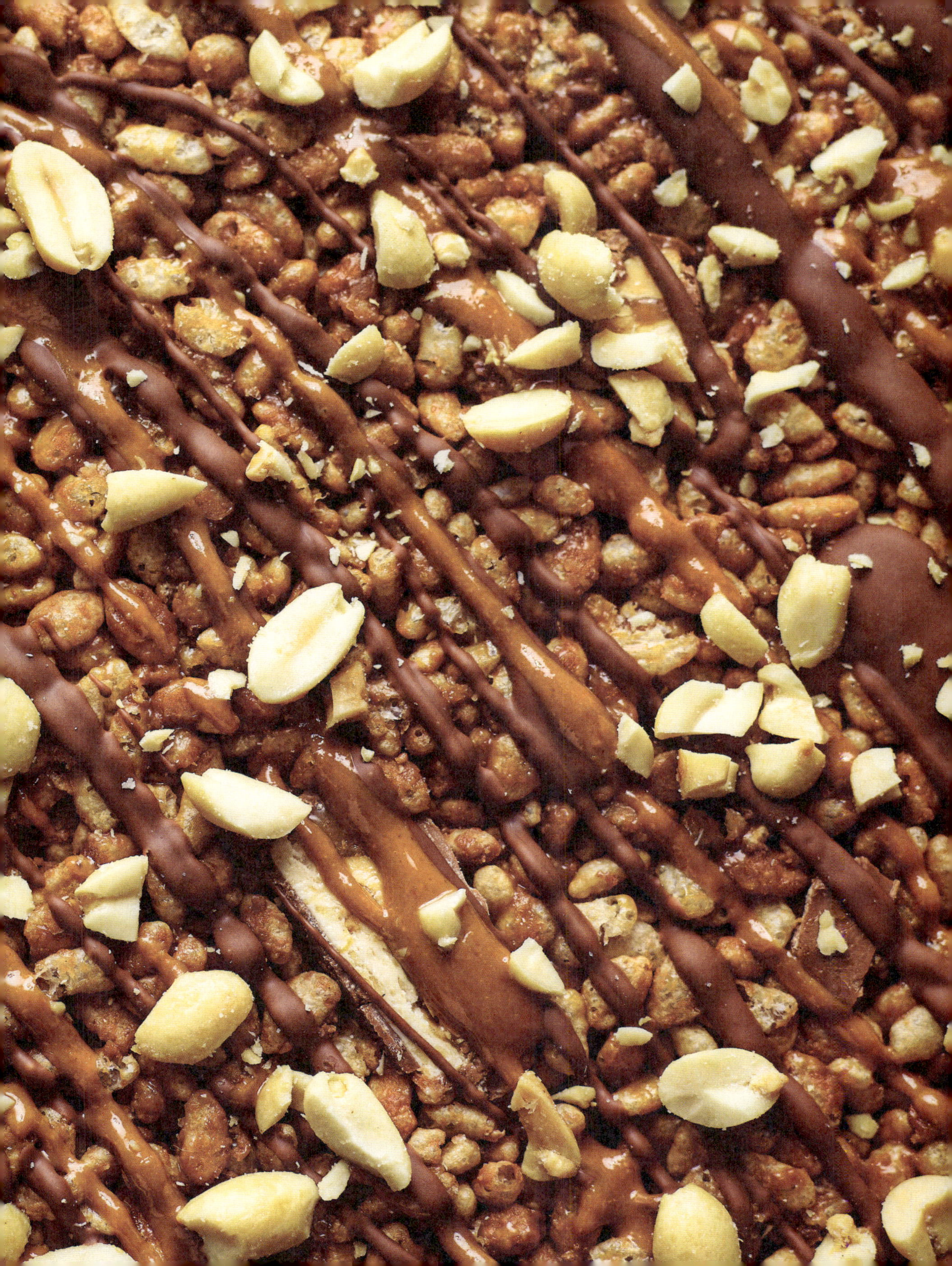

Raspberry Bakewell Cake

SERVES 12
TOTAL TIME: 1 HOUR

I was a waitress for eight years. I started out running food and drinks at 14 and finished just as I graduated university and began to work for myself full time. One of the restaurants I worked in bought some of their puddings from a little lady who lives on a canal, and she made the best Bakewell tarts. At 14, I had only ever tried the Bakewell tarts that come in a foil tin, and they were nothing like a slice of this soft cake with a jammy middle – it was beautiful. I became hooked on Bakewell flavours and so I came up with this cake. I am sure this is not something new, but sometimes the best cakes are those that don't need a lot of fuss.

210g (7½oz) salted butter, softened, plus extra for greasing
210g (7½oz/scant 1¼ cups) light brown soft sugar
3 medium eggs
1–2 tsp almond extract
150g (5½oz/1½ cups) ground almonds (almond meal)
70g (2½oz/generous ½ cup) self-raising (self-rising) flour
200g (7oz) raspberries, plus extra to serve
a handful of flaked (slivered) almonds
2 tbsp demerara sugar
clotted cream or vanilla ice cream, to serve (optional)
icing (powdered) sugar, to serve

EQUIPMENT
20cm (8in) round cake tin (pan)
baking parchment (optional)—mixing bowl
wooden spoon

1. Preheat the oven to 180°C (160°C fan/350°F/gas mark 4) and grease or line a 20cm (8in) round cake tin (pan).

2. Cream together the butter and sugar in a mixing bowl together until pale and fluffy. Now add the eggs one at a time, beating between each addition. When all the eggs have been added, add the almond extract and mix again. Fold in the ground almonds and flour to create a smooth batter, then gently fold in the raspberries. You want these to be evenly distributed through the batter but not too bashed up that they turn the cake pink.

3. Pour the batter into the prepared tin and sprinkle over the flaked almonds and demerara sugar. Bake in the oven for 45 minutes until springy and soft. Serve warm with clotted cream or cool with a good scoop of vanilla ice cream, a dusting of icing sugar and more fresh raspberries.

ALTERNATIVE INGREDIENTS
Raspberries: you can swap raspberries for strawberries, blackberries or blueberries

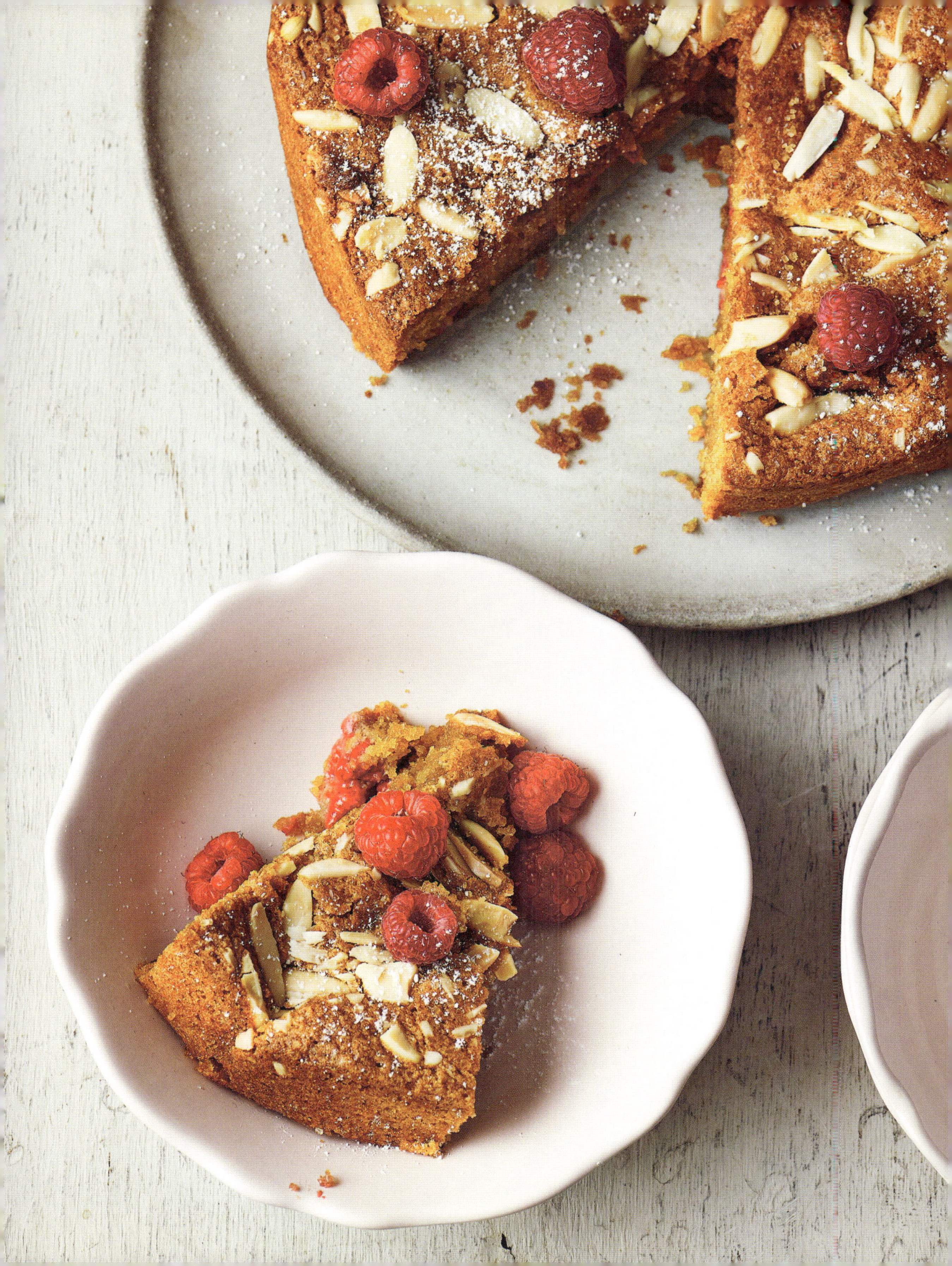

The Perfect Comfort Dinner

Whether it's just for you, a special someone, or a gathering of friends or family, use these simple tips to create the perfect comfort food experience.

MUSIC

Music isn't just for when guests arrive. It's for you, too. Turn the music on before you even reach for the ingredients in your fridge. Find something that feels nostalgic, just like the food you're about to prepare. Music should be something you enjoy, and there's no wrong way to choose your soundtrack, just like there's no right or wrong way to cook. For me, I love listening to old school country music and Elvis Presley from the 1950s. It's a constant companion through every season. I listen to more country during the summer and lean into the '50s tunes as the winter months settle in. The music should be soft, something you can gently sway to while still feeling relaxed. It should feel like a backdrop to your cooking, not something that makes you flustered or anxious. When you're lost in thought, even in the car, you instinctively turn down the music to focus. So, create that same calm atmosphere in your kitchen. Let the music help you connect with the cooking process.

DRINKS

Once the music's on, pour yourself a drink – a little treat that helps you unwind and brush off the day. This is your time to cook something with love, peace, and relaxation. For me, that's a glass of wine, signalling the start of 'me time.' The first sip feels like the moment when the stress melts away. Whether it's a Diet Coke, elderflower soda, or sparkling water, make that drink your own. Add a simple garnish: a wedge of lime to your Coke, cucumber to your elderflower soda, or a few mint leaves to your sparkling water. If wine is your choice, reach for your favourite wine glass (and we all know a thin stem and a delicate glass makes wine taste even better!). If you're into long drinks like a G&T, cocktail, or iced tea, find an ice-cube tray that excites you; big cubes, small cubes, fun shapes – even a quirky straw! Little details make it feel special and indulgent, making the moment a treat.

LIGHTING

Finally... Lighting! Whether you're cooking for yourself or having guests over, the right lighting can make all the difference. If you can, dim the lights, or if that's not an option, turn off the overheads and bring in lamps with warm bulbs. Candles add a soft glow, and fairy lights can add that extra touch of warmth. A golden, welcoming light will make everyone feel at ease. When the environment feels calm and beautiful, the food always seems to taste better. For a special touch, light a scented candle an hour before guests arrive. Place it by the door, it's the perfect way to set the mood before they step inside.

Let these little details fill your kitchen with comfort, they'll transform the ordinary into something extraordinary.

THE PERFECT COMFORT DINNER 215

Index

A

almonds
   my boozy carrot cake 196
   raspberry Bakewell cake with vanilla ice cream 212
   the perfect almond cake 188
anchovies
   kale & chicken Caesar salad 176
   summertime tomato stew 121
apples
   seasonal fudgy apple cake 204
artichoke hearts
   sausage & artichoke pasta 125
avocado
   avocado & smoked salmon on toast salad 174
   carnival salad 158

B

balsamic vinegar
   mango & kiwi salad with basil, balsamic & pine nut dressing 161
bananas
   banoffee pie in a cake 208
BBQ sauce
   BBQ tofu & chips 94
   slow-cooked BBQ pulled pork 111
beans
   butter bean & broccoli alfredo 39
   carnival salad 158
   chorizo & butter bean stew 143
   creamy sausage & bean bake with a crunchy topping 45
   love at first bite cannellini beans with dollops of pesto 55
   sea bass with mixed beans 22
   spicy jerk-style chicken, black beans & rice 25
   summery bean stew with burrata 137
beef
   beef & horseradish stew 146
   blue cheese steak & potatoes 102
   cheeseburger nachos 92
   deconstructed lasagne 133
   peppered steak with whisky sauce 27
   Sloppy Joe pasta 40
   slow-cooked brisket tacos 117
   taco Tuesday pan dinner 56
   warming meatballs & onion gravy 114
blueberries
   orange & blueberry loaf cake 187
brandy & fig cake 200
breadcrumbs
   baked sausage & tomato gnocchi 68
   creamy sausage & bean bake with a crunchy topping 45
broccoli
   butter bean & broccoli alfredo 39
   green goddess winter pie 36
   peri peri salmon, potato & broccoli traybake 76
   school night chicken & broccoli pasta bake 116
brownies
   gooey brownies in one go 190
buffalo sauce
   comfort mac & cheese with a buffalo twist 138

C

caramel
   banoffee pie in a cake 208
   peanut & caramel crispies 209
carrots
   carnival salad 158
   maple-roasted duck leg & veggie traybake 62
   my boozy carrot cake 196
cheese
   blue cheese steak & potatoes 102
   cheeseburger nachos 92
   cheesy garlic-stuffed chestnut mushrooms 86
   cheesy pesto chicken bake 64
   chorizo, manchego & red pepper traybake 84
   comfort mac & cheese with a buffalo twist 138
   creamy pesto, mushroom & courgette pasta 28
   creamy spinach & turkey meatballs 83
   deconstructed lasagne 133
   garlic & Parmesan crispy potatoes & trout 101
   goat's cheese, fig & Parma ham salad 152
   Greek herby roasted lamb sharing platter 71
   green goddess winter pie 36
   peachy summertime salad 163
   spicy tomato orzo with toasted pine nuts & feta 16
   summery bean stew with burrata 137
   taste of Greece salad 177
   taste of Italy salad 157
   watermelon, halloumi & mint salad 178

chicken
    cheesy pesto chicken bake 64
    chicken broth with mini meatballs & pasta 126
    chicken pot pie 21
    chicken shawarma-style traybake 74
    chimichurri chicken salad 167
    creamy 'marry me' chicken 108
    Friday night red Thai curry 31
    garlic butter & lemon chicken orzo 112
    garlic butter spatchcocked chicken 65
    honey & mustard chicken thighs 80
    juicy spiced chicken legs 53
    kale & chicken Caesar salad 176
    my kinda one-pot paella 129
    peanut crunch salad 173
    school night chicken & broccoli pasta bake 116
    simple coconut curry 134
    spicy jerk-style chicken, black beans & rice 25
chickpea & salami salad with a lemon twist 170
chillies
    cheeseburger nachos 92
    spicy tuna salad with pesto croutons 168
    taco Tuesday pan dinner 56
chimichurri chicken salad 167
chives
    creamy salmon salad with dill & chive dressing 154
chocolate
    gooey brownies in one go 190
    thick chocolate chip cookie bars 202
    white chocolate & nut blondies 199
chorizo
    chorizo & butter bean stew 143
    chorizo, manchego & red pepper traybake 84
    gambas pil pil 32
    my kinda one-pot paella 129
    sea bass with mixed beans 22
coconut
    creamy coconut cake 192
    gyoza noodle soup 144
    simple coconut curry 134
cod
    Parma ham-wrapped cod with sweet potato traybake 79
courgettes
    creamy pesto, mushroom & courgette pasta 28
cream
    creamy 'marry me' chicken 108
cucumber
    peanut crunch salad 173

D
dill
    creamy salmon salad with dill & chive dressing 154
duck
    maple-roasted duck leg & veggie traybake 62

E
eggs
    haddock kedgeree with jammy eggs 42

F
figs
    brandy & fig cake 200
    goat's cheese, fig & Parma ham salad 152
fudge
    seasonal fudgy apple cake 204

G
garlic
    cheesy garlic-stuffed chestnut mushrooms 86
    garlic & Parmesan crispy potatoes & trout 101
    garlic butter & lemon chicken orzo 112
    garlic butter spatchcocked chicken 65
    maple-roasted duck leg & veggie traybake 62
gnocchi
    baked sausage & tomato gnocchi 68
gyoza noodle soup 144

H
haddock kedgeree with jammy eggs 42
herbs
    chimichurri chicken salad 167
    Greek herby roasted lamb sharing platter 71
    honey & mustard chicken thighs 80
horseradish sauce
    beef & horseradish stew 146

K
kale & chicken Caesar salad 176
kiwi fruit
   mango & kiwi salad with basil, balsamic & pine nut dressing 161

L
lamb
   Greek herby roasted lamb sharing platter 71
   Mother's Day lamb 89
leeks
   green goddess winter pie 36
lemons
   chickpea & salami salad with a lemon twist 170
   garlic butter & lemon chicken orzo 112
   lemon, olive oil & thyme cake 184

M
mango & kiwi salad with basil, balsamic & pine nut dressing 161
maple-roasted duck leg & veggie traybake 62
mint
   watermelon, halloumi & mint salad 178
mushrooms
   cheesy garlic-stuffed chestnut mushrooms 86
   chicken pot pie 21
   creamy pesto, mushroom & courgette pasta 28
   Sloppy Joe pasta 40
mussels
   on the coast 'Rock' mussels 122
mustard
   honey & mustard chicken thighs 80

N
noodles
   gyoza noodle soup 144
   spicy peanut butter noodles 48
nuts
   white chocolate & nut blondies 199

O
olives
   Greek herby roasted lamb sharing platter 71
   summertime tomato stew 121
   taste of Greece salad 177
onions
   caramelised onion pasta traybake 88
   warming meatballs & onion gravy 114
orange & blueberry loaf cake 187

P
pancetta
   prawn & pancetta risotto 50
   pumpkin risotto with bacon & walnut crunch 130
   summer potato salad 162
Parma ham
   goat's cheese, fig & Parma ham salad 152
   Parma ham-wrapped cod with sweet potato traybake 79
   peachy summertime salad 163
   taste of Italy salad 157
pasta
   caramelised onion pasta traybake 88
   chicken broth with mini meatballs & pasta 126
   comfort mac & cheese with a buffalo twist 138
   creamy pesto, mushroom & courgette pasta 28
   deconstructed lasagne 133
   garlic butter & lemon chicken orzo 112
   Georgie's creamy prawn orzo 52
   nostalgic mini pasta shape soup 140
   rosé prawn pasta 18
   sausage & artichoke pasta 125
   school night chicken & broccoli pasta bake 116
   Sloppy Joe pasta 40
   spicy tomato orzo with toasted pine nuts & feta 16
peaches
   just peachy summertime salad 163
peanut butter
   peanut & caramel crispies 209
   spicy peanut butter noodles 48
peanut crunch salad 173
peppered steak with whisky sauce 27
peppers
   chorizo, manchego & red pepper traybake 84
   Friday night red Thai curry 31
   my kinda one-pot paella 129
peri peri salmon, potato & broccoli traybake 76
pesto
   cannellini beans with pesto 55
   cheesy pesto chicken bake 64
   creamy pesto, mushroom & courgette pasta 28
   pesto & halloumi traybake 73
   spicy tuna salad with pesto croutons 168

pine nuts
  mango & kiwi salad with basil, balsamic & pine nut dressing 161
  spicy tomato orzo with toasted pine nuts & feta 16
pineapple upside down cake 195
pork
  slow-cooked BBQ pulled pork 111
  teriyaki pork chops 98
potatoes
  BBQ tofu & chips 94
  blue cheese steak & potatoes 102
  garlic & Parmesan crispy potatoes & trout 101
  Mother's Day lamb 89
  peri peri salmon, potato & broccoli traybake 76
  summer potato salad 162
prawns
  gambas pil pil 32
  Georgie's creamy prawn orzo 52
  haddock kedgeree with jammy eggs 42
  prawn & pancetta risotto 50
  rosé prawn pasta 18
  pumpkin risotto with bacon & walnut crunch 130

R
raspberry Bakewell cake with vanilla ice cream 210
rice
  haddock kedgeree with jammy eggs 40
  my kinda one-pot paella 127
  prawn & pancetta risotto 48
  pumpkin risotto with bacon & walnut crunch 128
  spicy jerk-style chicken, black beans & rice 23

rosé prawn pasta 18

S
salami
  chickpea & salami salad with a lemon twist 170
salmon
  avocado & smoked salmon on toast salad 174
  creamy salmon salad with dill & chive dressing 154
  peri peri salmon, potato & broccoli traybake 76
sausages
  baked sausage & tomato gnocchi 68
  creamy sausage & bean bake with a crunchy topping 45
  nostalgic mini pasta shape soup 140
  sausage & artichoke pasta 125
sea bass with mixed beans 22
spices
  chicken shawarma-style traybake 74
  juicy spiced chicken legs 53
  my boozy carrot cake 196
  simple coconut curry 134
spinach
  creamy spinach & turkey meatballs 83
  green goddess winter pie 36
  peanut crunch salad 173
sweet potatoes
  Parma ham-wrapped cod with sweet potato traybake 79

T
teriyaki pork chops 98
tofu
  BBQ tofu & chips 94

tomatoes
  baked sausage & tomato gnocchi 68
  carnival salad 158
  chorizo & butter bean stew 143
  deconstructed lasagne 133
  Sloppy Joe pasta 40
  spicy tomato orzo with toasted pine nuts & feta 16
  summertime tomato stew 121
  taste of Greece salad 177
  taste of Italy salad 157
tortillas
  cheeseburger nachos 92
  slow-cooked brisket tacos 117
  taco Tuesday pan dinner 56
trout
  garlic & Parmesan crispy potatoes & trout 101
tuna
  spicy tuna salad with pesto croutons 168
turkey
  creamy spinach & turkey meatballs 83

V
vanilla
  simply vanilla cake 191

W
walnuts
  pumpkin risotto with bacon & walnut crunch 130
watermelon, halloumi & mint salad 178
whisky
  peppered steak with whisky sauce 27

INDEX 219

220 ACKNOWLEDGEMENTS

Acknowledgements

To the wonderful team at Quarto, wow. To my Publishers, Eleanor and Charlotte for always believing in me and knowing exactly how to bring my vision to life. Lewis for all you did with *Country Comfort*! To Claire, our Art Director, for understanding that sometimes we just need more pictures. To Dan, our photographer, who captures the warmth, cosiness and comfort in every shot (flick through the book, it speaks for itself). To Saskia, our Food Stylist, for making every dish look as mouthwatering as it tastes. To Em, my Manager, for being my speaker and advocate always and to my Literary Agent, Oscar, for picking up the phone when I said, 'I have an idea'; and somehow within a week, *Comfort in One* was no longer just a dream.

This team has made this book everything I hoped it would be, and I can't wait for it to be enjoyed in kitchens across the world.

To My Mum and Sister
My biggest cheerleaders, my safe place, my forever constants. Mum your unwavering support, your endless love, and the way you've always believed in me. You've been my rock through every high and every low, always ready with words of encouragement, a hug or just the gentle reassurance that everything would be okay.

And to my sister, my built-in best friend, my partner in crime, there's no one else I'd rather navigate life with. You've lifted me up when I doubted myself, cheered the loudest for every win (big or small) and reminded me time and time again that I could do anything I set my mind to.

This book and everything I have done, is just as much yours as it is mine, because without your love, support and belief in me none of this would be possible. I love you both beyond words.

To My Fiancé
Well, all that home cooking must have worked, because you decided to marry me!

Thank you for being my best friend, my taste tester (whether willing or unwilling), and for always pretending to be impressed when I tell you, 'this might be my best recipe yet!'. Your patience as I take just one more picture or video of our dinner, your willingness to try every kitchen experiment, and your ability to handle my chaotic cooking style (to ignore the washing-up pile) without running for the hills, those are true acts of love.

But more than that, thank you for always believing in me, supporting me, laughing with me and making life even more wonderful just by being in it. I can't wait to feed you for a lifetime.

About the author

Hari Beavis is a *Sunday Times* bestselling author and digital content creator, known for sharing her love of country living and comforting home-cooked meals with her online community. Her passion for food and rural life shines through in her Quiet Little Life videos, where she invites her audience into her world of cosy interiors, delicious dishes, and the beautiful English countryside.

Spending her happiest moments at home with her chickens, Hari has built a devoted following who turn to her for inspiration, whether in the kitchen or in curating a slower, more intentional lifestyle. Her debut cookbook, *Country Comfort*, makes home cooking effortless and accessible, empowering a new wave of home cooks. Hailed by The Times as 'Gen-Z's new favourite chef,' Hari continues to redefine modern comfort food for a new generation.

ABOUT THE AUTHOR

Quarto

First published in 2025 by Carnival
an imprint of The Quarto Group.
One Triptych Place, London, SE1 9SH
United Kingdom
T (0)20 7700 9000
www.Quarto.com

EEA Representation, WTS Tax d.o.o., Žanova ulica 3,
4000 Kranj, Slovenia www.wts-tax.si

Text © 2025 Hari Beavis
Photography © 2025 Dan Jones
Illustrations © 2025 Ryn Frank Ltd
Design © 2025 Quarto Publishing Plc

Hari Beavis has asserted her moral right to be identified as the Author of this Work in accordance with the Copyright Designs and Patents Act 1988.

All rights reserved. No part of this book may be reproduced or utilised in any form or by any means, electronic or mechanical, including photocopying, recording or by any information storage and retrieval system, without permission in writing from Carnival.

Every effort has been made to trace the copyright holders of material quoted in this book. If application is made in writing to the publisher, any omissions will be included in future editions.

A catalogue record for this book is available from the British Library.

ISBN 978-1-83600-905-4
EBOOK ISBN 978-1-83600-906-1

10 9 8 7 6 5 4 3 2 1

Book Designer: Claire Rochford
Food Stylist: Saskia Sidey
Food Styling Assistants: Caitlin Macdonald,
  Emma Cantlay and Eden Owen-Jones
Illustrator: Ryn Frank Ltd
Photographer: Dan Jones
Photography Assistant: Rosie Alsop
Prop Stylist: Max Robinson
Publisher: Eleanor Maxfield
Senior Designer: Isabel Eeles
Senior Editor: Charlotte Frost
Senior Production Manager: Rohana Yusof

Printed in Guangdong, China TT042025

MIX
Paper | Supporting
responsible forestry
FSC® C016973